*Outsourcing*

Outsourcing has become one of the key restructuring tools for companies seeking to boost their growth and business performance. As the outsourcing phenomenon has mushroomed, so a range of academic studies have sought to define and describe a unifying theoretical model. *Outsourcing: Design, Process, and Performance* draws upon managerial, economic, sociological, historical, and psychological perspectives to bring about a new understanding of how outsourcing design and the outsourcing process feed into the performance of firms. Blending empirical insights from a range of international cases and large-scale statistical tests with existing theoretical perspectives, the author argues that a negative curvilinear relationship exists between outsourcing and firm performance. A critical analysis of current outsourcing strategies, together with a discussion of future trends, offers a new agenda for academic researchers and business managers alike.

MICHAEL J. MOL is Senior Lecturer in Strategic Management, University of Reading Business School. He is also Visiting Researcher at the Management Innovation Lab, London Business School.

# Outsourcing

## Design, Process, and Performance

MICHAEL J. MOL

CAMBRIDGE
UNIVERSITY PRESS

CAMBRIDGE UNIVERSITY PRESS
Cambridge, New York, Melbourne, Madrid, Cape Town, Singapore, São Paulo

Cambridge University Press
The Edinburgh Building, Cambridge CB2 8RU, UK

Published in the United States of America by Cambridge University Press, New York

www.cambridge.org
Information on this title: www.cambridge.org/9780521682787

First published 2007

Printed in the United Kingdom at the University Press, Cambridge

*A catalogue record for this publication is available from the British Library*

ISBN 978-0-521-86410-7 hardback
ISBN 978-0-521-68278-7 paperback

For my big little brother

# Contents

# *Figures*

# Tables

# Boxes

# Acknowledgments

This book partly draws upon various research projects on outsourcing I have undertaken since 1995, including my M.Sc. and doctoral dissertations, an earlier book, and a range of articles and co-authored articles and book chapters on sourcing strategy that have appeared in this time period. Therefore I am heavily indebted to the co-authors with whom much of this work was written for their inputs. They include (in chronological order) Bob de Wit, Eric van Drunen, Otto Koppius, Jacques Schreuder, Robert Goedegebuure, Rob van Tulder, Paul Beije, Piet Pauwels, Paul Matthyssens, Lieven Quintens, Sjoerd Loeffen, Joost Breggeman, Masaaki Kotabe, Dries Vermeulen, Sonia Ketkar, Hans van Oosterhout, and Ariën Ritskes. Each of them has contributed in one way or the other to the learning process that culminated in this book.

Among these people, I would like to single out Masaaki "Mike" Kotabe as someone who has greatly supported and mentored me in my study of outsourcing. Much progress has come while working on joint projects with Mike and during my stays at Temple University. I am very thankful for the ideas and opportunities which he has provided.

Thanks and appreciation are due to the many respondents who have helped in various research projects by being interviewed or by completing questionnaires. I have received useful feedback on ideas from a large number of practitioners as well. This feedback strengthened me much in the conviction that academically generated knowledge can be of relevance to practitioners, if properly framed and packaged. The Dutch Association for Purchasing Management (Nederlandse Vereniging voor Inkoop) served as an intermediary on several occasions as did the Dutch Association of Generic Suppliers (Nederlandse Vereniging voor Algemene Toelevering). Statistics Netherlands (Centraal Bureau voor de Statistiek), particularly Robert Goedegebuure, provided very useful data, on which many of the empirical tests described in this book are based. KPMG helped us financially and in other ways in executing a survey on business process outsourcing, which is also appreciated.

The book was written while I was an Advanced Institute of Management (AIM) Research Fellow at London Business School. I would like to thank AIM, its sponsor ESRC, and LBS for providing me with the funding and opportunity to work on this book. Special thanks go to Julian Birkinshaw, with whom I have had the great pleasure to work since 2004 on an exciting new research agenda around management innovation. Julian provided me with both the time and the encouragement to take on this writing project, for which I am very grateful. Other institutions that provided substantial sponsorship for some of the research contained in this book are the Japanese Ministry of Science and Education (through Meiji University) and the Carnegie Bosch Institute at Carnegie Mellon University. Oxford's Said Business School was kind enough to provide a writing facility. Various research assistants helped in completing the empirical work discussed here, including Joost Breggeman, Tom Buijs, Bartjan Cornelissen, Ralph Tercic, Michael Fenn, and Sjoerd Loeffen. I would like to take this opportunity to thank them for their work.

I would like to thank various AIM, LBS and University of Reading colleagues for useful discussions around outsourcing and for feedback they provided on some of the ideas contained in this book. They include (in alphabetical order) Mark Casson, Panayotis Dessylas, Nicola Dragonetti, Gary Hamel, Srikanth Khannan, Zella King, Costas Markides, Klaus Meyer, Peter Moran, Phanish Puranam, Mari Sako, Abigail Tierney, and members of the innovation group. Other friends and colleagues who have over time provided very useful comments on my ideas include (in alphabetical order) Jos Benders, Eric Gedajlovic, Pursey Heugens, Isabelle Maignan, Ram Mudambi, Arjen Mulder, Janet Murray, Gwen Tecson, Bart Vos, Finn Wynstra, and Ed Zajac. I apologize in advance to those individuals I have forgotten to mention here. Finally acknowledgment for feedback should go out to yesterday's enemies who are today's friends, namely the many journal and conference reviewers who refereed the key ideas that have gone into this work and helped to shape these ideas further. Obviously I take full responsibility for any remaining errors and omissions. Special thanks go to the four people who were willing enough to read the entire manuscript and comment on it in great detail: Peter Cook, Mike Kotabe, Lieven Quintens, and Wendy van der Valk. Their contributions have really improved the contents and readability, for which I am grateful.

I would like to thank the staff at Cambridge University Press for their very helpful attitude and encouragement during the writing of this book. Thanks go in particular to Katy Plowright, who helped to get this book started, and to Lynn Dunlop, Philip Good, Paula Parish, and Chris Harrison for their support and encouragement during the writing process.

Finally, on a personal note, I would like to thank little Joakim just for being there as he is and the lovely Dolores for being such an inspiration to me (and for playing the tedious part of other half of a book-writer, of course). Without them the words on this paper might have come into being but surely with much less joy. As we say: thank you, *gracias* and *dankjewel*.

# 1 | *Outsourcing*

O
N February 14, 2005, the *New Yorker* published an article with the remarkable title "Outsourcing torture: the secret history of America's 'extraordinary rendition' program." In the article it was argued that the US government deliberately chose to leave the questioning of its terror suspects to other countries like Syria, in order to evade the limitations posed by US human rights laws. These other countries are believed to be less stringent regarding torture and hence, by outsourcing, the US government could obtain more information (a "better product" in a sense). Outsourcing, a word unheard of just twenty years ago, has clearly gained entry into the vocabulary of ordinary people. In the business world such pervasiveness is already taken for granted. A simple search of the Financial Times / Business.com website generated 10,506 published articles during the year 2005 alone. It is hard to find managers who do not have an opinion of outsourcing and even harder to find an individual who is completely unaware of it.

People all across the world are today feeling the impact of outsourcing. Consumers in the United States increasingly deal with suppliers of the firms who sell them products and services, rather than with the firms themselves, for instance when they call service centers. Managers in Germany are faced with tough decisions about whether to restructure their firms by outsourcing more manufacturing and services activities, often to low-wage countries. People who want to buy property in Bangalore, India, face steep local prices as a consequence of the business process outsourcing (BPO) boom. Some politicians are scrambling to find protective measures that raise the costs of outsourcing and help protect local employment, at least in the short run. Research institutions and consultants produce large numbers of reports that document the outsourcing trend and contain bold predictions concerning its future and often equally bold statements about its benefits for companies.

Outsourcing has indeed become one of the key restructuring tools for companies, with a promise to improve the fate of fledgling firms or to increase further the performance of firms that are already leading their industries. Stock markets, for one, seem to appreciate outsourcing. For instance, Oxford Metrica, an independent advisor, recently presented a study of outsourcing by asset managers in Europe with a combined $2,325 billion of managed funds.[1] It involved outsourcing of all kinds of non-core investment activities, including risk management, product development, and information technology. The outsourcing firms' share prices responded with an average price increase of some 10 percent. The logic presented by these firms was one of "core competences," which may be defined as "the collective learning in the organization, especially how to coordinate diverse production skills and integrate multiple streams of technologies" (Prahalad and Hamel, 1990: 82). By outsourcing these activities, they could free up managerial time and better "demonstrate an understanding of strategic issues." As ABN Amro's Chief Operating Officer commented in the report: "Outsourcing our fund administration and investment operations will enable us to support our business more effectively and to focus on the investment process. We have put in place a structure for future growth." The study noted that none of the benefits ascribed to outsourcing by the asset managers were realized benefits. Rather, they were intentions. It did not comment on the possible effects on industry competition either.

Important trends in management practice eventually get studied by academics, though not necessarily in a timely fashion, and outsourcing is no exception. Although there are some earlier studies, it is only in the last ten or so years that academics have produced a steadily increasing number of publications on the topic, in which a wide variety of outsourcing decisions in industries and countries across the globe have been examined. Whatever these studies may disagree on, they all concur in concluding that outsourcing is becoming an ever more pervasive and important phenomenon and that the nature of outsourcing is changing at some pace. It is within this context that this book attempts to contribute to our understanding of outsourcing, specifically how it impacts the performance of firms.

---

[1] http://www.bankofny.com/htmlpages/data/value_outsourcing.pdf (accessed on August 19, 2005).

## What is outsourcing?

All the agreement about increased outsourcing levels conceals real differences among practitioners and academics over what the term outsourcing actually entails (see Linder, 2004). Let us consider some of the following definitions and discussions of outsourcing. Loh and Venkatraman (1992: 9) believe IT outsourcing is "the significant contribution by external vendors in the physical and/or human resources associated with the entire or specific components of the IT infrastructure in the user organization." Lei and Hitt (1995: 836) think of outsourcing as simply "the reliance on external sources for the manufacturing of components and other value-adding activities." Gilley and Rasheed (2000: 765), though not providing any conclusive definition themselves, suggest outsourcing does not occur when organizations have no choice but to acquire a particular good or service from an external source. Linder (2004: 27) defines it as "purchasing ongoing services from an outside company that a company currently provides, or most organizations normally provide, for themselves." Accountants have looked at it as "the transfer of an internal service function to an outside vendor" (Friedberg and Yarberry, 1991: 53). In the fifth version of the *Shorter Oxford English Dictionary*, published in 2002, outsourcing does not feature at all, which serves as testimony to its relatively recent origins and possibly to the robustness of British institutions as well. The Wikipedia, in a rather shaky and inconsistent discussion of the topic, defines it as:

the delegation of non-core operations or jobs from internal production to an external entity (such as a subcontractor) that specializes in that operation. Outsourcing is a business decision that can be made for quality or financial reasons. A subset of the term (offshoring) also implies transferring jobs to another country, either by hiring local subcontractors or building a facility in an area where labor is cheap. It became a popular buzzword in business and management in the 1990s.[2]

Clearly, if anything, there is agreement to disagree. This raises the question how we should define outsourcing. I see the variety of definitions in use as being subsidiary to one of these three descriptions:
1. Outsourcing refers to those activities that are undertaken by outside suppliers.

---

[2] http://en.wikipedia.org/wiki/Outsourcing (accessed on August 2, 2005).

2. Outsourcing refers to the transfer of activities and possibly assets from a firm to an outside supplier.
3. Outsourcing refers to those activities that are undertaken by outside suppliers but could also be undertaken by the firm.

The third description is particularly problematic in my view. Gilley and Rasheed (2000), who are among its proponents, never clarify whether they imply the technical or the economic ability of firms to undertake an activity. If we take it that it refers to the firm being *technically* able to undertake an activity, this is clearly not very meaningful because any firm could hire the people and obtain the assets to undertake most activities, short of rocket science. Discussions of outsourcing thus would be restricted to the very small set of activities for which it is not possible to procure the people or assets to produce them, for instance because doing so is illegal or because they are extremely rare. But few firms are in need of rocket scientists. If, on the other hand, we interpret this description as referring to whether the firm is *economically* able to undertake the activity, we enter into circular reasoning, for outsourcing would then refer to those activities that are best, or rather most economically, outsourced. This leaves us with sparingly little room for further analysis of outsourcing as a phenomenon. Furthermore it reduces the costs and benefits of outsourcing to a binary variable – either costs outweigh benefits or vice versa – which takes away from the range of intermediate positions that exist from very beneficial through somewhat beneficial and from somewhat costly to very costly. So this third description either reduces outsourcing to a set of activities too narrow to be meaningful or defines it in a circular sense.

Clearly, the first and second descriptions are more useful, though they too present their own problems. The second definition, which is what practitioners often seem to understand by outsourcing, refers to a transfer. But at what stage does a transfer begin or end? Is an activity or asset that was "outsourced" ten years ago, i.e. transferred to an outside supplier, still outsourced today? If not, then when did it cease to become outsourced and start to become something else, perhaps "purchased"? Some twenty-five years ago many firms, like banks, produced their own database programs for a variety of applications. Now they no longer do so but instead rely on outside software producers like Microsoft or Oracle. In lay terms this would perhaps be seen as a form of procurement, not outsourcing, but this definition appears to suggest it is outsourcing. If it is not, some cut-off point must be introduced, which is likely context-specific and hence for which no universal definition can be provided. The first description, while being very broad in scope and objective, does not help to distinguish among any of the forms of using external suppliers. In other words, it treats as being equal the purchase of off-the-shelf components with that of a highly customized service such as legal advice. It also makes no reference to when an input was externalized, or indeed whether it was ever performed in-house.

Therefore neither of these two descriptions by itself helps us to understand the outsourcing phenomenon in its entirety. Combined, though, they provide a powerful piece of equipment for outsourcing research for they help us think about outsourcing as a state and outsourcing as a process. Outsourcing as a state, henceforth referred to simply as *outsourcing*, I define as *the procurement of goods and services from external suppliers* (following Kotabe and Mol, 2005). To say that something is outsourced therefore means it is at present being procured from external suppliers. The counterpart of outsourcing is *vertical integration*, which refers to goods and services that are produced internally or procured from other units within a corporate system. Also note that, unlike some authors, I do not believe outsourcing necessarily refers to services or to information technology activities alone, much as it never strictly referred solely to goods when services outsourcing was not much of a topic of discussion yet. Firms, in other words, can outsource or integrate any sort of activity, in the same way that the US government outsourced torture.

The second description leads to what I will refer to as the *outsourcing process*, defined as *a range of actions within a clearly identifiable time-frame that lead to the transfer to outside suppliers of activities, possibly involving the transfer of assets including people as well, that were previously performed in-house or procured from other units within a corporate system.*[3] In the context of the outsourcing process to say that something is being outsourced means that there is an ongoing transfer process. The counterpart of the outsourcing process is the

---

[3] The use of a legal entity, the corporate system, as a deciding criterion is arguable in some ways. For instance, some firms operate internal markets, in which case internal sourcing may not be too dissimilar to outsourcing. And other firms have quasi-integrated some of their external suppliers. Yet this demarcation is a necessary step for further analysis, if one wishes at all to generalize beyond individual cases.

*insourcing process*, which thus occurs when previously externally procured goods and services are taken in-house. By defining these terms,
there is now room for both a static and a dynamic analysis of the
outsourcing phenomenon. The reader who is not yet convinced of the
usefulness of this distinction is encouraged to at least read the next
paragraph.

## A further qualification

This definition arguably does not capture other important dimensions
of the sourcing phenomenon, most notably the nature of the relation
between the outsourcer and the supplier on the one hand and the
geographic scope of this relationship on the other. Some would for
instance argue (Nooteboom, 1998; 1999) that outsourcing only occurs
when the relationship is not strictly arm's length and some form of
specification or customization takes place. This argument starts to run
into the ground when one considers that real arm's length relations
barely seem to exist and, even more importantly, recognizes that there
is no natural cut-off point to determine what is and what is not
specification (Hennart, 1993). Almost by definition we find a mix of
specification and non-specification. Even the global currency trading
market has recently been shown to be a social constellation (Knorr-
Cetina and Preda, 2005). Ordering a book via Amazon using the
"express delivery" option entails a form of specification too.
Therefore we find a wide range of degrees of specification, which
makes it hard to determine a cut-off point.

   This does not mean that the analysis of the nature of buyer–supplier
relations in outsourcing therefore becomes irrelevant. I will discuss the
issue of outsourcing relations, and also that of geographic scope (international outsourcing or global sourcing), at length at a later stage, most
notably in chapters 5 and 6. At this point it suffices to say that I do
believe both dimensions are related to outsourcing (as evidenced by
Mol, 2001) and that while they do not help us determine whether
something is (being) outsourced, they do reflect upon the great variety
of forms of outsourcing, both in terms of a variety of relations and in
terms of a variety of geographical settings. And like the decision
whether to outsource or to integrate activities, the way outsourcing
takes place and its physical location can potentially have implications
for the performance of firms.

## *Two forms, three forms, many activities*

Further evidence that outsourcing is not a uniformly identified phenomenon comes from responses I have received from academics and practitioners on my proposed definition of outsourcing. They suggested my definition amounts to "externalization," "external sourcing" (a term preferred by Murray, Kotabe, and Wildt, 1995) or "vertical disintegration" (a term used by Jacobides, 2005), but not to outsourcing. In addition they said outsourcing is but one form of externalization, external sourcing, or vertical disintegration. Some said there are two forms, outsourcing and purchasing; other that there are three forms including outsourcing, purchasing, and subcontracting. Finally, people have commented that it is not very useful to treat the different outsourced activities, including IT, manufacturing, BPO, maintenance, repair, and operations, and R&D outsourcing as one and the same. All of these remarks warrant a response.

My definition of outsourcing explicitly incorporates all forms of outsourcing, and includes purchasing. Purchasing is generally seen as a straightforward process, where simple specifications lead to deliveries according to these specifications. The definition also includes subcontracting. Subcontracting is sometimes used in the context of projects of limited duration. It is also used in situations where buyers drive the supply process and mostly operational information is exchanged. And the definition includes what is perhaps best called strategic outsourcing, when buyer and supplier exchange higher-level information and objectives in order to create competitive advantage.

One way to conceptualize these three forms of outsourcing is through Thompson's (1967) classical categorization of interdependence mechanisms.[4] Purchasing comes closest to pooled interdependence, when "each part renders a discrete contribution to the whole and each is supported by the whole" (Thompson, 1967: 54). In purchasing, suppliers fulfill a discrete function and no communication is needed between ordering and delivery. Subcontracting looks like sequential interdependence, when parts "make contributions to and are sustained by the whole organization ... But, in addition, direct interdependence can be pinpointed between them, and ... the order of

---

[4] I am grateful to Peter Cook for suggesting this parallel.

that interdependence can be specified" (Thompson, 1967: 54). In subcontracting, buyer and supplier depend on each other and need to continuously communicate about operational matters, but the buyer still takes a clear lead. And strategic outsourcing is reciprocal, when "the outputs of each become inputs for the others ... each unit is penetrated by the other ... with each unit posing contingency for the other" (Thompson, 1967: 55). Here buyer and supplier work together more closely, what one partner does has serious implications for the other partner, and joint objectives may arise at the relational level.

These two or three forms of outsourcing, depending on whether one sees subcontracting as a viable separate form, are managed differently and carry different performance implications. Analytically, purchasing is less interesting than subcontracting or strategic outsourcing. Yet all three form part of the wider picture discussed in this book. There are two key reasons for this choice. First, there are important overlaps between the three (or two) forms, such that it will empirically be very difficult to separate one form from the other. These forms are little more than ideal types. Second, it is only by contrasting the more complex forms with the less complex ones that we gain real insights. So while the reader may indeed prefer external sourcing or vertical disintegration as the overarching term for what is discussed in this book, it is important to keep considering all three forms.

A further point is whether the different activities that are outsourced can be analyzed together. Would it not be better to treat outsourcing of software as a different phenomenon from outsourcing of market research? The answer to this question is twofold. One part of the answer is that these are different outsourced activities, which score differently on important characteristics. But the other part of the answer reads that these different forms of outsourcing can be explained by similar concepts and variables as a host of research has shown. In other words, there are differences of degree and in operationalization among these outsourced activities, but eventually the considerations driving them are quite similar.[5] Therefore there is merit in discussing the different outsourced activities together.

---

[5] Note that the question whether outsourcing is best discussed at the activity or the firm level is another one. It is discussed at length in chapter 3.

## A very brief history of outsourcing

It would obviously be a mistake to believe that outsourcing is somehow a recent phenomenon simply because its frequency of use has ballooned, or even to believe that the word outsourcing does not have any forerunners. Clearly outsourcing is similar in meaning to words like subcontracting, contracting out, contracting (Domberger, 1998), external sourcing (Murray, Kotabe, and Wildt (1995), and farming out (Doig, Ritter, Speckhals, and Woolson, 2001). While there is no need to define each of these terms at length, they often seem to differ from outsourcing by their use in a particular context, such as manufacturing or construction, by their reference to a particular type of outsourcing, or by the background of the user of the term. But there is little denying that both the practice and the academic study of management suffer from some repackaging of old phenomena into new terminologies (Abrahamson, 1997; Barley and Kunda, 1992) and in that sense outsourcing is neither very different from the above terms nor guaranteed any eternal popularity of itself. Therefore some understanding of historical developments and inter-temporal changes in outsourcing is useful prior to proceeding with a discussion of contemporary outsourcing strategy.

Outsourcing is in fact as old as the hills, or at least about as old as organizations themselves are. The kinds of businesses Adam Smith (1976) described very much relied on an interorganizational division of labor and subcontracting of production activities. His classical views presented the economy as consisting of markets in which an endless number of firms contracted endless numbers of activities to each other without transactional frictions or prima-facie motives for firms to grow beyond a single employee. Wilson (2005) describes how subcontracting existed from the very beginning of industrialization in Britain and how subcontractors were responsible for a range of management tasks.

To better understand outsourcing *circa* 2007, however, it helps to zoom in on changes in outsourcing in the twentieth century in general, and on three specific waves of outsourcing that have occurred over the past twenty-five years in particular. Broadly speaking, there was a rather substantial level of outsourcing in the early twentieth century, which was followed by strong vertical integration strategies that persisted into the 1970s and perhaps even the 1980s, and which themselves were replaced again by substantial outsourcing. This outsourcing trend has now been going on for at least twenty-five years, although it perhaps did not move into top gear until the 1990s. In our input–output analysis for a set of sectors of the Dutch economy, for instance, we found substantial rises in inter-sectoral trading patterns dating back as far as 1977 for some sectors (De Wit, Mol, and van Drunen, 1998).

In the early twentieth century contracting out was already a rather common phenomenon. Nishiguchi (1994) discusses the rising levels of subcontracting in Japanese manufacturing during the 1920s. Chandler (1977), in his work on the "visible hand" of management, sketches how there was a system of local contracting out in the United States, in which familiarity, and indeed family membership, played a major role. Such familiarity provided interpersonal trust in business contracts, thus allowing risky transactions to take place (see Lamoreaux, Raff, and Temin, 2003).

As the century progressed, however, firms changed their strategies substantially, in part forced by altered geopolitical conditions. Levels of vertical integration increased over time. The classic example of vertical integration is the Ford Motor Company. Its model of production has been referred to as "Fordism" (Piore and Sabel, 1984) and consisted of integrating into the firm not just assembly activities and production of components but even the extraction of iron ore and car dealerships. The thinking behind this strategy was that Ford could increase its scale and market power by owning all the activities required to produce a car and hence produce at low cost while excluding competing firms from its own channels (Chandler, 1977). General Motors is said to have taken the Fordist model even further than Ford itself and for a long time Fordism was the dominant production model in the automotive industry (Piore and Sabel, 1984).

Firms outside the automobile industry followed similar strategies. Unilever, for instance, maintained all kinds of agricultural facilities, including rubber plantations. Vertical integration levels appear to have risen until well into the second half of the twentieth century. One report (Ruhnke, 1966) stated that vertical integration levels might well continue to rise for another fifteen years and associated various advantages with vertical integration, including availability of supplies, control over quality and distribution, greater uniformity towards customers, and more coordination between activities. Clearly the dominant logic (Prahalad and Bettis, 1986) of the 1960s and 1970s was not geared towards outsourcing. Instead large firms sought to grow even larger, through related, but also much unrelated, diversification (Lamoreaux, Raff, and Temin, 2003).[6] By this time, however, enhancing the firm's scale was no longer a universal recipe for success. In fact, in retrospect most analysts are rather critical about unrelated diversification and the formation of conglomerates (Lamoreaux, Raff, and Temin, 2003). A different response gradually emerged, in the form of more decentralized and market-like relations, in which outsourcing played a role, if not the *key* role (Lamoreaux, Raff, and Temin, 2003; Langlois, 2004).

The current outsourcing wave broadly started in the 1980s and appears to have been triggered by a number of interrelated processes and beliefs, and has been captured by various publications. As so often seems to be the case in management, the popularity of outsourcing as a strategy first increased in the United States and only subsequently in other countries. As has been well documented elsewhere (for instance Ettlie, 1988) the United States found itself under considerable competitive pressure from European countries like Germany but particularly from Japan. In analyses of the "Japanese miracle" in practitioner and academic outlets (Pascale and Athos, 1981; Williamson, 1991a; Womack, Roos, and Jones, 1990) much was made of the ability of Japanese firms to obtain inputs at lower costs and higher quality by much more frequent use of outside suppliers. Firms like Toyota and Matsushita were seen as important examples of strategic outsourcing and the *keiretsu* structure they operated as something worth copying (Dyer, 1996). Thus one can argue that major shifts in outsourcing by firms like General Motors, which outsourced entire component divisions, were at least partly a response to the perception that Japanese firms were successful because they outsourced a larger part of their production activities.

A second, related shift took place when firms started to think differently about the basis for competitive advantage. During the vertical integration era much was made of the importance of scale and bargaining power (hence their central role in Porter's influential 1980 book). By integrating more activities into the firm, its scale of operations and

---

[6] Lamoreaux, Raff, and Temin (2003) provide a fascinating critique and rebuttal of Chandler's (1977) hypothesis that a dominant organizational form, in the shape of the large corporation, has emerged and that its dominance will not be challenged. They argue that there is not now, nor perhaps ever will be, such an end to business history.

bargaining power would increase only further, so it was argued (Harrigan, 1986; Porter, 1980). The management philosophy that now took root, however, was one where "sticking to your knitting" (Peters and Waterman, 1982) and building a firm's competitive advantage around its core competences (Hamel and Prahalad, 1994; Prahalad and Hamel, 1990) were seen as crucial. This new philosophy clearly favored outsourcing over integration as its implication was made out to be that those activities that do not fit in the knitting and are not related to core competences are best outsourced (Quinn, Doorley, and Pacquette, 1990; Quinn and Hilmer, 1994).[7] In chapter 7, I will discuss the issue of core competences and outsourcing strategy in more detail and provide a critique of the Quinn and Hilmer (1994) interpretation of core competences.

Third, another change occurred in the belief systems of managers, which complemented the philosophy of focusing on the core. Managers and academics alike began to profess a belief that it is possible to extract equal or even more than equal value from relations with all kinds of outside parties, including suppliers, and from interorganizational networks, including supplier networks. This belief has been expressed in a variety of publications (Doz and Hamel, 1998; Dyer and Singh, 1998; Powell, 1990; Uzzi, 1997) but also shows itself through substantial increases in various forms of interorganizational relations in practice (Barringer and Harrison, 2000). A further indicator is that many firms not only look at cost price as an indicator of a supplier's success but extend that either to total cost of ownership or even to the value produced by a relationship (van Weele, 2002; Wouters, Anderson, and Wynstra, 2005; Zajac and Olsen, 1993). Because managers' attitudes towards dealing with external suppliers have improved so much, they are now more willing to outsource goods and services to these suppliers. In many ways the default mode of operations has shifted from internal production to outsourcing. Concerns over appropriation of rents by suppliers and over suppliers'

---

[7] As we noted elsewhere (Kotabe and Mol, 2005), it is somewhat ironic that the positioning approach (Porter, 1980; 1985), which is generally referred to as the outside-in approach to strategy because it starts by analyzing the environment, advocates high levels of vertical integration, while the resource-based and competence approach, also known as the inside-out approach because of its initial focus on the firm's strengths and weaknesses, is more comfortable with high levels of outsourcing.

abilities to move up the value chain, while still present, have become less important and have been replaced by the new dilemma of how to get the most out of supplier relations and networks (Mol, 2005).

A fourth factor can be found in the development of new technologies that enabled outsourcing, most prominently new information technology (IT) but also transportation technologies. In their classic article Malone, Yates, and Benjamin (1987) argued that IT lowers the costs of transacting between an outsourcer and a supplier, so much so that outsourcing becomes a more viable option because its lower production cost levels easily offset the higher transaction costs associated with the externalization of production.[8] Although IT itself was much older it was not until the mid 1980s that useful IT like electronic data interchange (EDI) was developed to facilitate outsourcer–supplier communications, radically improving the ability of buyers and suppliers to coordinate inter-firm processes. In the 1990s this development took flight further with the development of Enterprise Resource Planning systems such as those of SAP and Peoplesoft that replaced the earlier Materials Requirement Planning systems and now included a range of interorganizational features, the development of e-mail, the World Wide Web and other long-distance communication technologies, and various file-sharing protocols. The rise of new, low-cost transportation technologies, such as freight containers, has also allowed for more physical decoupling of activities, thus opening up the possibility of outsourcing from physically remote locations. With low transportation costs, a faraway supplier can be integrated into a firm's supply chain more easily.

Fifth, the world has witnessed large changes in international trade regimes and trade flows over the past twenty years. The United States has particularly seen an increase in traded volumes with South Asian and East Asian countries, most prominently China and India. The nature of imports from these countries is also changing gradually to include higher-skilled goods and services. Western European countries, while perhaps not having seen such substantial increases in Euro-Asian trade, have benefited much from the opening up of the Iron Curtain, EU enlargement, and the wave of trade and foreign investment this has produced. As noted before, increases in international trade appear to coincide with

---

[8] Although others subsequently argued differently, as will be discussed in more detail in chapter 6.

increases in outsourcing. This mechanism has been studied in more detail by economists (McLaren, 2000) who seem to believe outsourcing and international trade are very closely related phenomena, if not two sides of the same coin. Indeed, easier access to foreign suppliers at substantially reduced transaction cost levels makes it much more attractive to start using foreign suppliers and engage in international or global outsourcing (Kotabe, 1992) of goods and services. As a larger and more diverse supply base becomes available, outsourcing becomes a more interesting option and hence easing of international trade and investment regimes often does go hand in hand with outsourcing.

A sixth factor is the economic liberalization that has taken place in a variety of countries. As argued by Toulan (2002) for the case of Argentina, a byproduct of economic liberalization is that it produces the kinds of institutional reforms that make market transactions more feasible. As institutions in most countries have become more market-oriented they have produced the kinds of conditions that allow outsourcing to thrive. It is telling in this respect that scholars now undertake investigations to explain why the conglomerate form of organizing can continue to exist in developing countries (Khanna and Palepu, 2000). They argue that conglomerates like India's Tata exist by virtue of the presence of substantial institutional voids, as the lack of a viable alternative in the marketplace more or less forces firms to develop their own supply chains, including the production of many goods and services, inside the firm. Because developed countries now display fewer and fewer institutional voids, markets function so well that outsourcing has become plentiful.[9] Thus, I suggest, increases in outsourcing levels over the past twenty years have been aided by the presence of a role model in the form of successful Japanese companies, a shift in where firms believe their competitive advantage to lie, a shift in how firms perceive the value-added of relations with suppliers, technological change primarily in the form of new IT, and institutional change in the shape of more liberal trade regimes and more international investment on the one hand and increased economic liberalization on the other.

---

[9] This remark should not be interpreted as saying that most of today's outsourcing relations are anywhere near the classical market mechanism or indeed the arm's length model (Williamson, 1975) of transacting. Rather, the economy seems to be characterized by a sea of organizations (Simon, 1991), linked by a variety of contractual and relational mechanisms.

We have argued (Kotabe and Mol, forthcoming) that these increases in outsourcing levels contain three important recent waves of outsourcing. These are outsourcing of manufacturing activities, starting in the mid to late 1980s, outsourcing of IT, in the early to mid 1990s, and business process outsourcing from the late 1990s onwards. The first wave was primarily focused on outsourcing of manufacturing activities, some of it across national borders (Bettis, Bradley, and Hamel, 1992; Kotabe and Omura, 1989). Key examples of this trend were firms like Nike, which outsourced extensively to various East Asian countries (Quinn and Hilmer, 1994), and Benetton, which used a large network of local suppliers around Treviso (Piore and Sabel, 1984). Large manufacturing firms were also increasingly spreading their operations across the world and began to use external suppliers from a variety of countries, to exploit so-called best-in-world sources (Quinn and Hilmer, 1994). Supply chains, as a consequence, became more global and also much more complicated in nature. Products could now be created through the combination of inputs from perhaps ten countries or more. In addition some specialized suppliers like Flextronics emerged which could produce entire products including the assembly operations, implying firms could get by without owning any type of manufacturing operations if they so choose.

A second wave started to occur in the early to mid 1990s, when firms decided to get rid of their IT departments that had, over time, grown to a substantial size (Cross, 1995; Lacity and Hirschheim, 1993). This IT outsourcing wave spawned the growth of large IT providers, such as EDS and what is now known as Accenture, but also of a host of smaller specialist firms. IT itself had turned into more and more of a commodity and many firms started to show little interest in developing new information systems in-house. The rise of commercial applications for a wide range of firm activities, epitomized in Enterprise Resource Planning systems, also implied that a marketplace had developed where independent suppliers could make competitive offerings. British Petroleum attempted to outsource not just single IT components but also the entire IT architecture (Cross, 1995) by shifting management responsibility to one key supplier (the "main contractor" in a sense), which was supposed to manage several smaller suppliers (the subcontractors).

In recent years we have seen the rise of business process outsourcing in what has also become known as the "offshoring movement." The object has now broadened beyond just IT services to a range of other services, including those in accounting, human resources management, finance, sales, and after-sales, such as call centers. India is a primary target country, and has now produced a range of strong local business process providers such as Infosys and Wipro, but competition from elsewhere is on the rise. It is this third wave, of business process outsourcing, that is now generating much noise and many media headlines, in part because it has been suggested that the foreign suppliers of such business processes may be moving up the knowledge chain more rapidly than buyers were expecting. Therefore such knowledge transfer could in the long run undermine buyers' ability to differentiate themselves from their foreign suppliers in the marketplace. These hollowing-out concerns have, of course, previously been raised about outsourcing of manufacturing activities as well (Bettis, Bradley, and Hamel, 1992; Kotabe, 1998; Markides and Berg, 1988). It appears, though, that the public debate over offshoring is more about issues of employment and relocation than about what offshoring does to companies (Mol, 2004).

## Outsourcing and society

Although this book focuses on the organizational aspects of outsourcing, the phenomenon also has a tremendous impact on society at large. Hence it is worth briefly stipulating this impact here. As alluded to earlier, outsourcing, and particularly international outsourcing, is sending something of a shock wave through OECD countries at present. Outsourcing generally involves the transfer of jobs from one organization to another and from one location to another. This is an issue that clearly affects employees, trade unions, and governments. Outsourcing also affects consumers, and therefore more or less everyone, in a myriad of ways as it alters economic processes and customers' perceptions of their outcomes. For non-governmental and civic organizations outsourcing also changes their outlook, for instance because those organizations that concern themselves with child labor have to monitor not only Ikea or Nike but also their suppliers throughout the world. Outsourcing, therefore, is very much in the public domain these days. The fact that there now is a Complete Idiot's Guide to outsourcing epitomizes how much outsourcing has become of interest even to people who are not involved in it professionally.

Generally, it can be argued that all those parties are only just coming to terms with the outsourcing phenomenon. Political and public policy debates on outsourcing have flourished over perhaps the last three or four years.[10] In those debates, the key issue appears to be whether or not to install protectionist measures, not so much whether outsourcing as such is beneficial for firms (this seems to be an implicit assumption). It may take some more time for governments to develop policies around the questions of what can be done to help firms improve their outsourcing decisions and how firms' capabilities for outsourcing, though not necessarily their outsourcing levels, can be increased. While there is consumer resentment in various pockets, and some of that resentment comes to the boil from time to time, there is no well-coordinated consumer movement that could help firms understand what kinds of outsourcing behavior consumers find acceptable and what is clearly not acceptable to them. Unions have obviously realized what outsourcing can do to their members' job security and employment conditions. Yet their response is generally quite reactive, in that they resist outsourcing announcements but neither provide a clear alternative nor produce any foresight that might have made outsourcing a less than inevitable step. What is more, unions generally do not seem to represent very well the new type of flexible worker, or contractor, who often makes a deliberate choice to be outsourced (Barley and Kunda, 2004).

## Outsourcing: the great promise?

A natural interpretation of these increased outsourcing levels is that firms must have initiated these outsourcing processes for some good reason. Since an important objective, quite possibly the key one, of a firm is to obtain high levels of performance, increases in outsourcing are generally believed to be motivated by a desire to increase firm performance and indeed by a belief that outsourcing does increase firm performance.

In an interview with the Outsourcing Institute,[11] James Brian Quinn maintained: "[i]f you are not best-in-world in doing something, and are

---

[10]  Drawing upon personal experience here, the Dutch Ministry of Economic Affairs started seeking my advice in 2004, while the British Department of Trade and Industry followed suit in 2005. Both have only recently developed substantiated policies around outsourcing.

[11]  http://www.outsourcing.com/content.asp?page=01b/articles/intelligence/quinn_interview.html&nonav=true (accessed on August 25, 2005).

doing it in-house, you are giving up competitive edge. You could out-source to the best in the world, up the value and lower the cost." He also said that "[p]eople found out early in the outsourcing of hardware and services to set up the process of management properly. If they did that, then the company doing the outsourcing actually learned more from its new suppliers than it ever would have learned from having a sole source internally, unless it was best-in-world of that activity." In an article, Quinn (1999: 9) confidently concluded that "[t]oday's knowledge and service economy offers innumerable opportunities for well-run companies to increase profits through strategic outsourcing." It is also argued (Gottfrears, Puryear, and Phillips, 2005: 132) that "[o]utsourcing is becoming so sophisticated that even core functions like engineering, R&D, manufacturing, and marketing can – and often should – be outsourced." Malone and Laubacher (1998), in their description of structural changes in the economy, foresee the rise of the one-person business connected with other like businesses through outsourcing and appear to applaud it, ironically mirroring the neo-classical interpretation of Adam Smith's (1976) classical work on how the economy operates.

Obviously such strong claims, particularly when they have a perva-sive impact on practice, raise a need on the part of academics to scrutinize whether, why, how, and when there really is such a thing as competitive advantage through outsourcing. This book is centered on the question of *how outsourcing design and outsourcing process feed into the performance of firms*. In the process I will engage in a range of discussions around this issue. The relevance of this book for practice is based both on the importance of the theme to practitioners and on the method of the book, which is to blend empirical insights from a variety of cases with analytical thinking that extends beyond a single case. This is in sharp contrast to many other books that are primarily a summary of practical experiences and/or a guide on "how to do outsourcing" (like Brown and Wilson, 2005). From the academic perspective various aspects make this book distinct from other articles and books on outsourcing. First, I propose a complete model of out-sourcing grounded in multiple social science perspectives, rather than, for instance, just an economic contracting perspective (Domberger, 1998). Second, this book encompasses many different forms of out-sourcing, rather than just one, like IT outsourcing (Lacity and Hirschheim, 1995). Third, it analyzes all parts of the outsourcing process, rather than just management of supplier relations (Jenster, Pedersen, Plackett, and Hussey, 2005) or contract design (Domberger, 1998). This is not to say that these other books do not in one way or another contribute to the stock of knowledge on outsourcing. They do not, however, make the contribution that I am seeking here, which is to provide a multidisciplinary, theory-driven analysis of how various forms and stages of outsourcing impact overall firm performance.

## The structure of this book

Having described the central theme of this book, I now turn to its structure. In chapter 2, the current state of the literature is described and some of its shortcomings are identified. Building upon that overview, I propose a new perspective for looking at outsourcing and the performance of the firm in chapter 3. Specifically it is suggested that the performance of firms is a negative curvilinear, or "inverted U-shaped," function of their outsourcing levels. This implies the best financial performance, which I shall refer to as the "optimal point," is achieved when firms perfectly align their outsourcing levels with a set of predictor conditions. However, this does not imply that actual behavior displays perfect alignment. In chapter 4, I therefore look at the causes of misalignment through an in-depth investigation of the outsourcing process. This equates to an analysis of why firms outsource less or more than is optimal for them. Chapter 5 contains a discussion of how some firms get more out of outsourcing than do others, especially through differences in supplier management capabilities. Such firms raise the optimal point on the curve. Chapter 6 deals with changes in outsourcing predictor conditions, both inside firms and in their environments, that alter the optimal level of outsourcing. The focus is on technological and institutional change. In chapter 7, I move away from the somewhat mechanistic discussions presented to that point to look at the role managers play as decision-makers and to investigate how managerial agency helps to shape real-life outsourcing decisions. Chapters 8 and 9 present an outsourcing research agenda and the book's conclusions respectively. Table 1.1 summarizes the various chapters beyond this introductory chapter.

Readers who have a specific reason to pick up this book may like to be guided towards their areas of interest. Those readers with a practical

*Table 1.1. An overview of the book's chapters, their purpose, and contents*

| Chapter | Purpose | Contents |
|---|---|---|
| 2: What we know about outsourcing | Provide an overview of existing literature | Advantages and disadvantages; functional areas; industries and countries; conceptual perspectives; critique |
| 3: A new perspective | Introduce the book's main model on outsourcing and performance | Motivation; laying out the negative curvilinear perspective; its fit with theory and practice |
| 4: The outsourcing process | Describe outsourcing decision-making | Misalignment and its causes; bandwagoning; people and decision-making processes |
| 5: Shifting the curve | Describe why some firms outperform others regardless of outsourcing levels | Performance heterogeneity; internal causes; external span of control; modifying the span of control |
| 6: Shifts of the curve | Describe how actual and optimal outsourcing levels change over time | Technologies and institutions; changes in steepness of the curve |
| 7: Managing outsourcing | Provide practitioners with guidance on outsourcing | Revisiting core competences and strategic outsourcing; managerial intent and experimentation; strategy |
| 8: Outsourcing research agenda | Sketch interesting research directions in outsourcing | Theoretical challenges; extensions; methods |
| 9: Future trends and conclusions | Predict how outsourcing may change | Trends for the future; conclusions |

interest in outsourcing ought to direct their attention especially to chapters 3 and 7, though none of the book is technically inaccessible to the practitioner. Scholars with an interest in the economics of outsourcing will be most interested in chapters 2, 3, and 4. From a sociological and psychological perspective chapter 4 is most interesting, while chapter 6 takes in the macro-political environment in more detail (organizational politics are dealt with as part of the discussion on the outsourcing process in chapter 4 and elsewhere). Those researchers who are more interested in the management side of outsourcing, will want to look at chapters 3, 5, 7, and 8. The conclusions, in chapter 9, will be of interest to all readers. The book also has an appendix, which describes the various empirical research projects that informed this book.

# 2 | *What we know about outsourcing*

A COMMON refrain of scholars of management and many other areas is the lack of literature in the area they study in order to legitimize their own research. For outsourcing, such claims can no longer be valid. A search of the Business Source Premier database on the keyword "outsourcing" generated a staggering 2,669 peer-reviewed articles using outsourcing in their titles, keywords, or abstracts, 917 of which were published in 2004 and 2005 alone. In the non-peer-reviewed category a further 19,364 articles appeared. Furthermore the Library of Congress holds 337 books and documents for which outsourcing is a keyword.[1] Outsourcing, in short, is a hot topic academically. Clearly, in the presence of such a plethora of writings, any claim to newness cannot be based on having found an understudied topic. As the necessarily incomplete review of the literature contained within this chapter shows, many of the sub-areas of outsourcing are now quite populated with research studies as well. Carving out an original research contribution has, therefore, not become any easier over the years. In this chapter I will first look at some of the advantages and disadvantages of outsourcing as the literature has discussed them. This is followed by an investigation of the various business functions on which outsourcing research has focused. Then I will talk about what knowledge the study of various countries and industries has produced for our understanding of how context affects outsourcing. This is followed by a review of the key theoretical perspectives authors have brought to bear on outsourcing. Finally, the predominance of the micro-economic perspective on outsourcing, especially transaction cost economics, is critiqued.

---

[1] Both searches were performed on August 30, 2006.

## The advantages and disadvantages of outsourcing

The literature on outsourcing suggests that there are important advantages as well as disadvantages to outsourcing (Domberger, 1998; Hendry, 1995). In this section I will try to group first the advantages and then the disadvantages.[2] Obviously there is some overlap between individual categories. The advantages are (1) strategic focus / reduction of assets; (2) complementary capabilities / lower production costs; (3) strategic flexibility; (4) avoiding bureaucratic costs; and (5) relational rent. The disadvantages are (1) interfaces / economies of scope; (2) hollowing out; (3) opportunistic behavior; (4) rising transaction and coordination costs; and (5) limited learning and innovation. Often authors discuss some combination of arguments to support or reject outsourcing. Each of these arguments will now be discussed in detail.

### *Strategic focus / reduction of assets*

Through outsourcing activities a firm can reduce its total level of asset investment in manufacturing and other related facilities and technologies, which is one factor that speaks in favor of outsourcing. Outsourcing activities often involve a direct transfer of certain assets from the sourcing firm to its supplier, such as machinery, buildings, or stocks of products. The investments associated with these assets can either be redeployed in other activities or redistributed to shareholders. The former means that more investments can be made in those activities that are seen as highly strategic for the firm's future revenue streams. The latter will result in improvement of the firm's financial returns (e.g. return on assets), at least in the short run. Therefore stock markets usually react favorably to outsourcing since more-or-less similar absolute profit levels can be obtained with lower fixed investments, allowing for a return to shareholders of some of their investments (Domberger, 1998). Furthermore, outsourcing can help the management of a firm to redirect its attention to a smaller set of activities. Outsourcing makes a firm more nimble in the sense that the range of activities that need to be

---

[2] This section is a much extended description of the advantages and disadvantages that was first presented in Kotabe and Mol (2004). I do not claim to provide an all-encompassing review of all the advantages and disadvantages ever assigned to outsourcing, merely an overview of what are seen as the key arguments in the management literature.

coordinated through the bureaucratic mechanism decreases, thereby lessening pressure on management. Instead of having to possess and keep updated a wide range of competences, a firm can focus on its core competences. This is what is usually referred to as the strategic focus argument. The Oxford Metrica example, cited in chapter 1, demonstrates the pervasiveness of this argument in the world of practice.

## Complementary capabilities / lower production costs

Suppliers are often used as a means of lowering the costs of production. For example, procuring necessary components and products from suppliers in Southeast Asia on a contractual basis has been efficient for US companies (Kotabe, 1998). From a corporate point of view, it has allowed US companies to lower prices and, furthermore, reduce fixed cost from their manufacturing operations and thus lower break-even points for improved profitability. External suppliers are often highly specialized in the production of certain components or products, allowing them to produce at lower costs than the outsourcing firm owing to scale economies. Therefore a firm can lower production cost levels by outsourcing non-core activities (Quinn, 1999). Hendry (1995) also suggests that outsourcing improves contracting costs. Other research has linked outsourcing with improvement of cost levels, customer satisfaction, or risk levels (e.g. Monczka and Trent, 1991; Quinn, 1992).

## Strategic flexibility

A third argument in favor of outsourcing is that it increases the firm's strategic flexibility. By using outside sources, it is much easier to switch from one supplier to another (Nooteboom, 1999). If an external shock (e.g. a change in the business cycle) occurs, firms are better able to deal with it by simply increasing or decreasing the volumes obtained from an external supplier. If the same item were produced in-house, there would be not only high restructuring costs but also a much longer response time to external events. Semlinger (1993) shows that large European firms tend to use smaller suppliers as a flexibility reservoir. A similar argument has been made for industrial networks in Japan by Nishiguchi (1994), although he suggests that the core firms in these networks also share a responsibility for the long-term wellbeing of smaller suppliers and are therefore somewhat constrained in their ability to lower purchased volumes from these suppliers. This implies that even in the case of outsourcing, flexibility is not necessarily unlimited, on account of the embedded nature of relationships (Uzzi, 1997).

## Avoiding bureaucratic costs

There are costs associated with internal production that do not exist outside the firm. In particular, rising production costs are associated with internal production (D'Aveni and Ravenscraft, 1994). More generally there is a lack of a price mechanism and economic incentives inside a firm (Domberger, 1998). To the extent that such incentives are completely missing, firm efficiency will suffer as a consequence. Agency theorists (Alchian and Demsetz, 1972; Jensen and Meckling, 1976) have argued that employees in a firm may not be fully motivated to perform as efficiently as possible, because there are no pecuniary incentives to do so and there are problems with monitoring behavior. It is usually not possible to achieve the same level of output control inside a firm as can be achieved in relations with external suppliers, because of the inseparability of outputs obtained from team production (Alchian and Demsetz, 1972). Thus the decision to outsource can also be seen as an avoidance of these bureaucratic costs.

## Relational rent

In recent years a wide variety of authors have argued that certain relationships with external suppliers can deliver competitive advantage. Arguably, Dyer and Singh (1998), who introduced the concept of relational rent, have best captured this discussion. By outsourcing items and then building idiosyncratic and valuable relationships with suppliers, firms are able to innovate, learn and reduce transaction costs. In practice a similar trend has been observed in partnerships with suppliers. Toyota is perhaps the best-known example. It has been able to establish long-term relationships with suppliers that differentiate it from competing automobile manufacturers (Dyer and Nobeoka, 2000). Relational rent can provide a competitive advantage that is sustainable because an existing buyer–supplier relation, which has a historical, social and often interpersonal context (Zaheer, McEvily, and Perrone, 1998), cannot be replicated easily by competitors.

Recently it has been argued that working closely with outside suppliers can lead to levels of innovation similar to internal operations. To the extent this is the case, one could argue in favor of outsourcing.

## *Interfaces / economies of scope*

A first argument against outsourcing springs from the relatedness of activities. Firms may benefit from internalizing production, rather than outsourcing it, through scope economies (D'Aveni and Ravenscraft, 1994). Firms are a value chain (Porter, 1985) in which multiple activities are united. If there is room for optimization between these activities, then there can be reason to internalize them in order to manage the interfaces optimally. Kotabe (1992) has suggested that manufacturing firms, in their outsourcing decisions, ought to reflect on the interfaces among R&D, manufacturing, and marketing. If there are important interfaces between activities, splitting them up into separate activities performed by separate suppliers will generate less than optimal results. Porter (1997) has similarly questioned the viability of the outsourcing trend in the 1990s by pointing at the need for firms to link the various activities in the value chain. It is argued that most value is created at these intersections, as this is the place where firms can differentiate themselves strategically from their competitors (Porter, 1985).

## *Hollowing out*

Another argument that has been brought to bear against outsourcing concerns its effects on the competitive distinctiveness of a firm relative to other firms. Firms that excessively outsource activities are hollowing out their competitive base (Bettis, Bradley, and Hamel, 1992; Kotabe, 1998). Once activities have been outsourced, it tends to become difficult to differentiate a firm's products on the basis of these activities. Furthermore, a firm could lose bargaining power *vis-à-vis* its suppliers because the capabilities of the suppliers increase relative to those of the firm (Bettis, Bradley, and Hamel, 1992). This implies that suppliers can demand better conditions, threaten to enter the outsourcing firm's markets, or even start competing head-on with the firm. Chesbrough and Teece (1996) have elaborated on the strengths and weaknesses of the virtual firm. Virtual firms are characterized by the fact that they do not produce anything internally and do not have any geographically fixed headquarters. The main objection that Chesbrough and Teece raise against this type of firm is that it has little to offer that could provide it with a form of competitive advantage. Porter (2001) has also argued that one of the reasons for the failure of Internet companies is their inability to deliver services that are distinguishable. In other words, the steep fall of these companies' stock prices and the many bankruptcies in the sector in the early 2000s can at least partly be attributed to the fact that they are virtual companies, as being virtual in their case is an indication of a lack of marketable capabilities.

## Opportunistic behavior

A third argument against outsourcing can be drawn from the transaction cost economics literature. External suppliers may behave opportunistically (Williamson, 1975) as their incentive structure differs significantly from that of the outsourcing/buyer firms. Opportunistic behavior helps a supplier to extract greater rents from the relationship than it would normally do, for example by supplying a lower than agreed product quality or withholding information on changes in production costs. These problems imply that firms that outsource need to monitor performance and provide incentives to suppliers to cooperate and share information, which could be a costly affair (Williamson, 1985). Therefore opportunism raises the costs of outsourcing in subtle, less visible ways (Masten, 1993).

## Rising transaction and coordination costs

The management literature has considered the problem of the span of control since at least the work of Fayol (1949), who states that any manager has a limited span of control with regard to his co-workers. Managerial time and capacity is limited and therefore has to be spread among many parties. Surprisingly, this issue has not come up much in academic discussions on sourcing. Firms are limited in their capacity to work with outside suppliers as partners and therefore have to prioritize outside partners. If they simultaneously gave time and attention to all outside suppliers, it would lead to very high coordination costs. Hendry (1995) has brought up the issue of the high coordination costs attached to excessive outsourcing. A similar perspective also appears indirectly in Dyer, Cho, and Chu (1998), who argue that firms need to think of their combined set of suppliers as a portfolio that needs to be segmented by the strategic potential of every relationship. Lying behind this need, then, is the problem of the limited external span of control available to firms managing these supplier relationships.

## Limited learning and innovation

As a fifth and final argument, the difficulty of learning and innovation through outsourcing stands out (Hendry, 1995). If the firm itself does not perform an activity, then how is it able to derive learning from it or to appropriate the innovations that may result from the activity? One form of learning that is deemed especially important for attaining tacit knowledge is learning-by-doing. Perhaps the supplier will acquire such tacit knowledge by performing the activity, but in this case the outsourcing firm is unlikely to be able to appropriate all the benefits. The issue of appropriation of innovation and rents is always a problem in buyer–supplier relationships (Nooteboom, 1999; Teece, 1986) because both parties will try to obtain as many private benefits as possible. Furthermore, it may become more difficult to innovate, given the lack of linkages or interfaces between activities discussed previously. Thus outsourcing may indeed lead to a limited degree of learning and innovation.

## Functional areas

The traditional area of study of make-or-buy decisions is in manufacturing operations. In fact, various cases of outsourcing of manufacturing inputs are now classics of business and management, perhaps none more so than the Fisher Body case. The Fisher Body case is, to the best of my knowledge, the only business case that has ever received the honor of being the topic of a full special issue in a serious academic journal (the *Journal of Law and Economics* in 2000). It certainly is the only case in the realm of make-or-buy decisions for which this is the case. Box 2.1 highlights the controversy over the best explanation for this insourcing decision.

Beyond Fisher Body there have been many other studies of outsourcing of manufacturing activities, including the production of car components (Monteverde and Teece, 1982; Walker and Weber, 1984) and of semiconductors (Leiblein, Reuer, and Dalsace, 2002). Obviously the physical properties of manufactured goods make it somewhat easier to

## Box 2.1. Fisher Body: one decision, two interpretations

In 1926 General Motors fully acquired one of its key suppliers, Fisher Body. The Fisher Brothers supplied body parts for GM cars. The traditional explanation of this insourcing decision, primarily by economists associated with the transaction cost economics framework, is that it was done to reduce so-called holdup problems, whereby Fisher Body could find means to hold GM hostage because of its crucial role in GM's production process (Klein, 2000; Klein, Crawford, and Alchian, 1978). By acquiring Fisher Body, GM could overcome these holdup problems, so these authors argue.

More recently, however, various authors have reinvestigated the Fisher Body acquisition and have come to question the logic assigned to this acquisition. They take issue with the portrayal of facts in the holdup story. In particular, they argue that this was not actually an acquisition but rather an increase in existing ownership by GM from 60 percent to 100 percent. The first 60 percent was purchased in 1919 when the problem described above did not then appear to exist (Casadeus-Masanell and Spulber, 2000). They also claim that there was no actual problem with transport distances and that the notion that the Fisher Brothers would have willingly used inefficient production methods is "not plausible" (Coase, 2000). Finally, they believe the motive for the acquisition was the impending departure of the Fisher brothers from the firm, and argue that while a holdup problem did not exist prior to the acquisition, one was created through the acquisition when the Fisher brothers could impose various conditions on GM under the threat of leaving the firm (Freeland, 2000). In this second interpretation, vertical integration is therefore not a response to the problem of holdup nor are organizations perfectly running machines with no or only marginal transaction costs. Although manufacturing outsourcing has been studied extensively, and is relatively tangible in nature, there are apparently still major differences among economists on how to explain such outsourcing decisions. These can be traced back to different theoretical perspectives and underlying assumptions.

assign values to characteristics like performance, technical change, delivery, and even quantity, that are much harder to measure for services. Furthermore, outsourcing of manufactured components is also typically an interesting decision from an analytical perspective, as various decision outcomes are feasible, though some will turn out to be better than others in retrospect.

There is a large and growing literature on the outsourcing of information technology (IT) activities, that by now probably at least matches the literature on the outsourcing of manufacturing activities. Loh and Venkatraman (1992) trace the initial iconic IT outsourcing deal back to 1989 when Kodak announced an outsourcing deal with IBM/Digital, although they also state some forms of IT outsourcing had been around much longer, as far back as the 1960s. The roots of EDS Revenues, for instance, go back to 1962 and the firm was acquired by General Motors in 1984. Activities that were typically outsourced in the early years include the operation of mainframe computers and the development of applications software. This makes it arguable whether the Kodak outsourcing deal was a landmark or just one further step in the evolution of the IT outsourcing process. Loh and Venkatraman (1992), in their discussion of the "Kodak effect," also show that other firms rapidly followed suit by imitating Kodak's decision. Lacity and Hirschheim (1993; 1995) similarly discussed the notion that IT outsourcing was driven by bandwagoning processes. Earlier work on IT outsourcing often talked about its strategic importance for firms (Huber, 1993; Willcocks and Kern, 1998). Others have studied which areas of IT were most prone to outsourcing, focusing on technological and organizational characteristics, and have looked at a variety of theoretical explanations for the phenomenon (Cheon, Grover, and Teng, 1995; Cronk and Sharp, 1995; Loh and Venkatraman, 1992). In recent times more attention has been paid to the outsourcing process, for instance how firms can obtain bids from suppliers that are low-priced yet lead to a sustainable relationship (Kern, Willcocks, and van Heck, 2002).

The amount of literature on outsourcing in other areas, while not negligible, is much more limited. There is some work on the outsourcing of maintenance, repair, and operations (MRO) activities. People have also written about the outsourcing of marketing and, especially, advertising activities. There is also some literature on the outsourcing of finance and accounting functions. The outsourcing of human resource management activities is another distinct trend, where it is argued that ever more complex and "important" activities are being outsourced. Many firms now outsource not only their payroll administration but also activities like training and recruitment. Two recently discovered areas of outsourcing are purchasing and research and development (R&D). The case of outsourcing purchasing is particularly interesting as it involves the handing of responsibility to an outside party for activities that are already undertaken by another outside party. That raises all kinds of questions on the consequences of such outsourcing, for instance about how specifications and requirements are decided and communicated, which research does not appear to have addressed yet.

Most recently a stream of literature on business process outsourcing (BPO) has started to emerge. Box 2.2 illustrates the variety of ways in which the BPO phenomenon is growing more important.

---

## Box 2.2. A serendipitous BPO provider

When the brothers Edwin and Jurjen Propsma ran into capacity problems with their marketing firm, which provided services like personalized mailings, they considered their options. At the outset all production was undertaken in the Netherlands, much of it by part-timers. These employees were not always available when called upon. Furthermore the production activities were relatively straightforward and the costs of performing them in a high-wage country like the Netherlands could not easily be justified. Because of existing family ties to Romania, they decided to start up a production subsidiary there in late 2004. The transition went particularly smoothly and the Propsma brothers were satisfied with the shift.

Having established themselves in Romania, they were entrepreneurial enough to realize that there was an existing large labor force of well-qualified and eager employees. This made them rethink the reason for their presence in Romania. They decided to diversify the activities of their subsidiary and to turn what was essentially an internal production facility into a service for potential customers. A new legal vehicle, DataMondial, was established in 2005 to provide business process outsourcing services to outside clients. DataMondial focuses strictly on those processes that can be made explicit and for which there is no room for interpretation. It also decided to work with medium-sized clients rather than large ones. In early 2006 DataMondial had some forty full-time employees in

Romania who were successfully providing BPO services to a few clients. This shows that unlike other forms of outsourcing, which are typically dominated by existing suppliers, the BPO market is still very much in development. This is all the more true for services that are provided to customers in non-Anglo-Saxon countries, for which a country like India is not necessarily the most logical or viable destination.

*Source:* Interviews; http://www.datamondial.nl/.

### Industry and country contexts

Given that the car industry and the United States appear to have shaped so much of our thinking on outsourcing, it is useful to investigate to what extent other industries, especially outside manufacturing, and other countries are similar or different. I will first tackle developments in various industries and then look at outsourcing in other countries.

*Industries*

The key change in the banking industry in recent decades has been the introduction of new information technologies, including, in recent years, those based on the Internet. It is therefore unsurprising that banks have been strongly associated with IT outsourcing. Huber (1993) documented the monumental shift in thinking that took place at Continental Bank but that spread equally elsewhere. In the 1980s banks built up substantial IT departments, including many programmers, in a belief that IT was a strategic asset and that IT systems therefore needed to be built in-house. Over the 1990s most banks realized that IT was increasingly becoming a commodity and that off-the-shelf software could be sourced at much lower costs from outside suppliers. There was also a generational gap between internal IT departments and their software products and external suppliers and their off-the-shelf software. As a consequence off-the-shelf software, though it had not been written to purpose, often outperformed "legacy software" developed internally. As evidenced by the Oxford Metrica report cited in chapter 1, the financial services industry has now taken this outsourcing thinking a step beyond just IT and concluded that outsourcing of a wide range of activities could be beneficial.

Leiblein, Reuer, and Dalsace (2002) discuss important trends in the semiconductors industry. They suggest that some firms are increasingly choosing to outsource manufacturing activities while holding on to design activities. In our own work on almost 8,000 manufacturing firms in the Netherlands (Mol, Schreuder, and Goedegebuure, 2001) we looked at the three broad types of manufacturing industries proposed by Woodward (1965), namely small-batch industries, process industries, and large-batch/mass production industries. We demonstrated that of these three types, process industries, with their heavy reliance on inputs in the form of raw materials, displayed the highest absolute outsourcing levels throughout the 1990s, as measured by external sourcing divided by turnover. Large-batch/mass production industries came second, while small-batch industries, which are characterized primarily by high levels of manual labor, outsourced least. When, however, we looked at the outsourcing process, the trend was different. Large-batch/mass production industries started to outsource many more activities during the period between 1993 and 1998, while the other two types of industry also raised outsourcing levels but did so much more slowly. In the Netherlands large-batch/mass production industries, which can alternatively be referred to as assembly industries (Kotabe, 1998), include electronics, cars and car components, and bicycles. In other work (Mol, van Tulder, and Beije, 2005) we showed that these same industries are also less likely to use international sourcing because of the complications of coordinating supply chains across borders in these industries.

## Countries

Unlike what some outside observers of the Japanese contracting system have concluded, firms in Japan at present do not seem to outsource as much as their American counterparts (Kotabe, 1998) and they still differ in the way they outsource (Dyer, Cho, and Chu, 1998; Helper and Sako, 1995). Moreover, Japanese firms appear to be much more concerned than their American counterparts about the potential loss of knowledge and competitive advantage associated with outsourcing (Kotabe, 1998). Where they do outsource, Japanese firms generally prefer the "strategic sourcing" approach (Nishiguchi, 1994), involving more information exchange with suppliers, cooperation, and perhaps parallel sourcing (Dyer and Nobeoka, 2000; Richardson, 1993).

In France, outsourcing appears to have taken a slower pace than elsewhere. For instance, Dragonetti, Dalsace, and Cool (2003) report on a sample of firms which outsource only 10 percent of their sales, with outsourcing defined as all activities that have ever been transferred to outside suppliers, whether this occurred recently or some time ago. However, Barthélemy and Geyer (2001) report in a study of IT outsourcing in France and Germany that French firms were slightly more likely to engage in outsourcing than their German counterparts and that, in addition, outsourcing more often involved the transfer of assets and people for them. In Germany, research conducted at the Fraunhofer Institute (Kinkel and Lay, 2003) among German manufacturing firms revealed sharp increases in outsourcing levels as well as an intention to increase these levels further. The report also notes that German firms have some way to go, coming from relatively high levels of vertical integration, with internal production accounting for 62 percent of all value even in IT in 2001 and higher percentages still in other areas. Kinkel and Lay further point at the negative effect that outsourcing appeared to have in Germany on innovation, flexibility, and resilience although the impact on costs and capacity was positive. These findings are reflective of, and perhaps help explain, the unwillingness of German firms to engage in outsourcing.

McCarthy and Anagnostou (2004) document the large increases in outsourcing levels among manufacturing firms in the United Kingdom. They also link increased outsourcing to the supposed demise of the manufacturing sector in the UK by showing how outsourced activities tend to crop up in other parts of the economy in official statistics. Hence, manufacturing actually plays a larger role than such statistics suggest. Other research on the UK has focused on the development of tools for managing outsourcing. Tayles and Drury (2001) for instance offer a decision-making diagram that helps firms decide when to outsource. Willcocks and Kern (1998) discuss how IT outsourcing relations are moving towards partnerships and how to shape such relations. For Italy, Bonazzi and Antonelli (2003) also report a trend towards more outsourcing, specifically for Fiat. In Italy, the outsourcing trend is encapsulated in the well-known industrial districts, implying most outsourcing takes place within the confines of these districts.

Our own work on the Netherlands (Mol, 2001; 2005; de Wit, Mol, and van Drunen, 1998) shows that the outsourcing discourse there took on a shape quite similar to that in the United States. Partly this was due to a direct influence through translations of articles like that of Quinn and Hilmer (1994). Outsourcing levels in manufacturing industries rose rapidly in the Netherlands over the 1990s (Mol, 2005) but outsourcing extended far beyond manufacturing to include areas like IT and engineering. Other colleagues have documented the trend towards developing partnership relations with suppliers in an effort to increase innovation (Nooteboom, 1998; Wynstra and Weggeman 2001). For Denmark, Pyndt and Pedersen (2006) have documented the outsourcing trend, especially how global sourcing is becoming ever more pervasive.

## Conceptual perspectives

A variety of conceptual lenses have been applied to outsourcing. For each of these I will briefly discuss the underlying concept and in some cases touch upon empirical findings. Any division between conceptual perspectives contains a degree of arbitrariness and some authors may simultaneously belong to other perspectives.

### *Transaction cost economics*

Among the conceptual perspectives applied to the study of outsourcing, one stands out from the crowd because of its frequent application, the relatively strong empirical support for some of its hypotheses, and its contentiousness. Transaction cost economics (TCE, see Coase, 1937; Williamson, 1975) is concerned with the boundaries of the firm and the make-or-buy decision is probably its hallmark application (Williamson, 1991a). Although there have been multiple interpretations of what transaction costs are and how they influence firm behavior (Buckley and Casson, 1976; Coase 1937; Rugman, 1981), the most widely cited and critiqued framework, particularly in the outsourcing area, is that of Oliver Williamson (1975; 1981; 1985; 1991a; 1991b). Williamson maintains that any economic transaction can be characterized by two types of cost. First, there are the costs of producing a service or component. These production costs are generally lower in markets than they are in organizations because the allocative efficiencies of markets will produce some inter-firm division of labor. Second, Williamson distinguishes transaction costs, which have usefully been defined by Arrow (1974) as "the costs of running the economy." Transaction costs are therefore very broad in scope, even to the extent of being something of a container category. Transaction costs are usually higher in markets because of the need to use a variety of monitoring mechanisms, in order to counterbalance the possibility that opportunism may arise. Hence outsourcing decisions are essentially a balancing act between the benefits of markets, lower production costs, and their costs, in the form of higher transaction costs.

Since Williamson's theory uses the market as the default mode of a transaction, often referred to as governance structure by Williamson (1995), it aims to explain when and why markets fail. Only under conditions of market failure will firms revert to internalization (the make option). Williamson (1981) then suggests the likelihood of market failure hinges upon the presence of three or four conditions and the interaction between two of these. Markets are said to fail when the assets required to produce a service or component are highly specific to that component or service, i.e. when the opportunities for redeploying these assets in other settings are limited or non-existent. If asset specificity is high, the price at which a supplier will be willing to engage in that transaction will be exorbitant because the supplier lacks opportunities to employ these assets differently should the contract end or go awry.

The second condition is volume uncertainty. When there is uncertainty over the business conditions surrounding a transaction, it will be equally difficult to find a supplier that is willing to invest in that transaction, as the supplier needs to deal with costly demand shocks. In earlier formulations of his argument (Williamson, 1981) a similar role was attributed to technological uncertainty but Williamson (1995) later retracted that, partly in the face of empirical evidence to the contrary (e.g. Walker and Weber, 1984). Technological uncertainty is now said to play no significant role in determining outsourcing levels. A further complication is the interaction that is said to exist between uncertainty and asset specificity. Some interpretations of the transaction cost argument go so far as to say that uncertainty has no direct effect but only affects outsourcing decisions when it occurs simultaneously with asset specificity. This is what David and Han (2004) found in their meta-analytical study of transaction cost articles. A more recent meta-analytical study seems to counter this finding though, and stresses direct effects over interactions (Geyskens, Steenkamp, and Kumar, forthcoming).

A third variable influencing outsourcing decisions according to Williamson (1981) is the frequency with which a transaction recurs. When a transaction is rare, there is little sense in setting up productive capacity in-house. The Olympic Games come to mind as a one-off event for which it is preferable to contract out almost all activities. When, on the contrary, a service or component is required more or less continuously and for the foreseeable future, integration makes more sense. A fourth variable, though one that has only received scant attention in empirical tests of transaction costs is ease of measurement. Barzel (1982) suggests that the easier it is to monitor the behavior of suppliers, the more likely it is that outsourcing will occur.

## Resource-based view

In the 1990s a new perspective on strategic management was presented, in the form of the resource-based view (RBV), which takes internal strengths and weaknesses as the starting point for an analysis of firms' competitive strategies (Barney, 1991; Wernerfelt, 1984). This perspective holds that competitive advantage is a function of the extent to which the resources controlled by the firm are valuable, rare, inimitable, and hard to substitute (Barney, 1991). The RBV predicts that firms sitting on a rich resource base may internalize an activity without losing competitiveness, as the relative advantages of outsourcing to independent suppliers are small. For those firms that are less well prepared internally, outsourcing may be more viable and necessary although it has been noted that outsourcing is not a problem-solver (Lacity and Hirschheim 1995). If a firm is not able to solve a problem, it may also be unable to solve it in conjunction with a supplier (Doig, Ritter, Speckhals, and Woolson, 2001). A perspective somewhat related to the resource-based view is that of dynamic capabilities. A dynamic capability is "the firm's ability to integrate, build, and reconfigure internal and external competences to address rapidly changing environments" (Teece, Pisano, and Shuen 1997: 516). In a firm where such capabilities are present there is reason for integrating activities into the firm. Thus having numerous and strong resources and capabilities that are needed for an activity reduces the likelihood the activity will be outsourced (Barney 1999; Leiblein and Miller 2003). Obviously the most relevant comparison in determining how many capabilities a firm has for an activity is with its potential suppliers, not with competing firms.

## Core competences

A more practitioner-oriented, and probably less theoretically grounded, perspective is that of core competences. The core competence approach shares many assumptions and ideas with the resource-based view of the firm but has taken on a different role in the outsourcing discourse and thus warrants separate treatment here. Since I have already discussed the core competence perspective in chapter 1 and will return to it in some detail in chapter 7, I will only briefly summarize it here. The core competence approach was developed by Hamel and Prahalad (Hamel and Prahalad, 1994; Prahalad and Hamel, 1990). They essentially argued that firms build their competitive advantage around a set of core competences, such as miniaturization in the case of Sony. Once these core competences have been established, firms should build their activities around them in order to exploit them as much as possible. The core competence argument has been applied to outsourcing by Quinn (Quinn, 1992; Quinn and Hilmer, 1994), who argues that firms ought to outsource non-core activities to best-in-world suppliers.

## Micro-economics

Another perspective on outsourcing that has developed in recent years is micro-economics. Current work in this area is primarily focused on the application of micro-economic models to firm returns and efficiency analysis (Grossman and Helpman, 2002; Shy and Stenbacka, 2003), including the recent development of Cournot models (Mol and Vermeulen, 2003; Nickerson and Vandenbergh, 1999; Shy and Stenbacka, 2005). These models mostly look into the effect of existing competition on outsourcing, the subsequent effect of outsourcing on competition and prices, and the resulting surpluses for consumers and producers. They show outsourcing is most useful in the context of commodity markets and has the effect of strengthening price-based competition (Cachon and Harker, 2002) since external suppliers are more likely to provide standardized solutions, reducing the possibilities for successful differentiation from competitors. Although these models are useful illustrations of basic arguments, for instance that outsourcing levels will tend to be higher when there is much competition between firms (Cachon and Harker, 2002), they do not provide much detail on how this process takes place or real empirical data that exemplify the arguments.

## Industrial organization

In the industrial organization (IO) and "positioning" tradition (Porter, 1980; 1985), outsourcing has not been tackled very often, but its counterpart of vertical integration has received much attention. IO scholars have traditionally been rather skeptical about the potential benefits of outsourcing. In this tradition, vertical integration is usually associated with the presence of scale advantages (Harrigan, 1986; Stigler, 1951) or is seen as a means to increase bargaining power (Porter, 1980). Harrigan (1986) developed the notion of "taper integration" to capture part-integrated, part-outsourced components and services. According to Harrigan, integration levels depend on factors such as demand and infrastructure uncertainty, industry volatility, bargaining power, and corporate strategy needs. More recently, Porter (1997) has argued that outsourcing, while being a popular solution, is sometimes chosen a little too rashly. Porter (1985; 1997) has always stressed the importance of the interfaces between activities in the value creation process (see also Kotabe, 1992). Outsourcing tends to make it harder, and sometimes altogether impossible, to exploit these interfaces between activities as the activities are organizationally, and often physically, decoupled.

## Agency theory

Another well-known perspective in organizational economics is agency theory (Jensen and Meckling, 1976). In outsourcing, agency theory has been used to sketch the relations between the outsourcing firm and its supplier. It has been argued that the outsourcing firm can be seen as the principal who commissions an assignment from the agent, the supplier (Milgrom and Roberts, 1992). Thus outsourcing can be studied as a problem of aligning the interests of the outsourcing firm and its supplier. The central thesis of the problem is that outsourcing becomes more feasible if contracts allow for the alignment of interests. When interests remain misaligned, vertical integration is a better option. Because agency theory's focus is on relations between owners and employees (Jensen and Meckling, 1976), though, it also details the problems associated with such vertical integration, specifically how employment contracts inside firms ought to be set up.

## Real options

A relatively recent addition to the list of perspectives on strategic management is that of real options (Kogut and Kulatilaka, 1994). Its proponents argue that a firm's strategic choices can be couched as real options to undertake some future action, much as financial options provide the owner with the right to buy or sell a financial asset at some point in the future. Kogut and Kulatilaka (1994), for instance, view the decision to build identical plants in two countries as a real option that provides the right to transfer production between these sites, in case of currency fluctuations, political turmoil, or other forms of uncertainty. In the context of outsourcing, Leiblein and Miller (2003; see also Leiblein, 2003) have suggested that the make-or-buy decision can also be framed as a real option, where outsourcing and vertical integration are undertaken to create a platform for future investments and strategizing. The larger the uncertainty surrounding decision-making, the more valuable such options will become. According to Leiblein and Miller (2003) two chief forms of uncertainty are in technologies and product demand.

## Institutional voids

An approach that primarily draws upon national institutions to explain firm behavior is the institutional voids framework (Delios and Henisz, 2003; Khanna and Palepu, 2000; Toulan, 2002). Institutional voids can be understood as gaps in a country's institutional provision. Such gaps force firms to adapt their behavior in ways that they would otherwise not have pursued. Its primary thesis in the context of outsourcing is that the greater the number of institutional voids, and the more serious these voids are, the more firms will tend to integrate activities vertically (Khanna and Palepu, 2000). An example would be a regime with insufficient provision of property rights, which leads to vertical integration (Teece, 1986). Because institutional voids undermine the effectiveness of markets, they increase the transaction costs (Williamson, 1985) associated with outsourcing. They therefore make strategies of diversification, including unrelated diversification, and vertical integration more feasible (Khanna and Palepu, 2000). As a consequence, emerging countries often feature more business groups operating in diverse industries, such as India's Tata, a well-known conglomerate with activities as varied as consulting, automobile production, and now BPO provision. It is also argued that as the level of institutional voids decreases, so the level of outsourcing increases (Toulan, 2002). The gradual break-up of Korea's *chaebols*, and to some extent Japan's *keiretsus* as well, is often cited as evidence that if a country develops economically and its level of institutional voids decreases, the viability of business groups is undermined. The institutional voids framework therefore provides a useful basis for a cross-national comparison of outsourcing levels.

## Costly contracting

Grossman and Hart (1986) elaborate on a theory of costly contracts. Their argument is that vertical integration occurs when it is costly to write complete contracts, and more specifically when specific rights cannot be assigned to either party (buyer or supplier). Grossman and Hart propose that it is important to understand the benefits of organizing transactions inside firms and that transaction cost economics, while being helpful in specifying the costs of the marketplace, does not spell out such benefits of organizations. The main benefit of organizations (integration) is the fact that contractual specification of specific rights is no longer necessary. Their main conclusion is that integration is optimal when one firm's investment decision is relatively important compared to that of another firm, in which case the former firm will choose to integrate or acquire the latter firm. If both parties' decisions are more or less equally important, they will not integrate.

## Relations and learning

Another perspective stresses the importance of relations with suppliers, specifically how firms can learn from these (Dragonetti, Dalsace, and Cool, 2003; Lane, 2001). These authors argue that there may be complementarities between outsourcing firms and their suppliers, an argument also proposed by others (e.g. Dyer and Singh, 1998), and that outsourcing is motivated by a desire to draw upon such complementarities to learn new capabilities inside the outsourcing firm. Firms' supplier networks hence form an important source of learning (Lane, 2001; Lorenzoni and Lipparini, 1999). Through outsourcing, firms can transfer some of the investments in new knowledge, while reaping the benefits of this knowledge. Brusoni, Prencipe, and Pavitt (2001) perhaps best summarized this view, when they talked about "why firms know more than they make." Brusoni, Prencipe, and Pavitt (2001) convincingly make the case that, especially in industries where products are not simply the sum of their underlying components, like in their case of airplane engines, firms can outsource many activities without falling foul of the well-known hollowing-out problem (Bettis, Bradley, and Hamel, 1992). The relations and learning perspective also makes the point that under conditions of high uncertainty, particularly technological uncertainty, it makes more sense to outsource (Dragonetti, Dalsace, and Cool, 2003; Gulati, 1995) since it allows firms to disengage from the risk of betting on the wrong new standards and technologies (Afuah, 2001).

## Social networks

The literature on social networks has perhaps touched upon outsourcing only indirectly but it still contains some lessons of interest for the study of outsourcing. One of the points of departure of this literature is that markets are not as prominent as standard economic theory would want us to believe (Richardson, 1972) and that it is actually better to think of markets as "islands in a sea of firms" (Simon, 1991) than vice versa. Another point that has been made is that economic approaches, particularly transaction cost economics, tend to hold an undersocialized view of markets and an oversocialized view of firms (Granovetter, 1985), which leads these approaches to attribute powers to markets and solution mechanisms to firms they may not actually have. The social networks response is to argue that relationships between firms and their suppliers are "embedded" in wider inter-firm networks (Granovetter, 1985; Uzzi, 1996; 1997). Such embedded relationships may produce positive performance effects over market-like, arm's length relationships, because they can draw upon additional resources, are built upon shared conventions, allow for building of trust, and expedite search processes (Uzzi, 1997). For outsourcing, the (indirect) implication would seem to be that when firms and their suppliers are well embedded, the relative advantages of outsourcing over vertical integration increase.

## Different perspectives?

At first sight these perspectives appear to differ significantly from one another. Yet one can easily link some of them. TCE and RBV considerations, for instance, appear to strengthen one another (Leiblein and Miller, 2003; Williamson, 1999) and recent literature has started to integrate RBV, knowledge, and competence considerations into outsourcing decisions (Barney, 1999; Leiblein and Miller, 2003; Poppo and Zenger, 1998) in addition to transaction cost reasoning. Broadly speaking, one can argue that most of these approaches fall under the header of *economizing*, a term proposed by Williamson (1991a) to describe a perspective that predicts governance modes are chosen in the pursuit of efficiency. Williamson (1991a) contrasts this term with *strategizing*, which he uses to refer to the industrial organization perspective of Porter, Harrigan, and others that presents the attainment of a strong market position and associated bargaining power and monopoly rents as key objectives. Yet both strategizing and economizing are micro-economics perspectives, differing in how they view outsourcing as an economic process, but not in whether or to what extent they consider outsourcing to be an economic process. Of the above, perhaps only the networks and relationships/learning approaches can be said to differ substantially from the micro-economic view.

## A critique

This overview has shown there is at present a clear preference in the literature for the micro-economic view of outsourcing, most prominently by the application of transaction cost economics but also through a range of other approaches. This raises two questions in particular: (1) What have we learned by using the micro-economic view? (2) Does its predominance stand in the way of uncovering other interesting and practical knowledge of the outsourcing phenomenon. As I will argue below, the short answer to the first question is: much. The short answer to the second question is even shorter: yes.

TCE has been shown to provide a reasonably powerful explanation of make-or-buy decisions in a wide range of studies (David and Han, 2004; Geyskens, Steenkamp, and Kumar, forthcoming). It is now recognized widely enough in the scholarly community to provide some shared understanding of the mechanisms through which asset

specificity, uncertainty, and frequency are believed to influence outsourcing levels, and how misalignment between these factors and outsourcing levels can undermine performance.

As such the dispute is not centered on whether or not TCE provides
some explanation for outsourcing levels but more on (1) whether the
causal mechanisms it applies and the behavioral assumptions it makes
while doing so are valid; (2) whether additional variance can be
explained outside of the TCE framework; and (3) whether the TCE
framework is over time becoming less relevant empirically.

The first issue has been dealt with at length by a variety of authors.
Granovetter's (1985) contribution is perhaps best known since it
attacks not just TCE but all of micro-economics. Granovetter argued
that economists hold an undersocialized view of markets and treat
actors in markets as mostly anonymous in nature, whereas in reality
there are important social mechanisms in any type of market.[3] Ghoshal
and Moran (1996) extensively critiqued the behavioral assumptions
underlying the TCE framework, especially the starting assumption that
because others can be opportunistic any contract design ought to
depart from the possibility that opportunistic behavior will occur.
There is further criticism of TCE's notion of "self-interest-seeking
with guile," which can be extended to economic theories of organization in general, because it presumes a more self-centered view of
individuals than may be warranted (Ghoshal, 2005). The counter-
argument in particular is that individuals, including managers, are
at least as social and cooperative as they are self-interest-seeking
(Ghoshal, 2005). But criticism of TCE has also come from within the
economics profession. Simon (1991) argued that the modern economy
is anything but a market but rather represents a sea of organizations,
connected to other organizations in various ways, thereby echoing
Richardson's (1972) point. Thus economics, and TCE in particular,
should not assume that the market is the default option.

The second issue concerns extensions beyond TCE that authors have
deemed necessary and fruitful. Barney (1999), in making the case for a
capabilities-based view of boundary decisions, pointed at the difficulty

---

[3] One could, at present, perhaps make an argument that some of the literature that
followed Granovetter (1985) equally has a blind spot for anything that cannot be
fitted under the network or embeddedness header, thereby largely ignoring managerial agency, intra-organizational aspects, and the role of supply and demand in
the creation of networks.

of analyzing highly dynamic industries through a TCE lens. Holmström and Roberts (1998) discussed a series of empirical observations that neither TCE nor Grossman and Hart's (1986) contracting perspective was able to explain. Kogut and Zander (1992) proposed that additional explanatory value could be obtained by looking at the positive aspects of organizations, in particular their ability to leverage the internal knowledge base, rather than just the possible deficiencies of markets. By failing to analyze organizations and their value-adding processes seriously, TCE does not do sufficient justice to this alternative to the market (Kogut and Zander, 1992). All of these extensions claim to be able to pinpoint additional variance in outsourcing decisions.

The third issue revolves around the extent to which TCE logic is being outpaced by developments in the real world of firms and managers. Williamson himself (1995) retracted earlier arguments on the role of technological uncertainty, which was previously assumed to lead to less outsourcing. Moreover, Quinn, Baruch, and Zien (1997) have argued that under conditions of rapid technological change it is much better to seek outside suppliers, as has Afuah (2001). Some doubt has also been cast on the role of asset specificity, since high-trust supplier relations can also be characterized by high levels of asset specificity (Dyer and Singh, 1998; Gulati, 1995). In recent work (Mol, 2005) I found that R&D intensity, which in IO accounts (Harrigan, 1986; Porter, 1980) and to some extent also in TCE (Teece, 1986; Williamson, 1985: 141–144) is associated with vertical integration, was no longer a negative predictor for outsourcing and appeared to have become a positive predictor. In all, this seems to suggest that some of the predictions put forward by TCE may have fitted better in the slow-moving world of the 1970s, populated by large and vertically integrated firms, than they do in today's world of nimbler and more dynamic firms which increasingly rely on outside network partners to produce value-added, and for which industry boundaries become increasingly blurred.

Since my intention is not to provide an extensive critique of economics or any branch of it (in fact I will be partly building on it in the next chapter), I will take a pragmatic and not a normative stance on TCE and other economics approaches and assume that despite the shortcomings discussed above, we can learn something from their application, though clearly not everything we need. This leads us, however, to a much more fundamental concern over how the outsourcing literature has developed over time. Because of the dominance of one particular explanation (transaction cost economics), other explanations have not gained as much currency as they should have, as TCE is always used as the yardstick. Ironically, this is particularly true in the management area and perhaps less so in economics, where Williamson's TCE forms but one branch of explanation. In leading management journals it is quite impossible to present an argument on outsourcing without invoking the TCE framework. Those who do use other approaches (e.g. Leiblein, 2003; Leiblein and Miller, 2003; Poppo and Zenger, 1998) always use TCE as their default explanation. If TCE indeed provided the perfect explanation of outsourcing, this would be unproblematic. Unfortunately, it does not. If we can safely assume that TCE explains 30 percent of the variance in outsourcing behavior, a number that has been thrown up by some of its proponents, that leaves 70 percent unaccounted for and creates a pressing need to allow for alternative explanations that build from different sets of assumptions. Furthermore, analyses of outsourcing have tended to focus particularly on make-or-buy issues, as this is the domain of TCE, at the expense of process accounts of outsourcing.

## The social costs and benefits of outsourcing

In chapter 1 the social effects of outsourcing were briefly discussed. None of the conceptual lenses discussed above makes much mention of the social costs and benefits of outsourcing decisions. Such costs come about because outsourcing may involve the transfer and physical moving about of employees, the need to outplace them or the payment of release costs when people are fired as part of outsourcing decisions. Practical experience indicates such costs may be substantial. Moreover, there may be not only direct costs like these but also indirect costs, for instance in the form of a drop in motivation of the remaining employees. The frameworks mentioned above do not look at such costs explicitly, though it might be argued that they present either "switching costs" or "transaction costs" in some frameworks. This is clearly something of an omission.

I am not aware of studies that specifically tackle the social costs of outsourcing but some broad generalizations may hold true. First, the decision to start outsourcing an activity, i.e. to engage in an outsourcing process, will invariably produce social costs. Second, such costs decrease the relative benefits of outsourcing, and hence are likely to act as either a brake on or a deterrent to outsourcing. Thus, because social costs are present, firms will either delay a decision to outsource an activity or avoid such a decision altogether. In other words, the social costs of outsourcing may be producing resistance to outsourcing. Third, social costs will depend heavily on the context in which the firm operates. Some key variables that likely increase social costs are the nature of laws around employment and dismissal, the enforcement of such laws, the presence and strength of labor unions, the openness of the economy, and the behavior of similar firms. The larger the social costs associated with outsourcing, the lower one would expect outsourcing levels to be, other things being equal.

At the same time, outsourcing can also be said to produce societal benefits, in so far as it produces more efficient forms of organizing. Since the prime growth engine of capitalist societies is innovation (Baumol, 2002), innovation in organizational forms contributes substantially to economic growth (Birkinshaw, Hamel, and Mol, 2005; Teece 1980). Hence outsourcing may be a necessity if a country wishes to keep up with other countries. Of course, it is questionable whether more outsourcing always leads to more efficient forms of organizing, as will be discussed in the next few chapters.

## Conclusion

I conclude this chapter by noting that a rich but fragmented literature has been developed on various forms of outsourcing and to some extent also in a variety of industry and country contexts. There are also various theoretical explanations of outsourcing in use, though one (transaction cost economics) has figured far more prominently than others. In the next chapter, I will address the issue of how we can make sense of this fragmented knowledge-base and the apparent contradictions in current literature, focusing on applying the various pieces of knowledge to the question how outsourcing is related to firm performance.

# 3 | A *new perspective*

I F the present state of the literature teaches us anything, it must be that there is a variety of activities that can be outsourced. The challenge I will set myself in this chapter is to find a common denominator for the outsourcing of various activities, by focusing on the shared space, or relatedness, between them and providing a perspective that helps to discern how the outsourcing of various activities has an impact on overall firm performance. I will start this chapter by identifying what I believe to be a major weakness of the outsourcing literature, its inability to predict performance at the firm level based on overall outsourcing levels. I will then propose the construct of "outsourceability," defined as the degree to which it is beneficial to outsource a given activity. Since there are differing degrees of outsourceability across activities, it makes sense to outsource some of these activities while integrating others into the firm. Firms that get all their outsourcing decisions right are in a sense optimizing their performance. It will be shown that deviations from this optimum are costly, in such a way that at the firm level the outsourcing–performance relation takes on a negative curvilinear shape. Finally I will discuss some empirical and practical evidence to support this new, negative curvilinear perspective.

## Why a new perspective is needed

There are broadly three groups of puzzles that can act as motivators for the creation of a new perspective on outsourcing and firm performance. These are, respectively, practical, theoretical, and methodological puzzles. I see the practical puzzles as crucial in raising the theoretical puzzles, for what is the value of a theory in management studies that does not reflect practical decision-making, and will therefore discuss them conjointly before proceeding with the methodological issues. From a practitioner's perspective a large range of questions can be raised on outsourcing. How many activities should I outsource? Which activities should I outsource? How does the number of activities to be outsourced change over time? When should an outsourcing process be initiated? From which suppliers should I outsource these activities? What relational investments should I make in these suppliers? How often and when should I contemplate outsourcing levels? To which locations should I outsource these activities? How should I internally manage outsourcing? How will various stakeholder groups respond to outsourcing? How should I measure and evaluate the results of my outsourcing strategy? How do I deal with the positive and negative feedback that outsourcing may generate among my organization's constituents? How do I minimize the social adjustment costs associated with outsourcing? What is the best way of managing the outsourcing process? How does the nature of the decision-maker affect outsourcing outcomes? How does previous outsourcing decision-making affect my present set of choices? How can I use outsourcing to change the industry's rules of the game?

As discussed in the previous chapter, the academic literature is at present quite strong in explaining some of these questions, particularly the question of which activities are best outsourced and which are best integrated. Relatively elegant theories have been designed to explain the outsourcing phenomenon. However, the literature ignores many of the other questions, particularly those that are not easily addressed from a micro-economic perspective. As a consequence the academic response to the set of questions practitioners deal with is unnecessarily restricted. Some of these questions are better addressed using socio-logical, psychological, historical, political, or managerial perspectives. But an overall approach to outsourcing that includes such perspectives is missing. Such an approach should obviously build upon micro-economic models and theories but ought not to be restricted to these. Hence this perspective has to be newly created and somewhat eclectic and pragmatic in its selection of inputs.

Another way to approach this issue is to look at strategic management as a field of study, and at organization theory more generally as well, and wonder how much of the knowledge generated in that field has been applied to outsourcing. Boundary decisions are firmly within the domain of strategic management, as discussions in the field on the theory of the firm appear to claim (Barney, 1999; Foss, 1999; Teece, Pisano, and Shuen, 1997; Williamson, 1991a), because it is generally believed there is some type of (sustainable) competitive advantage that firms can obtain from making such decisions. But of the many approaches to strategy (Mintzberg, Ahlstrand, and Lampel, 1998) only a small minority appear to have been applied to outsourcing issues with any regularity. And of the wide variety of approaches mentioned in the *Handbook of Organization Studies* (Clegg, Hardy, and Nord, 1996), how many have been brought to bear upon aspects of outsourcing? In other words, perhaps it is time to stop treating outsourcing as strictly an *economizing* (Williamson, 1991a) phenomenon and to start looking at outsourcing as also an organizational phenomenon. Although it is undoubtedly in part an economizing phenomenon, the set of questions that practitioners can raise extends far beyond economizing and governance decisions, and so should the set of theories academics use to investigate the phenomenon. Through this book I hope to make some small contribution to this cause.

Short of inventing an entire new theory two routes are possible for making such a contribution. One is to look at problems to which no theoretical solution has as yet been found. The managerial questions above serve as a list of such problems. Though some of these questions have been tackled in the literature, others have not. The second route is to look at existing theoretical solutions that have not previously been applied to the problem area. In other words, are there ideas and theories out there that have proven their usefulness in other areas but not yet in outsourcing? By matching problems with solutions (Cohen, March, and Olsen, 1972) innovative combinations may be obtained (Hargadon, 2002) that could potentially help to shed more light on the outsourcing phenomenon.

From a methodological perspective the great majority of the many previous tests on outsourcing and performance levels in the literature (Capon, Farley, and Hoenig, 1990; D'Aveni and Ravenscraft, 1994; Gilley and Rasheed, 2000; Murray, Kotabe, and Wildt, 1995; Leiblein, Reuer, and Dalsace, 2002) can be improved upon, for one of three reasons or a combination of these. First, quite a large part of the literature uses performance effects of a single transaction or a single activity to abstract to the outsourcing–performance relation in general. Hence it presupposes that what applies to the use of third-party logistics, for instance that this type of outsourcing improves the performance of supermarkets in the United Kingdom, applies equally well to the decision to outsource part of the R&D function by pharmaceutical firms based in

Switzerland. Clearly those types of generalization place researchers in rather dangerous territory unless they have a clear theory to support them. Since most of the literature is indeed concerned with only one activity or one set of activities, any performance findings and normative implications based on these are barely useful both from the perspective of the practitioner and from the perspective of theorizing on outsourcing and performance. Thus authors of these studies face a choice between two evils. They can claim universal validity, based on reference to an underlying theory, without actually having tested whether what they find for one activity simultaneously holds for other activities, even within the same firm. Or they can decide not to claim universal validity, implying their findings only speak to their specific empirical context.

Second, these studies test for linear effects of outsourcing on performance. Unless one specifies a range in which such linear effects hold, which authors generally do not seem to do, this amounts to a test of whether firms should outsource everything, when the effect is positive, because more outsourcing is going to lead to higher performance, or alternatively integrate everything, when the effect is negative. This is clearly a rather crude way of thinking about outsourcing, particularly if one generalizes to all of a firm's activities, as it would imply that a firm ought to be either an empty shell or fully integrated. It is also by definition incorrect since it is legally impossible to integrate all activities and logically impossible to outsource all activities (Mol and Vermeulen, 2003). The use of accountants to certify financial statements comes to mind as an area where integration is not allowed.[1] A firm that outsources all of its activities, a virtual firm in the truest sense of the word, has no decision-making center left to take such outsourcing decisions. Being truly virtual, as in fully outsourced, is therefore a logical impossibility. Hence there is both a lower limit to outsourcing that is higher than 0 percent of all activities that are needed to produce a firm's products and services and an upper limit that is lower than 100 percent of all activities. In other words, firms can strictly speaking never outsource all their activities, nor can they integrate all activities.

Third, most of the literature in this area uses cross-sectional data to undertake tests of performance. In other words, scholars examine whether today's outsourcing levels are somehow related to today's

[1] The link between Enron and Arthur Andersen illustrates that quasi-integration of accountants is not such a great idea either.

performance levels. That, however, neglects the very real possibility that it may take time for outsourcing levels and outsourcing processes to run their course. As various cases in this book show, some costs and benefits of outsourcing may emerge long after an initial decision is taken. There can be learning effects involved both on the production costs side, for instance because the supplier needs to train its employees, and on the transaction costs side, because trust between outsourcer and supplier is built over time. Similarly, increases in production costs and, especially, transaction costs can take time to come into effect. What is needed to test whether outsourcing affects performance is therefore not a cross-sectional test but some type of longitudinal test.

In all, there are therefore serious methodological problems with most of the current literature on outsourcing, although I would rate the third problem, which is caused by limited data availability rather than faulty conceptualization or testing, to be perhaps less of an evil than the first two. Combining this observation with the earlier discussion of the practical and theoretical puzzles, it seems that a new perspective on outsourcing and the performance of firms is needed because current research neither covers the entire range of relevant research questions nor uses a tool-set that is truly appropriate for the questions it does seek to answer.

## Outsourceability

I start building the perspective from the notion that activities differ from one another primarily, but not exclusively, along the lines of the various strands of literature discussed in chapter 2. Thus there are different degrees of asset specificity among activities. For a car rental firm like Avis, for instance, the cars it rents out may represent relatively low asset specificity as they have many alternative uses outside of Avis, whereas the information system it uses has a high degree of asset specificity because it was purpose-built. Similarly a firm's specific resource-based advantages will have a larger bearing on some activities than on others. If a bank is good at business concept innovation, because of in-house resources like a good marketer, this will increase the effectiveness of its marketing function but may not do much for purchasing. Thus different activities are more or less amenable to outsourcing. I capture such differences through the term *outsourceability*. The outsourceability of an activity is *the degree to which it is beneficial to outsource that activity*. Box 3.1 provides some illustrations of this concept.

## Box 3.1. Outsourceability: many variants

An activity can vary on the outsourceability dimension from very low to very high. For instance, most Western organizations would not, and should not from a performance point of view, integrate the construction of their offices. Perhaps a construction firm might choose to construct its own offices, but it would make little sense for a consulting firm, university, or manufacturer of watches to do so. The employees of a bank have little or no knowledge of construction and there is a wealth of potential suppliers who could help out. Such an activity has a very high outsourceability for these firms. Another example of very high outsourceability is the production of electricity, which firms gladly leave to utility companies. At the other end of the spectrum, it would certainly raise eyebrows if a firm chose permanently to outsource its CEO or managing director. For one, that individual is supposed to bring skills to the table that are specific to the firm, like knowledge and dedication. The CEO is supposed to help set a firm's strategy, which one would not trust outsiders to do well enough. In addition, there might be concerns about knowledge leakage. Of course, there might still be employees who would like to see their particular CEO outsourced or replaced, but that is an altogether different matter! And in some instances an interim CEO from the outside might be hired as a temporary cover or to manage during a crisis. In general though, the notion of outsourcing the CEO is so absurd it does not even get discussed. The CEO therefore has a low outsourceability.

The analytically and practically interesting examples are activities with medium outsourceability. A small car manufacturer which focuses on getting out new and exciting designs may choose to produce its own engines, but it may also choose to procure them from a larger firm. Britain's sports car producer TVR does the former while its smaller competitor Marcos uses engines of established producers like Volvo. A sports club with an on-site nursery, for parents to enjoy quiet exercising, can decide to run the nursery itself or to use a specialist nursery provider instead. Firms can outsource IT activities or integrate them (e.g. Poppo and Zenger, 1998). These medium outsourceability activities make for interesting practical examples, as there is a real choice to be made. They are also analytically interesting, because the performance outcome of outsourcing the activity may be either positive or negative. The car manufacturer may, for instance, find that by outsourcing its engine, it can produce a relatively cheap car. On the other hand, if it integrates engine production, the engine might be more fit for the purpose and the firm's customers might be willing to pay a premium to have a TVR engine over, say, a Ford engine. Activities of medium outsource-ability therefore are far more likely to show up in both practical and academic discussions of outsourcing. As discussed in chapter 1, for some people these are the only activities that justify the outsourcing label.

Another important aspect of outsourceability is its context-dependence. For instance, the earlier example of the construction of offices clearly holds for schools or universities in Western countries. But in 2005 the BBC broadcast a documentary called "African School" about the life of pupils and teachers of two schools in Masindi, Uganda. Some of the teachers saw the need for a new affordable private school in the town. The first step was to erect a new building for their school. Instead of contracting a construction firm, they started to build their own school, using whatever spare time they could find gradually to add to the building. In their context there was a lack of available finance for their start-up, which meant they could only buy more building supplies when they received their salaries, a well-known phenomenon in the housing market in developing countries. In addition there was no readily available supplier who could produce the building at a lower cost. And, in some ways, building the school created a bond among the teachers who founded it. Thus the context in which this new building was constructed lowered its outsourceability drastically.

*Source:* http://www.open2.net/africanschool/series.html (accessed on June 16, 2006).

As we have argued elsewhere (Kotabe and Mol, 2005) the outsourceability of an activity is a consequence of the activity's characteristics, the characteristics of the buying firm (in relation to those of its suppliers), the industry's characteristics including competitive positioning, the (national) institutional environment that constrains and enables a firm's strategies, and finally the interplay among all of the above. Thus, broadly, one can think of outsourceability as a consequence of past

*Table 3.1. Performance effects of outsourcing each of nine different activities*

| Activity | A | B | C | D | E | F | G | H | I |
|---|---|---|---|---|---|---|---|---|---|
| Performance gain from outsourcing | −4 | −3 | −2 | −1 | 0 | 1 | 2 | 3 | 4 |

experiences, present transaction traits, and future strategic intent. If we then look at the firm as a bundle of activities or a "nexus of treaties" (Aoki, Gustafsson, and Williamson, 1990; Williamson, 1995), some of which will be undertaken in-house and others outsourced, it becomes clear that this portfolio contains activities that are clearly best outsourced, activities that are best kept in-house, and a range of activities for which the best solution is not so clear-cut. In other words, outsourcing decision-making is a balancing act: in some instances outsourcing will be the preferred solution, while integration will come out on top in other cases. I will try to illustrate this using an example.

## A *simplified example*

Suppose a firm's value chain consists of nine activities, A through to I, each representing an equal proportion of that chain and all having varying degrees of outsourceability, as outlined in table 3.1. As discussed above, outsourceability can be thought of as the additional effect that a decision to outsource will have on a firm's performance. In this example, outsourcing activity C will have a negative effect of two units, compared to integrating it. Outsourcing activity E will not have any effect, that is it makes no difference whether it is outsourced or not, and outsourcing activity I will have a positive effect of four units. The numbers are, of course, strictly hypothetical; there is, for instance, no reason for them necessarily to be completely symmetric. For simplicity purposes, assume that all activities are of equal size and that there is a single decision-making center. Also note that the activities themselves may be profitable or not, regardless of whether they are outsourced or integrated. The focus in this example is exclusively on the performance losses or gains that stem from the decision to outsource or integrate the activity. This is consistent with practice, as even activities that are outsourced when they should be integrated (or vice versa) can continue to add some value to an end-product.

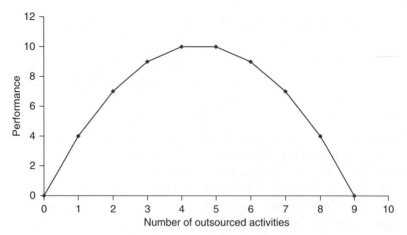

**Figure 3.1.** A simplified example of the number of outsourced activities and firm performance

In this much simplified example, what would be the consequences of outsourcing only activity I, the two activities I and H, the three activities I, H, and G, and so on until all nine activities are outsourced?[2] We would in fact obtain the pattern displayed in figure 3.1. Outsourcing no activities generates no net performance change, but so does outsourcing all activities. The best result, a performance gain of ten units, is obtained from outsourcing either four or five activities. The fact that it does not matter whether four or five activities are outsourced is of course driven by the absence of a performance effect from the outsourcing of activity E. The shape in this figure resembles what is called a *negative curvilinear* shape, otherwise known as an inverted U-shape.[3]

## The negative curvilinear perspective

This example and the form it produces lead us in an inductive manner to the thesis around which much of this book is built: *the performance*

[2] For simplicity's sake, I also assume here that the firm will outsource activities in order of outsourceability, that is it will not outsource activity F while integrating activity G or integrate activity C while outsourcing activity B. The realism of this assumption will be addressed in what follows.

[3] Because of the limited number of data points, the nine activities, there is, of course, not an exact curvilinear shape in place in this figure.

*of a firm is a negative curvilinear function of its degree of outsourcing across all of the activities in its value chain.*[4] This statement begs for some explanation. First, it is necessary to remember that the degree of outsourcing implies the extent to which goods and services are procured from independent outside suppliers. In other words, it asks the question: "Of all the value that goes into a firm's product or service, what percentage is obtained from outside suppliers?" This does not imply that an individual activity must be either completely outsourced or completely integrated. Some activities will only be partially outsourced, what is called "tapered integration" (Harrigan, 1986), for instance because partial outsourcing might keep internal employees more aware of competition or because two supply sources increase the reliability of supplies or product innovation. Related to that it is important to stress that this statement refers to the entire range of activities, not to any single activity or group of activities. For an individual activity, full outsourcing, tapered integration, or complete integration may be the outcome prescribed by the negative curvilinear perspective, depending on the outsourceability of that activity.

In addition, this statement does not imply that a firm's outsourcing level is the only predictor of its performance or even the most important one, as there is a vast range of performance predictors. Firms that build a unique resource base, for instance because their employees possess special knowledge, can outperform their competitors (Barney, 1991). Another predictor is the industry in which the firm operates, because some industries are more attractive than others (Porter, 1980). Firms that manage to produce more innovation, especially of the frame-breaking type, will generally perform better as well (Christensen, 1997). Larger firms may be able to extract more profits because of their bargaining power (Porter, 1980). And the reader may provide other examples based on her or his own insights, which would extend well beyond the scope of this book. The point is that outsourcing levels are a significant predictor of performance.

A short summary of the perspective is the following. If a firm integrates all activities into the firm, this will lead to poor performance because of the disadvantages of integration and the foregoing of advantages associated with outsourcing, for instance because this produces bureaucratic behavior or what economists call X-inefficiency. Hence as

---

[4] This notion was first introduced in Kotabe and Mol (2004; 2005).

the firm starts to outsource some activities its performance will initially increase as these activities produce a higher performance outcome when outsourced. At some point, however, the firm will be outsourcing activities that produce more or less the same performance when integrated as they do when outsourced. This is when the firm reaches a flex point in its outsourcing level. This will be referred to as *the optimal level of outsourcing*. The optimal level is without exception some intermediate level of outsourcing: it will never be when all activities are integrated or when all activities are outsourced. Beyond the optimal point, if the firm is outsourcing activities they will be activities that are better kept in-house. Thus by increasing its outsourcing level, it is now actually lowering its overall performance. As it continues to outsource until all activities are outsourced, it will reach another low in performance. It is also very important to note that I do not claim that there is one optimal outsourcing level for which every firm ought to strive, for instance half of all its activities. Rather, *every firm has its own optimal level of outsourcing*. For some firms this may be 30 percent of their activities, for others it could be 85 percent. Also note that I do not want to suggest that firms actually know what is their optimal degree of outsourcing.[5] Nor is it the case that the optimal degree of outsourcing can be measured exactly by firms, which suggests that firm cannot even be supposed to know their optimal degree of outsourcing.

In conclusion, *a firm ought to outsource some, but never all, of its activities*. This is, of course, a highly intuitive conclusion, as we see no firms that do not comply with that notion. At the same time it is a non-trivial conclusion for two reasons. First, it points to the need always to maintain a balance in outsourcing policy, which on the basis of the literature review does not seem to be a generally embraced principle in either academia or practice. Second, the negative curvilinear perspective actually specifies the costs of outsourcing too much or too little, by indicating what performance gap is produced by the integration of an activity that ought to be outsourced (and vice versa). But it does not only that; it also concludes these costs are non-linear in nature, which implies any statement or empirical test that specifies a positive or negative linear performance effect of outsourcing at the firm level, or indeed no direct performance effect at all, is incorrect. Although an

---

[5] This issue of the cognition of optimal outsourcing levels will be revisited in chapter 7, in the discussion on experimentation.

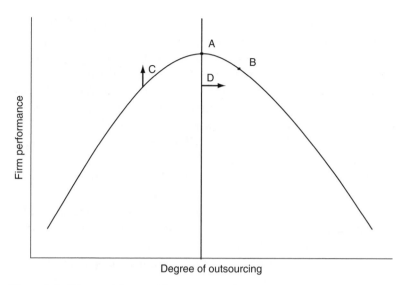

**Figure 3.2.** The negative curvilinear perspective

empirical test may show a linear effect, this is little more than an artifact of the measurement range applied in the study. For instance, the study may contain only firms that integrate too much. Even in this case, a curvilinear shape will produce a better empirical fit. Figure 3.2 contains a graphical summary of this discussion. At point A, firms will achieve optimal performance. Point B, where a firm outsources too much, will be discussed in chapter 4 along with its counterpart, where a firm integrates too much. Arrow C, factors that increase an individual firm's performance curve, will be the focus of chapter 5. Arrow D, an increase or decrease of the optimal amount of outsourcing over time, will be featured in chapter 6.

Obviously this curve is a highly stylized portrayal of how any individual firm's performance responds to changes in its outsourcing level. For instance, some firms will have a wide range of activities that should definitely be integrated and a much smaller range of activities that should be outsourced. If this is the case, the area to the left of the optimal point will actually be much larger than the area to the right and the curve will not be symmetric. The reverse can also hold true, for firms that require many activities that are best outsourced. Similarly firms will vary in the extent to which they rely on activities for which it is not very clear-cut whether outsourcing or integration is the best solution. Those firms which have many such activities will display a fairly flat top of the curve. Another point to note is that the degree of outsourcing itself is not as continuous as portrayed here but instead takes place in steps, depending on the size of an activity. A large activity presents a large step on the outsourcing dimension, for instance from 60 percent to 64 percent. As a consequence a saw-tooth pattern may be obtained. For an activity where tapered integration is a possibility there is no step, as any part of the activity may be outsourced. If all of a firm's activities are amenable to tapered integration, which seems rather hypothetical, there will be no discontinuities.

And a final and important disturbance of the neat curvilinear pattern is produced by interactions among activities. If a particular activity is outsourced or integrated, this may have a bearing on the outsourceability of another activity. For instance, the outsourcing of production activities can potentially undermine a firm's ability to engineer new products, so these engineering activities may also have to be outsourced, perhaps to the same supplier. Alternatively, some other internal activities may benefit from the outsourcing of production because they now receive more management attention. Marketing comes to mind as a possible example. Thus various interaction patterns between activities are possible. All of these interactions will tend to make any specific firm's outsourcing–performance pattern look less like a negative curvilinear shape and more like a seemingly random shape.[6] Ironically this interaction between activities is precisely one of the reasons why an analysis of outsourcing at the firm level, above and beyond single transactions, is fruitful.

The formal mathematical formulation of the negative curvilinear perspective reads:

---

[6] Normally that will imply that the slope of the curve changes in magnitude, i.e. that flatter and steeper parts alternate. But, in extreme cases, this interaction effect may also produce a local optimum below the overall optimal performance level, when a specific activity with high outsourceability is outsourced or integrated but which causes strong changes in the performance of another activity in the opposite direction. Coming back to the production and engineering example, this happens when production is outsourced, which in itself is a good move, but the performance losses in engineering outweigh the gains in production.

$$y = ax^2 + bx + c$$

where $y$ = performance of the firm; $x$ = level of outsourcing by the firm (between 0 and 100 percent); $a$ ($<0$) and $b$ ($>0$) are parameters and $c$ is a constant, all determined at the level of an individual firm.

The constant $c$ represents the effects on the performance of the firm produced by other factors than the outsourcing decision, i.e. it represents where the curve is located vertically. As discussed before, other factors combined form a far more important predictor of performance than does outsourcing. Parameter $b$ determines what degree of outsourcing is optimal, i.e. where the curve is located horizontally; and parameter $a$ determines both the direction (negative) and the steepness of the curve. For those with a mathematical mind it is easy to see that the optimal level of performance is reached where $2ax + b = 0$. While I will not play around with this formula in any detail, I will discuss in later chapters what it means to see a shift in any of the parameters and how such a change will affect the effectiveness of a firm's outsourcing strategy.

## Fit with current theory and practice

Thus far I have presented the negative curvilinear perspective much as if it was an entirely new and unproven perspective on outsourcing and performance. This raises two questions. To what extent is this perspective new and does it build upon existing theory or is it in disagreement with it? And is there any evidence from practice and from empirical tests to confirm this perspective? I will now tackle both questions in some detail because the answers allow us to position this perspective in the wider literature and to assess its practical applicability. To the best of my knowledge, no one has previously proposed that the outsourcing–performance relation takes on this specific shape and in that sense this perspective is certainly novel. A similar argument has been made in other areas though, specifically in the area of corporate diversification strategy. Here it has been argued that the best degree of diversification is an intermediate one and that the performance impact of the degree of diversification takes on a negative curvilinear perspective, implying firms ought to be neither too focused nor too diversified. Markides (1995) provides a succinct summary of this point, including a discussion of the advantages and disadvantages of diversification.

There are, however, various arguments that can be brought to bear against this perspective. From a TCE perspective, one important objection to the negative curvilinear perspective and the performance effects it describes is that it does not focus on individual transactions but rather on *outsourcing as a firm-level construct*. In other words, in the above it was implicitly assumed that one can assign an overall level of outsourcing to a firm. In the TCE tradition, scholars would argue that the proper level of analysis is the transaction and not the firm, though the transaction in most empirical analyses based on TCE seems to be replaced by activity (e.g. Leiblein, Reuer, and Dalsace, 2002; Walker and Weber, 1984).[7] So why do I maintain that the firm level is an appropriate level of analysis and, if it is, does that also mean that the transaction is an irrelevant level of analysis?

First, as argued above, it is possible to conceive of *firms as bundles of transactions* or nexuses of treaties (Aoki, Gustafsson, and Williamson, 1990; Williamson, 1995). In other words, if one were to aggregate analytically all the transactions a firm undertakes, admittedly a rather arduous task, an overall firm level of outsourcing would result. And the top of the curve, what was referred to as the optimal level of outsourcing earlier, will be located where all transactions (the governance structure) are perfectly aligned with the antecedent conditions, primarily asset specificity, uncertainty, and frequency. In that sense the negative curvilinear perspective is entirely consistent with the basic premises that transaction cost economics makes on how governance structures are made to fit with antecedent conditions. However, that still leaves unaccounted the question of misalignment, to which I return in depth in the next chapter.

The second issue is whether it is always appropriate to single out transactions for analysis. In other words, under what conditions is disaggregation of firms into individual transactions an appropriate

---

[7] The outsourcing of an activity can, of course, be the consequence of a single transaction but does not need to be. Generally, therefore, the activity is already a more aggregate level of analysis than the transaction. The problem with analyzing a transaction rather than an activity is that data availability on transactions is often limited. There are some exceptions where actual transactions are the focus of the analysis, such as the MAT database on IT outsourcing transactions in the Netherlands (e.g. Snijders and Tazelaar, 2005), but these require substantial data-gathering exercises. One can therefore make the same criticism of much of the empirical transaction costs research, i.e. that it does not actually analyze the transactions that the underlying theory describes, but aggregates of transactions.

analytical procedure? Generally speaking there are instances where transactions are related to one another. Williamson (1995) argues that clustering of transactions may be necessary when this is the case. It would then become an open empirical question how often transactions are indeed interrelated. But if one accepts the notion that firm resources and routines come into play in governance decisions, as Williamson (1999) seems to do, transactions would almost by definition become interrelated because a firm's resource base and its routines are very much shaped by the activities it undertakes in-house (Nelson and Winter, 1982). In other words, it is very hard indeed to analytically separate single transactions in a strict manner.

A further question is whether it is empirically correct to look at outsourcing as a series of individual decisions. In other words, do managers take only individual outsourcing decisions or do they develop an outsourcing policy that extends beyond a single transaction? This question has not been dealt with in much detail by TCE proponents. Certainly some of the managers I have interviewed indicated that outsourcing policies, extending beyond individual transactions, were in place inside their firms. TCE proponents may believe that decision-makers ought to take each decision individually. But, reflecting Ghoshal's (2005) points, I believe theory ought to focus on describing the world as it is, not on trying to make that world look more like the theory that describes it. So until there is more proof that the transaction is the only level at which outsourcing decisions are taken in practice, we ought to at least hold open the option that higher levels of analysis, such as the firm, can also provide an appropriate basis for theorization around outsourcing.

Inside economics some criticism has also been uttered relatively recently over the use of single transactions as the unit of analysis. Milgrom and Roberts (1992: 32–33) argue that it is very difficult to attribute the costs of bureaucracy and hierarchy to transactions because these costs occur across the entire range of transactions. Holmström and Roberts (1998) provide various examples that counter the notion that single transactions are the best way to analyze firm boundary decisions, including a single-source contracting arrangement between Nucor and the David J. Joseph Company, which holds not because of advantages in single transactions but rather through mutual dependence at the relationship level. The relational focus, which supplants transactions as the unit of analysis, has also become prominent in management studies (Dyer and Singh, 1998) and I will deal with it in greater detail in chapter 5. The relationship level also clearly comprises more than a single transaction.

I conclude that although there are some clear frictions between empirical work in the TCE tradition and the perspective proposed here, there is no fundamental incompatibility between them, because firms can be seen as bundles of transactions. Performance effects that are found for single transactions (or activities) can be aggregated to obtain firm performance. For any specific activity there may still be a linear performance effect in either direction or no direct effect at all, but, as argued above, the performance effects of a specific activity should and can never be generalized beyond their context. From a strategic management point of view, studies of outsourcing at the firm level thus actually become more desirable, rather than less, because of the more useful performance implications they generate as well as the possibility of developing an *outsourcing strategy* or policy, not just executing a series of analysis events.[8]

More generally and beyond TCE there is no inherent conflict between various theories of outsourcing and the negative curvilinear perspective I propose here, since this perspective is (a) not a theory of when outsourcing occurs (it is in fact not a theory at all but rather a model), and (b) can incorporate a variety of explanations as to when outsourcing occurs. To overstate the point, but only somewhat, the perspective proposed here is more or less agnostic when it comes to the why of outsourcing. It willingly accepts there are various reasons why outsourcing may occur. For instance, if a firm's resource base or its competitive positioning and bargaining strength are co-determinants of what is an appropriate level of outsourcing, then these co-determinants are simply included in determining the optimal level of outsourcing. A variety of conceptual mechanisms have an impact on the optimal

---

[8] What makes the existing tests of the performance effects of outsourcing that base themselves on a single activity even less useful from the perspective of analytical generalization is that authors generally sample those activities for which the performance differential between integration and outsourcing is relatively small or even negligible. Thereby they are far less likely to find significant performance effects of outsourcing than would be the case if, say, they investigated the performance effects of outsourcing the firm's CEO (most likely negative) or of outsourcing the construction of the firm's offices (most likely positive). Thus it can be argued this research has already sampled for a lack of a direct performance effect by its choice of activities.

outsourcing level. When a firm exactly matches all its outsourcing decisions with the relevant antecedent conditions, in other words when it makes only perfect outsourcing decisions, it will reach the optimal level of outsourcing in this model. A theory of outsourcing, on the other hand, would propose a limited number of fixed variables to help explain the outsourcing phenomenon. As will be shown in other chapters, the negative curvilinear model used here can form the basis for explaining a number of things beyond outsourcing levels, such as the timing and magnitude of outsourcing processes, the management of supplier relations, and how empirical changes in outsourcing levels come about.

If all of the factors mentioned in these conceptual mechanisms matter, does that imply I propose that "anything goes" when it comes to explaining outsourcing and that no clear categorization of determinants can be developed? Not quite. There are two useful categorizations of the determinants of outsourcing. The optimal outsourcing level can be said to be a consequence of (a) the firm, its industry and country context, and its transaction set, or of (b) the firm's historically determined situation, its current set of transactions, and its future strategic intent. The first dimension was discussed at length in chapter 2 when existing literature was reviewed. The second dimension can be justified from the view point of the conceptual perspectives themselves. Some of these perspectives use a historically generated situation, such as the accumulation of resources in the resource-based view. Others look at the present situation, such as transaction cost economics in its focus on current transaction characteristics. And others describe outsourcing in terms of its future potential, like the real-options perspective. Table 3.2 attempts to capture both categorizations and ranks a variety of

*Table 3.2. A categorization of the perspectives on outsourcing design*

|  | *Firm* | *Context* | *Transaction* |
|---|---|---|---|
| Past | Resource-based view | Social networks | |
| Present | Costly contracting<br>Micro-economics<br>Core competences | Industrial organization<br>Institutional voids | Transaction cost<br>economics<br>Agency |
| Future | Real options<br>Relations and learning | | |

conceptual mechanisms within these categories. Obviously, this is to some extent a stylized presentation of these perspectives and some of them belong to multiple categories, like relations and learning which has a past and present aspect as well as a future one. None the less, it presents some interesting cues for the study of outsourcing and these will be discussed at later stages.

In terms of evidence for this perspective through empirical testing, there are admittedly not many tests as yet. Our own test of manufacturing businesses in the Netherlands (Kotabe and Mol, 2005) serves as the primary empirical confirmation of the negative curvilinear perspective. In chapter 8 I will address in greater detail the need for additional empirical tests of this perspective. But a more detailed description of the empirical test in Kotabe and Mol (2005) may serve as a primer. In that paper we build up a conceptual argument that is largely in line with this chapter and hence produce the hypothesis that performance will be a negative curvilinear function of outsourcing levels.

We then use a sample of over 1,100 manufacturing businesses in the assembly industry, including sectors with many and large firms, like vehicles, electronics, and machinery. For each of these businesses we calculate its 1995 outsourcing level, measured as all external purchases divided by turnover. This is of course entirely consistent with outsourcing as defined in this book. Performance we measure as 1998 return on value added, calculated as net profits divided by internally produced value. Thus we obtain a measure of performance that looks at how profitable the firm is in those activities it still undertakes, consistent with the idea that outsourcing ought to lead to a concentration on those activities in which a firm holds competitive advantage. Return-on-value-added measures have a long history in vertical integration research (see, for instance, Balakrishnan and Wernerfelt, 1986). Ordinary least squares regression is applied to test and confirm the hypothesis.[9] Also note that we apply a three-year time-lag, which not only removes concerns over reverse causality, when the predicted variable causes the predictor variable, but also allows for all benefits and

---

[9] Apart from the direct curvilinear effect, the paper also reveals an indirect effect. It turns out that business uncertainty acts as a negative moderator on the negative curvilinear effect. This implies that as uncertainty increases, the curve will become steeper. In terms of the formula presented earlier, parameter *a* becomes even more negative when there is much uncertainty. As a consequence the costs of deviating from the optimal decision are larger for firms in uncertain environments.

costs of outsourcing to come fully to fruition. A simple cross-sectional, time-invariant, analysis would, for instance, not allow for the inclusion of costs that occur as a consequence of contract renegotiation or of future benefits like the development of interorganizational routines between the outsourcer and the supplier.

A possible criticism that could be made of our study is that we have no way of describing how the aggregate performance consequences flow from many individual activity-level (transaction-level) decisions. It could be argued that while the theory suggests that firms will make optimal decisions across all activities, the aggregation that takes place here does not allow for a direct test. Yet why would a firm outsource an activity that is "obviously" best integrated while not outsourcing an activity that is "perhaps" best integrated? For instance, why would a bank outsource its CEO while constructing its own office? In other words, the likelihood of "making a mistake" is strongly negatively correlated with the performance impact of that mistake, unless one is going to assume a random-walk decision-making process, but none of the theories on outsourcing does that nor is there much reason to believe it reflects the world of practice. From a more pragmatic point of view some firms will make such mistakes, but the use of statistics eventually means mistakes in both directions will be included, which decreases the likelihood of a significant finding and means the estimation is conservative. In other words, if anything, the effect ought to be even stronger than this empirical test showed.

Beyond the paper discussed now (Kotabe and Mol, 2005) I am not aware of any other empirical tests of what is being proposed here. But I will venture to say there is ample practical evidence to support the negative curvilinear perspective. In the management literature, various practitioners have pointed to the limits to outsourcing (Brück, 1995; Doig, Ritter, Speckhals, and Woolson, 2001; *Financial Times*, 2005c). These authors essentially argue that outsourcing can take a wrong turn and that even if outsourcing is a useful strategy, too much outsourcing is not a good idea. Doig, Ritter, Speckhals, and Woolson (2001: 25), for instance, argue that "[f]arming out in-house operations has become a religion. Now it must be tempered by reason." Brück (1995: 29) argues somewhat similarly to the earlier discussion in stating that "every company must find its own optimum level of integration." He also suggests that (1995: 30) "[c]ompanies that outsource production simply because they are not cost-competitive must be prepared to be overtaken by more efficient competitors, or even by suppliers entering the market in direct competition." Brück (1995) quotes from a research project undertaken inside McKinsey that looked at outsourcing and vertical integration inside different German manufacturing industries. It turned out that, in some of these, outsourcing produced superior performance, while in others integration did. This is of course entirely consistent with the notion of a negative curvilinear effect, as some industries may be outsourcing too much, finding themselves at point B in figure 3.2, and others not enough. Hence increases in performance sometimes come from more outsourcing and at other times from less outsourcing.

As described earlier a majority of firms in all OECD countries has started to outsource more and more activities in the recent past. Some countries, industries, or firms may have been slower to join in than others but there is an unmistakable and undeniable trend. The discourse around outsourcing is both a cause and a consequence of this trend. That discourse has been markedly positive, although the tide may slowly be starting to turn a little. One piece of evidence for a pro-outsourcing bias is the way the advantages and disadvantages of outsourcing are discussed. Almost without exception, outsourcing is discussed in leading business media in terms of *benefits and risks* (see, for instance, *Financial Times*, 2005b). That suggests that outsourcing as such will deliver benefits but that these benefits may be suppressed or become negligible. It also suggests that outsourcing does not entail inherent drawbacks, just risks. For any decision-maker who needs to defend an outsourcing decision, that thesis is clearly convenient. The decision will generate benefits but there is, of course, always a risk that these benefits will not materialize. A possibility that is to be ruled out *a priori*, however, is that outsourcing is the wrong decision (wrong design) from the outset. That frees the decision-maker and whoever else was involved in the decision of all possible blame. Another example is a recent practitioner article, the summary of which reads (Lynch, 2004: 44):

There are many good reasons to outsource logistics and supply chain activities. But outsourcing is not necessarily the best answer for every situation. The key to making the right decision about whether to perform an activity in house or turn it over to an outside provider is to carefully assess the pros and cons of both options – and then make the choice that's best for you.

Unfortunately the article itself (Lynch, 2004) then goes on to spend six pages on the advantages of outsourcing, while paying a little attention to its risks, and only two sentences on reasons to keep logistics activities in-house, or what would be disadvantages of logistics outsourcing. Outsourcing, in other words, is the default option of the day.

Although, then, they mostly appear to sing its praise, newspaper and other media reports have also addressed the limits of outsourcing. Box 3.2 provides an example. In discussions I have had with practitioners, they too generally mention the benefits of outsourcing but are also willing to admit that there is some natural limit to how much their firm can and should outsource. This shows that managers, even when they operate based on a strong dose of intuition, generally tend to have some feeling for how many and which activities they should be outsourcing. Many managers seem to grasp intuitively that there is an inherent need for balancing outsourcing and vertical integration. As I will discuss in the next chapter, however, managers usually come by their decisions through a limited set of decision-making rules and hence they seldom take perfect decisions across a wider range of choices. Thus in the balancing process they tend to make mistakes.

Another way to look at the empirical viability of the negative curvilinear argument is to check the robustness of the finding I presented in the earlier example. To what extent is it subject to strong assumptions

---

## Box 3.2. British Rail / Railtrack / Network Rail: in need of maintenance

There is evidence in practice to suggest that superior outsourcing designs do not necessarily lead to effective outcomes. When the operations of the British national rail operator British Rail were privatized by the Conservative government of John Major in the early 1990s, the infrastructure provider was renamed Railtrack and outsourced maintenance activities through long-term contracts with a number of independent companies. Such a scheme had been successful for other public transit systems, for instance in the USA and Australia (Domberger, 1998). Railtrack itself went bankrupt in the late 1990s, causing embarrassment not just for the Conservatives but also for Tony Blair's New Labour government, which had embraced the privatization with some vigor, in part because of widespread dissatisfaction with British Rail. Railtrack's successor,

Network Rail, inherited its relations with maintenance contractors.[10] One of these contractors was Jarvis, a company that came under heavy scrutiny in 2002 and 2003 over its involvement in a number of railroad accidents, including one at Potter's Bar which took seven lives and a derailment at London's busy King's Cross station.

British media blamed this on Railtrack's inability to manage relations with independent suppliers properly, a problem its successor Network Rail inherited. Other causes that were discussed related more to the loss of maintenance capability during the outsourcing process and transfer. Whereas British Rail had its own measurement equipment, Railtrack had to rely on its suppliers to execute its measurements. These suppliers then presented it with findings and recommendations for maintenance. Because Railtrack did not have an in-house capacity for verifying the correctness of these findings, it had trouble negotiating good deals with suppliers. It was also very hard for Railtrack to evaluate *ex post* whether the work had been performed effectively. Railtrack therefore had to rely heavily on its suppliers to tell it whether they had done a good job. This naturally encouraged suppliers to be positive in their self-reporting.

As a consequence Network Rail decided to gradually insource maintenance activities. Jarvis transferred its rail maintenance activities to Network Rail in October 2003. *The Economist* (2005), normally an unlikely source when it comes to criticism of markets, commented: "Network Rail has even managed to underspend its budget, now that it has brought maintenance in-house. That replaced the previous baroque arrangements of contractors and sub-contractors, all badly managed and risk-averse, which made the simplest engineering jobs longer and more complicated than necessary." Outsourcing maintenance activities may look like both a necessary and straightforward decision to implement but apparently these outsourcing processes are not that simple and not necessarily that effective either. This indicated the need for outsourcing to be implemented well.

---

[10] I do not mean to suggest that the management-outsourced maintenance activities are the only, or even the chief cause, of the failure of Railtrack. Indeed, the British Rail privatization has been the subject of much discussion and analysis. Many analysts seem to agree that the rail system was too complex, with interdependent components, simply to cut into pieces. After the privatization the individual components were incentivized and encouraged to perform optimally, without much regard for the performance of the system as a whole.

regarding the real distribution of activities along the outsourceability dimension? Note that if we rank activities according to their outsourceability, outsourceability will by definition rise as we go along because we use it as the sorting variable. Is it reasonable to expect the distribution that was used in the earlier example to hold generally? I would submit that it is, because it does not assume any peculiar distribution of the outsourceability of activities. Instead the outsourceability rises in a linear fashion, which seems intuitively correct. But even if we assume that outsourceability rises in a non-linear fashion, for instance when there are more-or-less three discrete zones with low, medium, and high outsourceability and not many activities that fall in between the zones, the shape that we obtain will (a) still have a single optimum, though that may be stretched out around the medium outsourceability zone, and (b) look similar in shape to a negative curvilinear outsourcing–performance relationship in the sense that it never increases as we move away from the optimal point. This shows that the proposed shape of the outsourcing–performance relationship is reasonably robust.

## Performance

In our empirical test we used the return-on-value-added measure, which looks at the firm's profitability per monetary unit of internal production. Obviously, firms measure their performance against a much wider range of criteria. For instance, one can look at the immediate effects of outsourcing on return on investment and stock market prices (both are normally positive) or on return on sales (which is negative). These are imbalanced financial measures although using some combination of them can provide a better idea of the effect of outsourcing on financial performance.

Beyond these financial measures, one can measure performance in a variety of ways. Murray, Kotabe, and Wildt (1995), for instance, include market share and sales growth among their performance measures. In their sample, outsourcing has a negative effect on these measures. From a marketing perspective these measures are much more useful than financial performance measures because they relate to marketing outcomes. And there appear to be some differences in perception between firms with different countries of origin as to the importance of various measures. Japanese firms, for example, tend to attach relatively greater value than US firms to market share and sales growth as important measures of their success on account of their longer-term perspective on firm performance (Kotabe, 1998). As a consequence they employ outsourcing to increase the effectiveness of their operations (Kotabe, 1998), not necessarily the efficiency with which operations are executed. Therefore outsourcing may not have an immediate positive effect on production cost levels for Japanese firms. Another way to look at outsourcing, not pursued as far as I am aware, would be to investigate how it affects a firm's chances of survival in the long run. This could help to relate outsourcing to notions of survival in institutional theory (Baum and Oliver, 1991; Scott, 1995).

But performance can take on an even wider meaning if one considers the effect of outsourcing on the firm's relations with internal and external stakeholders. This raises a host of possible questions. What does outsourcing do to a firm's relations with its employees for instance? How does outsourcing affect the nature of the work of managers and their job satisfaction? What is the effect of outsourcing and job transfer on local communities in which a firm operates? Is there an environmental benefit or cost associated with outsourcing? Does outsourcing affect the tax intake of governments? As researchers we have only scratched the surface of these questions and generally through anecdotal observations rather than systematic analysis. In chapter 8 this topic will be discussed more systematically.

## Conclusion

In this chapter I constructed a new perspective of outsourcing, which builds around the notion that firm performance is a negative curvi-linear function of a firm's overall outsourcing level, producing an optimal level of outsourcing. In the process it was discussed how a variety of theories can help us understand why this perspective makes sense. But various questions were left unanswered for the time being, perhaps most obviously the issue of whether firms ever truly optimize their outsourcing levels, and if not, why not. I will return to this question in the next chapter.

# 4 | *The outsourcing process*

MUCH of the description in the previous chapter focused on the structure of outsourcing and, perhaps more correctly, on the vertical structure of firms. The negative curvilinear explanation relates that vertical structure to a firm's performance levels. Hence the previous chapter, as well as the literature discussion in chapter 2, did much to cover design and performance but little to help understand the outsourcing process. In this chapter I try to provide more detail of the decision-making processes that lead to changes in outsourcing levels, what was defined as the *outsourcing process* in chapter 1, as well as the timing and magnitude of these outsourcing processes. In doing so, I will draw much more heavily on social sciences other than economics, especially the organization theory and strategic management versions of history, sociology, psychology, and political science.[1] Three core concepts that are used in the process are misalignment, inertia, and bandwagoning. In all, this chapter helps us to understand how outsourcing is driven not just by a set of structural determinants that are optimally processed by some anonymous brain but also by a variety of social processes. It begins by answering the question of why firms would locate anywhere other than at point A, for instance at point B, in figure 3.1.

## The meaning of misalignment

Alignment and misalignment have been the subject of study in a variety of settings. In the area of management information systems, studies of alignment have focused on the extent to which information systems are

---

[1] Clearly many interpretations of these fields in organization theory and strategic management are themselves substantially less sophisticated in theory and method than the work that occurs in these fields themselves. That is a necessary and perfectly acceptable trade-off of depth for breadth and applicability.

aligned with firm strategies (Henderson and Venkatraman, 1989). In organization theory, specifically contingency theory (Donaldson, 2001), alignment refers to the fitting of elements of organizational structure, such as degree of centralization, to a set of contingency variables, such as firm size. In transaction cost economics, alignment refers to choosing a governance structure such that it fits with the characteristics of a transaction (Williamson, 1985). Hence firms are said to be misaligned when the governance structure of a transaction is not in line with the transaction's characteristics (Masten, 1993). My use of the term alignment comes closest to the TCE version, as alignment is choosing the firm level of outsourcing that best fits the variety of outsourcing determinants. *Alignment occurs when firms choose their level of outsourcing such that they are located at the top of their performance curve and exactly fit outsourcing levels to outsourcing determinants.* As follows from earlier chapters, my definition of alignment differs from TCE in that it looks at firms as the unit of analysis, not transactions, and takes into account a variety of outsourcing determinants, including, but not limited to, those proposed by TCE.

But there are various deviations from perfect alignment that cannot be explained through the economizing view of outsourcing. First, why do incumbent firms remain vertically integrated for so long in the face of substantial change in their technological and institutional environments that shifts the balance between transaction and production costs to allow for more outsourcing (Afuah, 2001; Malone, Yates, and Benjamin, 1987)? The US automotive industry, for instance, remained vertically integrated for a long time until the fact that Japanese competitors were successfully relying on *keiretsu* alliances with external suppliers was openly recognized as one of their key success factors (Cusumano, 1985; Womack, Jones and Roos, 1990). That is not in line with the perfect alignment thesis, as it implies American automotive companies ought to have responded earlier.

Second, why is it that the process of outsourcing often appears to take on a punctuated equilibrium model (Tushman and Anderson, 1986) in the form of long periods of limited change followed by industry-wide waves of sudden outsourcing, during which every manager wants to be seen to engage in outsourcing (Bettis, Bradley, and Hamel, 1992)? As Lamoreaux, Raff, and Temin (2003: 430) describe, "despite these cumulative unidirectional, almost linear, trends [in falling transportation and communication costs], the degree of hierarchical coordination in what have conventionally been regarded as the center parts of the economy has followed a pronounced hump-shape pattern over time." Once the Detroit Big Three realized that Japanese firms were playing the game differently, they quickly and collectively copied Japanese practices of substantial outsourcing and more cooperation with suppliers, albeit with mixed success (Dyer, 1996; Kotabe, 1998). The most recent wave has seen many firms, including the British banking industry, simultaneously transfer call-center activities and other business processes to India and other faraway destinations.

Third, and perhaps most importantly, why is it that the initial promise of lower production costs, which often triggers outsourcing decisions, so often falls short when all is said and done, or is more than compensated by unexpected transaction costs (Doig, Ritter, Speckhals, and Woolson, 2001; Hendry, 1995)? Apparently, there is something that makes it difficult for managers to weigh the short-term and long-term benefits of outsourcing activities and causes them to make "wrong" decisions, in that outsourcing levels are not fully aligned with transaction (and firm) characteristics.

There are many instances of misalignment in the world of practice. Misalignment occurs when there is no perfect alignment; in terms of the model presented in chapter 3, when firms do not locate at the top of their curves. Misalignment happens, therefore, when firms locate either to the left or to the right of the optimal point, i.e. when they outsource too much or do not outsource enough. In strictly empirical terms, it would be very unusual to find any firm that is located exactly at the top of its curve. Thus it is highly common that some degree of misalignment occurs. What is more unusual though is to find a lot of misalignment in business firms, especially a lot of misalignment maintained over longer time-periods (Masten, 1993). Masten argued that those firms that are most likely to survive do not necessarily have to get all decisions right, but the organizations that get a greater percentage of their decisions right are more likely to survive.

There are two types of misalignment, being too integrated and outsourcing too much. It is useful to consider some examples of each type. Looking first at firms that are too integrated, a case can be made that many manufacturing firms were too integrated coming into the 1980s (Quinn, Doorley, and Pacquette, 1990). Firms like Detroit's

Big Three, General Motors, Ford, and Chrysler, performed many activities in-house that were profitably outsourced by Japanese competitors like Toyota. Since they had always followed the model of vertical integration championed by Henry Ford, they were left performing some activities for which a market of external suppliers clearly existed and for which they themselves were rather poorly equipped. The same can be said for a host of other manufacturing firms across the Western world, some of which now no longer exist. One interviewee told me: "When I started working here some 35 years ago, we produced everything in-house, even screws." As the firm found itself being outpaced by lower-cost producers, it grudgingly and slowly submitted to more outsourcing. It was also sold and reorganized on a few occasions, which increased the speed of the outsourcing process.

Which firms can be said to have outsourced too much? Arguably many of the dotcom firms, whose market values rose steeply during the late 1990s but then dropped even more quickly in the first years of this century, were almost virtual firms. While not all of these firms went bankrupt solely, or even primarily, because they outsourced too much, it has been widely observed (e.g. Hamel, 2002) that many dotcom firms operated from a very limited basis for competition since their lack of activities undertaken in-house provided them with insufficient points of distinction. As Chesbrough and Teece (1996) put it, being virtual should not be equated with being virtuous. The earlier example of Fisher Body (box 2.1), where General Motors decided it needed to integrate its supplier at a high cost, shows that too much outsourcing is not a new phenomenon either.

Therefore it seems fair to conclude that too much misalignment not only leads to severe performance losses but may eventually even spell bankruptcy for firms. The amount of misalignment a firm can afford itself, however, is very much going to depend on the nature of competition in the industry and one's perception of it. Where competition displays many imperfections, as arguably still is the case for many industries today, firms can afford to be misaligned somewhat. It is also important not to overestimate the effect that one range of decisions, on outsourcing, has on the overall performance of the firm. Just as much as increasing outsourcing is not a panacea for improving a firm's competitive position, outsourcing too much, by itself, is unlikely to lead to a firm's downfall.

## The causes of misalignment

If the conclusion is that most, if not all, firms are misaligned with regard to their degree of outsourcing, the obvious question is why such alignment takes place. The answer to that question is somewhat less obvious. What might seem like a natural starting point in explaining misalignment, to draw upon the theories that explain alignment, rapidly turns into a dead-end street. For any theory predicting alignment is poorly positioned to explain misalignment. From the perspective of transaction cost economics or the resource-based view, the consequences of misalignment are clear, in the form of lower performance. But if one seeks to explain the causes of misalignment using TCE or the RBV, the only obvious conclusion is that managers make mistakes, a strong form of which is that managers are ignorant, because they do not adhere enough to the prescriptions, or "laws" to some, that these approaches produce. I do not find this to be a satisfactory answer, for it suggests that those who do not behave as we would expect are ignorant.[2] As social scientists we should hope to explain behavior in a slightly more sophisticated manner, by questioning whether theoretical advances and a widening of our perspective can help us better to understand the behavior.

To explain misalignment and outsourcing processes, then, I propose we turn to other branches of social science and management that are more insightful when it comes to those aspects of managerial behavior that are induced not by economic rationality but by individual or group processes. In a very general sense the outsourcing misalignment we find here can occur for three possible reasons: (1) firms simultaneously optimize their behavior along multiple dimensions, and do not just look at economic performance; (2) firms do not optimize their behavior at all but instead engage in satisficing (Simon, 1998), accepting a good, but not the optimal, solution; (3) behavior is not goal-oriented at all. If outsourcing levels are optimized along multiple dimensions, one would expect there to be clear additional goals for outsourcing decisions to be in place, for instance that these decisions need to add to, or at least not detract from, the firm's legitimacy. If satisficing rather than optimizing is what decision-makers do, one would expect outsourcing decisions to

---

[2] Ghoshal (2005) and Ghoshal and Moran (1996) have taken up this critique in much more detail.

be driven by broad heuristics rather than very detailed analysis. And finally, to the extent that outsourcing decisions are not goal-oriented at all, one would expect them to appear rather random and decision-makers ought to have a hard time defending their rationale.

There are various routes one can take to investigate whether these explanations are valuable and valid. Among the concepts that are of foremost interest here are inertia and bandwagoning. Broadly speaking, I propose *outsourcing processes at the level of an individual firm occur in a pattern where long periods of relative inertia are followed by short periods of relatively rapid change that are induced by the presence of various types of bandwagon pressures*. In that sense, the model followed here is not unlike the idea of punctuated equilibrium in technological innovation (Tushman and Anderson, 1986). The punctuated equilibrium model that Tushman and Anderson proposed implies that long periods of relatively slow technological change alternate with short periods of rapid or even disruptive (Christensen, 1997) technological change. In such periods the *modus operandi* of an industry is often turned on its head because the drivers of costs and benefits change along with the technology.

The first part of the punctuated equilibrium model is equilibrium in the form of organizational inertia. Inertia in outsourcing can be understood as a lack of change in outsourcing levels in spite of a need for change. For instance firms produce component A in-house since they have always been doing that, even though it is better to outsource, or procure service B from an external supplier because they have never produced it internally, missing out on an opportunity to exploit existing in-house resources. In organization theory inertia is the terrain of neo-institutional theorists, especially those in neo-institutional sociology (DiMaggio and Powell, 1983; Scott, 1995; Zucker, 1983). Why do organizations decide to stay their course, even when that course is not clearly (or even clearly not) beneficial?

Some of the answers to this question include related concepts too, including what has been described as escalating commitment by social psychologists, path dependence by economists, and a dominant logic by strategists.[3] Staw (1981) suggests that decision-makers, once

---

[3] Scott (1995) shows how institutional theorists across various areas of social science use highly similar concepts but define and explain them differently. This is clearly a case in point, although escalating commitment is an individual-level

committed to something, often have no way to retract mentally from their earlier commitments. Once a manager has dedicated much energy to improving and upholding an in-house activity, escalating her or his personal commitment to that activity over time, that manager is unlikely to want to outsource the activity, because doing so would also mean the severance of an emotional attachment and an admission of failure. In the world of practice such activities are often referred to as pet projects or "babies." A similar term used by economists is path dependence (David, 1985; North, 1991), which refers to the difficulty associated with moving from one technology (solution) to another because of the costs of switching. Once firms have invested much time and many resources (sunk costs) in an outsourcing relationship to try and make a supplier perform at a higher level, that makes it relatively unattractive to reverse an outsourcing decision and engage in an insourcing process, because these sunk costs will be lost without compensation. As Lamoreaux, Raff, and Temin (2003: 411) put it: "The search for more effective coordination mechanisms, in other words, will be path dependent in the sense that choices that business people make are likely to be affected by the ways they organized their activities previously and also by the particular range of options conspicuously available to them at that point in history."

In strategic management the notion of a dominant logic (Prahalad and Bettis, 1986), implying a well-established and broadly agreed set of industry- and firm-level rules on how to operate a firm, suggests that outsourcing can be seen, during specific time-periods, as the default option to solve a range of performance problems.[4] In other words, if the dominant logic in the industry is that outsourcing is the path to increased performance, the top management of firms in the industry may come to believe that outsourcing is a superior solution to integration. On that basis it can establish a policy which favors outsourcing over integration. At lower levels in the organization, where many smaller outsourcing decisions are taken, this may lead to numerous decisions that keep up outsourcing levels even when circumstances dictate outsourcing is no longer the best solution. The dominant logic is therefore hard to replace and in a sense becomes a part of the genes of management.

concept whereas path dependence and dominant logic at least initially referred to organizations or sets thereof.

[4] Prahalad and Bettis (1986) say that the dominant logic can be both a "knowledge structure" and a "set of elicited management processes."

The second part of the punctuated equilibrium model, rapid change, is not necessarily more important in explaining a firm's degree of misalignment in outsourcing, since misalignment can be just as much a consequence of no change in outsourcing levels as it can be of too much change.[5] It is, however, considerably more relevant to our understanding of the recent rises in outsourcing levels described in chapter 1 and witnessed by many observers (for instance, Sako, 2006). Why is it that when we see change in outsourcing levels in an industry, we see much and sudden change, rather than gradual change, and changes occurring in parallel across many firms in that industry? For instance, why did all British banks decide to outsource and offshore their support activities like call centers to BPO providers in India around 2003? And why (*Financial Times*, 2005a) did Europe's established airlines keep their catering in-house until the late 1990s and then suddenly decide to outsource their activities to either Gate Gourmet or Sky Chefs?

The answer to these questions ought to build upon the conditions under which the decision suddenly to increase outsourcing is taken. First, as in most decision-making, outcomes are subject to uncertainty, for instance uncertainty over business conditions or technologies, as Williamson (1975) highlighted. That uncertainty makes it difficult to decide not only *what* is the best course of action, because of information incompleteness, but also *when* that course of action should be taken. If uncertainty is the only condition surrounding outsourcing decision-making, it is still possible to take a decision that leads to the best outcome probabilistically through some sort of risk analysis or scenario exercise. For instance, in a simple example, if there is a 40 percent probability that outsourcing level A is optimal and a 60 percent probability that outsourcing level B is optimal, firms may choose an outsourcing level of $0.4 * A + 0.6 * B$. But beyond being surrounded by uncertainty, these decisions are also subject to causal ambiguity (Reed and DeFillippi, 1990). For several reasons, it is unclear whether outsourcing leads to improved performance. First, a certain type of outsourcing may not have been attempted very much before, as was the case with IT outsourcing in the late 1980s. Loh and Venkatraman

---

[5] In chapter 6 this issue will be discussed in more detail. Suffice it here to say that the circumstances may change, such that a previously optimal outsourcing level is now far from optimal. So even when an optimal, or almost optimal, outsourcing level is attained, this does not guarantee future alignment.

(1992) detailed how the type of IT outsourcing that first arose around 1986, featuring substantial transfers of assets and interorganizational relations that went beyond the arm's length model, was both new and radically different from established practices. Therefore, they argue, outsourcing was a management innovation (Loh and Venkatraman, 1992). As management innovation is a poorly understood phenomenon both in practice and in academia (Birkinshaw, Hamel, and Mol, 2005; Birkinshaw and Mol, 2006; Hamel, 2006), firms simply did not know what to expect from it.

Second, there is a substantial time-lag between the outsourcing decision and its eventual effect. A decision to outsource a service may generate production cost savings now but could lead to a lack of innovation (a transaction cost in the broad sense of the word) in the future. As March (2006: 204) argues, feedback-based adaptive processes, of which bandwagoning is an example, "do not necessarily result in the timely achievement of global optima" because of the properties of settings and human actors, as well as the properties of adaptive processes themselves. Settings may be too complex for decision-makers to find an optimum usefully. Unlike the example given in chapter 3, where a firm needed to have only nine activities performed, a real-life firm performs dozens if not hundreds or even thousands of activities, many of which are interlinked. This clearly makes it very hard to find the overall optimal outsourcing level. Individuals may be limited in their information-processing and decision-making abilities and prone to the use of heuristics. Any single decision-maker will only be able to interpret correctly a part of the signals surrounding an outsourcing decision. And adaptive processes occur slowly and without complete accuracy (March, 2006). Firms do not constantly reconsider all of their activities to decide whether to outsource or integrate them. Even when they reconsider an activity and decide to outsource or integrate it, it will take time to implement that decision, and it is hard to find the correct extent of outsourcing or integration.

A natural response to dealing with these factors that prevent highly rational and well-informed decision-making is to look for heuristics (Simon, 1998). Heuristics are shortcuts that allow decision-makers to come to a conclusion in the face of limited evidence. One such heuristic is to observe the decisions of other decision-makers and to mimic those decisions. Another heuristic could be to listen to what advisors see as proper decisions. These heuristics have been captured by the bandwagon effects described by Abrahamson and Rosenkopf (1993; 1997).[6] Abrahamson and Rosenkopf (1993) refer to bandwagon effects as the pressure to adopt or reject an organizational innovation created by large numbers of adopters or rejecters.

Outsourcing, like downsizing (Budros, 1999), may be thought of as a type of organizational innovation or management innovation since it changes the structure and operations of organizations (Loh and Venkatraman, 1992; Bonazzi and Antonelli, 2003). Adoption of outsourcing can be seen as an increase in outsourcing levels over a firm's historical levels, while rejection refers to a situation of no change in outsourcing levels. Although this definition clearly explains the nature of bandwagon effects, it may not necessarily be large numbers of adopters that induce these effects; it could equally well be the fact that some large, visible, or highly reputable organizations adopt a certain innovation (Haunschild and Miner, 1999). Not all outside peers will have equal effects on an organization's decision-making process.

Abrahamson and Rosenkopf (1993) distinguish between competitive and institutional bandwagoning, where the first refers to copying of behavior by competing firms and the second to caving in under the pressures of a variety of external actors. Loh and Venkatraman (1992) claim that the firms which initially engaged in IT outsourcing did so on their own initiative, thereby essentially engaging in an organizational experiment. When, however, Kodak announced a major and widely publicized IT outsourcing deal with IBM and Digital Equipment Corporation in 1989, firms that subsequently outsourced IT did so because they imitated Kodak's decision. Loh and Venkatraman (1992) thus framed this as the "Kodak effect". Abrahamson and Rosenkopf (1993) would refer to it as competitive bandwagoning. A competitive bandwagon effect will occur when an organization perceives that outsourcing is helping a large number of its industry competitors to overcome a performance gap and when the organization believes it can similarly improve its performance through outsourcing. The organization will mimic such behavior because it wants to obtain a

---

[6] Abrahamson and Rosenkopf (1993; 1997) are not the only authors to use the idea of bandwagoning, though their conceptualization is perhaps sounder than that of other authors. Knickerbocker (1973) applied bandwagoning to the foreign direct investment decisions of multinational corporations. Lacity and Hirschheim (1995) applied bandwagoning to IT outsourcing, though in a very informal sense of the word.

similar degree of success. As a further example, Toyota's successful and widely publicized outsourcing and supplier relations practices may have prompted other firms, however unrelated to Toyota in terms of industry or physical location, to copy its practices.

The second type of bandwagon, the institutional bandwagon, does not presuppose that actual performance gains can be attained from implementing an innovation like outsourcing, either by the firm or its competitors (Abrahamson and Rosenkopf, 1993). Rather, in this second type, the presence of institutional pressures is a necessary condition for a bandwagon to occur. Such institutional pressures to outsource may be exerted through a wide variety of sources including knowledge entrepreneurs, financiers (including shareholders), business schools, business associations, and training institutes (Abrahamson and Fairchild, 1999), to which governments and supply chain partners like customers and suppliers should probably be added. It can also occur because widespread adoption of outsourcing increases the legitimacy of outsourcing as a strategy (DiMaggio and Powell, 1983). Similar to the competitive bandwagon process, institution-based bandwagoning may induce outsourcing. The fact that many other firms engage in outsourcing may create isomorphic pressures on other firms, who will want to be seen to act similarly to their industry peers. But the presence of institutional bandwagons can itself also be an indirect consequence of observations of the competitive marketplace. For instance, the presence of highly visible and exemplary firms that successfully mount the outsourcing challenge, however unrelated to the firm itself, may lead outside institutions to promote outsourcing. Box 4.1 provides an example of a bandwagon process and its unintended consequences.

## Empirical illustrations of bandwagoning

Because the bandwagoning perspective of outsourcing is not well established in the literature, it is useful to provide some more extensive and detailed empirical illustrations of it. In 2003 we conducted interviews with a series of manufacturing firms in the Netherlands, focusing on the instruments and appliances and pumps and compressors industries.[7] These industries were chosen specifically because they had

---

[7] The methodology behind these interviews is described in much more detail in Mol and Kotabe (2006).

## Box 4.1. British Airways and Gate Gourmet: not catered for

In the airline industry it became customary to outsource onboard catering activities during the late 1990s and early 2000s. But the outsourcing of one activity can have a snowball effect on all kinds of other activities. On the morning of Thursday August 11, 2005 a strike broke out among some 1,000 Heathrow-based ground services workers working for British Airways (BA). The strike lasted for almost two days and led to the cancellation of hundreds of flights by BA and other Oneworld Alliance airlines. Because it came in the middle of the holiday season up to 100,000 passengers were left stranded all around the world. Most of those on strike, including the baggage handlers, did not have any disagreement with BA directly. Rather, the strike was their way of expressing solidarity with the 670 workers sacked by Gate Gourmet, BA's single-source catering supplier.

Gate Gourmet, an American-owned but Swiss-based catering firm, was in a long-drawn battle with the Transport and General Workers Union (TGWU) over pay and working conditions. When some of the TGWU's members started an unofficial strike on Wednesday August 10, thereby severely limiting the amount of food available on BA's flights, Gate Gourmet responded by firing 670 of around 2,100 Heathrow workers, including some who had not participated in the strike. BA was in great difficulties to reschedule all flights and ended up paying large sums of money to its passengers in the form of new flights, hotel rooms, and other expenses, as well as having to hand out Frequent Flyer miles to keep its regular customers happy. The estimated costs of the conflict for BA were around £40 million. Meanwhile BA's CEO, Sir Rod Eddington, could do little more than ask Gate Gourmet and the TGWU "to sit down as a matter of urgency." Over the weekend BA managed to restore some of its catering capacity although on many flights it could offer little but water. Hot food did not return to most flights until August 22.

The following week negotiations continued fruitlessly between Gate Gourmet and the TGWU but Gate Gourmet also opened separate negotiations with BA to renegotiate its multiyear contract with the airline. Gate Gourmet claimed to have lost £25 million at Heathrow alone during 2004 and suggested it would have to call in the administrators if the BA contract could not be renegotiated. Eventually a new contract was struck between BA and Gate Gourmet. Though details of that deal were never made official, it is believed to have increased the catering costs of BA at Heathrow by around £10 million. In the two weeks following the strike and before the new deals were announced BA's share price dropped by 3 percent, well above the 1 percent drop of the FTSE 100. BA and Gate Gourmet struck a new deal but it was not until December 2005 that the conflict was finally resolved and Gate Gourmet completely resumed its supply of food and drinks to British Airways. Gate Gourmet ended up paying some of its employees to leave while firing others, who were seeking compensation through the courts in return.

BA found out the hard way that its activities were more inter-dependent than hitherto conceived. That does not necessarily mean outsourcing was a completely wrong decision. But it implies that simply following the trend among airlines to outsource catering activities was probably not appropriate. This shows that band-wagons can produce outsourcing misalignment. BA's core customers expect it to deliver different service levels from Ryanair or Easyjet. If it decides to outsource an activity like catering, which is an impor-tant part of a flight in the eyes of the customer, such outsourcing has to be undertaken with great care. This may involve close monitoring and hands-on management of suppliers. It may also involve the creation of alternative sources, should one source (Gate Gourmet) no longer be able to deliver. Nishiguchi and Beaudet (1998) describe Toyota's response when a key Toyota supplier saw its manufactur-ing plant burn down. By using its supplier network and internal production capacity Toyota managed to get enough production back on stream within two weeks to overcome the problems. BA clearly had not given much thought to how a relatively simple production process, of food and drinks, could be backed up. Nor was the fact that its Oneworld Alliance partners also used Gate Gourmet particularly helpful in this respect. BA perceived the fact that every other airline was outsourcing catering at the time it took its own outsourcing decision as comforting. Instead it ought to have realized there were also certain risks involved with this decision and taken appropriate measures. The use of heuristics indeed proved to be costly in this case.

*Source: Financial Times*, 2005b, 2005d; http://news.bbc.co.uk/2/hi/business/4361746.stm (accessed on June 21, 2006).

rapidly increased their outsourcing levels, measured as external sourcing over turnover. We held semi-structured interviews, during which we asked firms specifically about the activities they had outsourced over the previous ten years and the process through which outsourcing took place. In table 4.1 below, an overview is provided of the firms in these two industries.

In the instruments and appliances industry a 7.1 percent increase in outsourcing was observed between 1993 and 1998. Respondents consistently described their products as being medium- to high-tech. They also talked about rapid technological change, particularly the increasing electronic content of their products, and shortening product life-cycles. One specific component that all six firms had outsourced during and after the time-period covered by our interviews was the printed circuit board (PCB). Respondents cited a combination of lack of scale and the benefits of using specialized, up-to-date external PCB suppliers, especially in light of the shortening product life-cycles. Respondent 2 (of firm 2) said: "in the world of electronics things move fast in components. Your components may be up-to-date during development but by the time you release the product, eighteen months down the road, some of them are already outdated."

In the pumps and compressors industry outsourcing increased by 6.7 percent between 1993 and 1998. In this industry, products were generally described as moving along more slowly and being less advanced technologically. Most change was related to the use of different materials depending on specific customer demand. Firm A had for instance recently completed its first pump made of titanium, because its customer pumped around an aggressive liquid that had previously destroyed a steel pump within two years. It outsourced much of the production of that pump to an Italian supplier who knew how to work with titanium. So in both industries we could observe some industry-wide trends around product development and outsourcing.

Some of the motives behind outsourcing decisions involved a comparison that broadly looked like an economizing motive, as TCE or the RBV would describe it. Many firms, for instance, suggested that they no longer integrated specific production processes because they were unable to use machines at full capacity, which then caused a production cost disadvantage *vis-à-vis* specialized outside suppliers as argued by TCE (Williamson, 1985). Respondent 3 (of firm 3), for instance, when talking about a specific process said: "but you have to guarantee a 98

Table 4.1. *An overview of the firms that were interviewed*

| | Firm 1 | Firm 2 | Firm 3 | Firm 4 | Firm 5 | Firm 6 |
|---|---|---|---|---|---|---|
| **Instruments and appliances** | | | | | | |
| Firm | Large multinational, market leader | Large multinational, cost focus | Large multinational, market leader | Small local firm, many exports | Small local firm, many exports, market leader | Small local firm, many exports, market leader |
| Outsourcing history | Traditionally highly integrated | Traditionally integrated | Traditionally highly integrated | Traditionally highly integrated | Traditionally integrated | Traditionally highly integrated |
| Outsourcing processes | Many and substantial | Limited but one large offshoring decision | Many and substantial | Substantial, part of corporate restructuring | Some, limited internal capacity | Many and substantial |
| Outsourcing examples | Competitors, icons | – | Competitors, similar firms | – | Similar firms | – |
| Information sources | Management literature, knowledge networks | – | Management literature, knowledge networks | Management literature | – | Outside experience, management literature, knowledge networks |
| Other involvement | Global headquarters | Divisional headquarters, suppliers | Divisional headquarters, consultants | Consultants | Joint-venture parents | – |

Table 4.1. An overview of the firms that were interviewed (continued)

**Pumps and compressors**

| | Firm A | Firm B | Firm C | Firm D | Firm E | Firm F |
|---|---|---|---|---|---|---|
| Firm | Large multinational, many exports | Large multinational, many exports | Medium-sized Dutch multinational, market leader | Large multinational, market leader | Small local firm, niche player | Large multinational, many exports |
| Outsourcing history | Traditionally highly integrated | Traditionally highly integrated | Traditionally not very integrated | Traditionally somewhat integrated | Traditionally highly integrated | Traditionally highly integrated |
| Outsourcing processes | Few | Some, more substantial after 1998 | Few, substantial | Some, substantial | Some, many after 1998 | Some |
| Outsourcing examples | Similar firms | – | – | Related firms, icons | – | Similar firms |
| Information sources | – | – | Management literature, knowledge networks | – | Management literature | Informal knowledge networks |
| Other involvement | – | Consultants | Suppliers | Global headquarters, consultants | Suppliers | Global headquarters, customers |

percent load on that machine, because if it is not at full capacity you can no longer compete with a company that only produces those components." He said that because the business unit could no longer do that, they had turned themselves into a "showcase manufacturer," with very limited internal production capacity. This example confirms the frequency argument in transaction cost economics, as this manager suggests that the low frequency with which the machinery would be used internally made internalization a less attractive alternative. It also refers to asset specificity, in that the manager recognizes the machinery is specific to the process, yet outside suppliers can combine the demand of multiple customers to overcome the frequency problem. Other firms, like firm 6, increased their reliance on external suppliers because they grew so rapidly that their internal resources and capacity were simply insufficient to keep up with that growth, an argument in line with how dynamic industries are described in the RBV (Barney, 1999). Firm E, after a management buy-out in 1998, drastically restructured its outsourcing policies along the lines of "core business" thinking. Outsourcing also involved all kinds of services activities for these manufacturing firms. Firm D, for instance, had outsourced all of its HRM activities, including selection, training, and development.

But more in line with the bandwagoning argument, sourcing managers also admitted to holding views that were sometimes at odds with the rest of the organization and that shaped the organization's decisions. Respondent 3 said about future outsourcing trends inside his firm: "it will only continue, but that's my personal vision of things." In firm 6, the role that the outside experience with outsourcing of newly arrived individuals played in breaking inertia was highlighted: "Look, when you work somewhere and you have always done things in a certain manner, you may develop the idea that you're the only one who knows how to get things done. And you have never seen something like that [outsourcing] before, but when you have seen it, you may be prepared to do it." In that same firm, the CEO thought outsourcing was very important and had turned it into a key policy. He wanted to implement it more quickly but internal resistance (outsourcing inertia) made that difficult. In firm B the replacement of the management team also led to drastic changes in the firm's outsourcing policies. The old management team, consisting of former consultants, heavily favored outsourcing, but the new team less so. Respondent A admitted to outsourcing often being a "gut feel" decision inside the company:

"You buy things and you make things. Then you start comparing. You walk around the plant sometimes and then I wonder, for example, is that still happening here?" This points to the role that instincts and heuristics seem to play in this type of decision-making.

When looking at how competitors' outsourcing policies affect the decisions that managers made, it turned out that many managers were actually unaware of the outsourcing policies of their direct competitors. Although they did cite competitive pressures in general as a key reason to outsource, with very few exceptions they did not make explicit comparisons between their own and their competitors' outsourcing strategies. After admitting that he knew next to nothing about the identities of competing firms and had no idea about what they outsourced, respondent 4 did say: "I think that cost pressures are a key motive for outsourcing." This not only shows that the behavior of direct competitors is not always observed by sourcing managers, but also points to the lack of coordination between various functions inside this firm. Given that sourcing strategy is all about coordination at the interfaces between functions (Kotabe, 1992), it casts some doubt over this firm's operations.

Quite a few firms in both industries looked at the practices of similar manufacturing firms that they did not compete with directly though. Often these similar firms were located in the same region of the country or were part of the same supply chain, attesting to the importance of local search in decision-making (Cyert and March, 1963). Respondent 6 pointed at the importance of using informal contacts with individuals working for such similar firms.

A third type of comparison we found was with iconic firms or industries. As perhaps should be expected the automobile industry featured heavily as an icon but interestingly so did the food industry. If managers used such outsourcing examples, they admitted this shaped their decisions. Firm D, as a supplier to the automobile industry, had already outsourced quite a few activities prior to 1993, which shows that industry's forwardness when it comes to outsourcing. The industry moved ahead of the major wave in outsourcing in the Netherlands, which occurred after 1993 (De Wit, Mol, and van Drunen, 1998; Mol, 2005).

Respondents also used outside information, primarily from a variety of knowledge networks and from popular management literature. They varied in the extent to which they found this information useful and applicable. Respondent E, a veteran with decades of experience in the job, suggested, for instance, that "what I find time and time again is that I do not see many new things there." Respondents 4 and 6 however, as relative newcomers, did use these sources a lot and in these cases they influenced decision-making as well. In the interview with respondent 3, we also discussed the role of the professional literature in shaping his thinking on outsourcing. After explaining that he does not keep up with the academic literature, he said that "I do read the management literature, you know, and it includes articles about whether or not to outsource." After being asked whether it shaped the firm's ideas on outsourcing, he responded by saying "Yes. And it also proves that we are quite far along." He had previously explained the firm was ahead of its competitors in how much it outsourced. We asked whether he and his colleagues visited professional conferences to gather ideas as well. He said: "No, not in order to take up new ideas but to observe." We asked: "To observe what others do?" and he replied: "Yes exactly and to see what the trends are."

Respondent 1, a sourcing manager at a subsidiary of a large technology firm, explained how he uses his contacts with academia to take in what he considered to be leading-edge knowledge. He said: "Well, I make sure that I see [names various Dutch professors in purchasing management]. I know all of them. After that I take in more practical information. I attend seminars, courses and I read, and that way you keep your sourcing knowledge up to date." Asked to expand upon his use of academics, he answered: "Well, the fact you are here now also shows I talk to those people a lot. Surveys and the like, I spend a lot of time on them. Partly because I enjoy it but also because it provides you with feedback." These examples show how the competition, the profession, and other institutions or fashion-setters serve as examples and information sources for firms' behaviors (Abrahamson, 1996; Abrahamson and Fairchild, 1999).

Various outside parties were involved in outsourcing decisions. Respondent 4 said of his interaction with consultants that they suggested that substantial cost savings could be obtained by outsourcing a specific activity. Our respondent indicated that in practice this was not easy to realize but the consultant "did shake things up in the long term. Someone comes calling from the outside and that's how other people became convinced and hence at a later stage, and perhaps earlier than planned, the prints [printed circuit boards] were outsourced as well.

Everything we had left was then farmed out as well." Firm D also used consultants, though mostly to listen to their argumentation in favor of outsourcing, to test whether these were valid arguments in its own situation. Suppliers and sometimes customers similarly exerted pressures to outsource. Firm C was regularly confronted with suppliers who suggested they might be able to lower its costs or improve its final products through outsourcing an activity. But respondent C also made clear that supplier offerings, knowledge networks, and popular management literature did not have much of a bearing on internal decision-making.

Firms in these industries varied on some other dimensions too. Businesses that were part of large multinational firms, for instance, had relatively analytical, though not formalized, outsourcing procedures in place, while smaller firms did not. These multinational firms were more likely to know their competitors' outsourcing strategies and were often able to draw some meaningful comparison with competitors. The larger multinational firms were also much more likely to engage in outsourcing, especially global outsourcing, and some exchanged information on outsourcing policies with colleagues abroad. For these firms, divisional or global headquarters were normally involved in outsourcing decisions, often to the extent that they dictated terms. Some managers were more-or-less instructed to start outsourcing more and had to find suitable activities themselves. This is an empirical confirmation of the argument provided in chapter 3 to counter some of the assumptions of TCE, that at least some firms operate outsourcing policies that extend beyond a single transaction or even a cluster of transactions. It shows that the firm or business can provide a valid level of analysis for outsourcing decisions.

Overall these industry cases, while obviously not providing any statistical significance, do appear to point at a link between the presence of competitive and institutional bandwagons and of outsourcing processes. Firm A and firm 5, for instance, were slowest on the outsourcing trail and also admitted to not really keeping an eye on outside developments. Firms that were most actively involved in knowledge networks and other possible sources of information and bandwagoning appeared to be among the quickest and most comprehensive outsourcers. It is clear from these cases that some heuristics are in use in outsourcing decision-making, in the form of bandwagon effects. Outsourcing decisions, then, are not only about economizing.

In a second empirical study of bandwagon effects we also found substantial statistical support for both types of bandwagon (Mol, van Oosterhout, and Ritskes, 2005). In 2004 we surveyed over 400 for-profit and not-for-profit organizations on their business process outsourcing decisions. This study intended to look at specific types of bandwagons in order to capture the bandwagon phenomenon in more detail. We included transaction cost and core competence arguments as possible alternative explanations and controlled for various other factors.

It turned out that observing competitor behavior was a positive predictor for decisions to outsource business processes. In addition, involvement of colleagues outside their own organization (fellow professionals) had a positive influence, while involvement of accountants had a negative influence. The effect of the profession fits in neatly with arguments on the role of professions in spreading managerial beliefs in neo-institutional sociology (in the tradition instigated by DiMaggio and Powell, 1983, but see also, for instance, Guler, Guillén, and Macpherson, 2002). That the involvement of accountants had a negative effect is perhaps surprising at first sight. It can be traced to their desire to assess organizations holistically. Outsourcing leads to disaggregation and hence complicates accounting activities, so we argue. This also shows that institutional bandwagons need not always lead to more outsourcing but could actually lead to less outsourcing too. At the same time we could not find confirmation for proposed effects of consultants, suppliers, or customers. On the latter two groups we (Mol, van Oosterhout, and Ritskes, 2005) concluded that because business processes do not directly affect supply chains, suppliers and customers might not be as interested in who executes these processes. One interviewee explained that customers did not press his firm to outsource more: "No, you just need to source more cheaply."[8] Consultants, who used to be among the major proponents of outsourcing, appear to have changed their tone in recent years and may have become somewhat more skeptical (Doig, Ritter, Speckhals, and Woolson, 2001). That perhaps explains why their involvement no

---

[8] This is in line with the typical notion of output control from TCE, which suggests that customers are not interested in how an end result is achieved, just in the result itself. Outside customers keep their suppliers at arm's length so it is argued (Williamson, 1985). In contrast, inside the firm, throughput control is used, which implies a predominant concern with how outputs are attained.

longer leads to higher outsourcing levels. It could also be that customers do not listen to their consultants as much anymore, perhaps being skeptical of the reliability of their statements.

In another paper (Mol, van Tulder, and Beije, 2005), we found that levels of international outsourcing are co-determined by communication flows among subsidiaries of multinational firms. It is quite common for managers located in different parts or different subsidiaries of a multinational firm to exchange all kinds of information since multinationals now operate as a network (Birkinshaw, 1997). Once they start exchanging information about possible supply sources this information makes it more likely that a foreign supplier will be evaluated positively and hence increases the likelihood that this supplier will be selected over other suppliers and that this supplier's offering will be rated above a competing internal bid in an outsourcing decision. The conceptual mechanism at work here is "search and evaluation" (Rangan, 2000). In international transactions, evaluation costs are particularly problematic because foreign suppliers are not normally a part of a firm's network. But another subsidiary located near the supplier can serve as an information intermediary and provide the focal firm with enough assurances the supplier is trustworthy and offers desirable services or other inputs. So the firm's internal network may also be a bandwagon source. This empirical evidence and related conceptualization has shown that outsourcing processes (changes in outsourcing levels) can be brought into motion through bandwagon effects, including both competitive and institutional bandwagoning.

## The human factor

Bandwagoning is an organization-wide phenomenon. This raises the question whether there are also factors at the level of the individual or small group that influence outsourcing. Do variations in decision-makers' backgrounds and preferences produce different outsourcing decisions? From anecdotal evidence we know that outsourcing processes can take on a prolonged character. Abrahamson (2004) describes how one particular activity at Cisco was transferred to an outside supplier, then brought back in-house, and later outsourced again. All the time there was much uncertainty over what needed to get done and how it had to get done. It seemed, so Abrahamson suggests, that every new manager brought a different frame of mind regarding the merits of outsourcing, leading to changes in outsourcing decisions whenever that person was replaced. In interviews, I have encountered similar cases of new management teams arriving that carried with them a different outsourcing philosophy. Among Dutch manufacturing firms such new teams are usually more amenable to outsourcing, leading to the outsourcing of components and services the old guard would not have considered outsourcing. Managers who have been around for a long time are often hesitant to make radical decisions. They also entered the profession at a time when outsourcing was far from a common refrain and vertical integration was a more popular strategy (Ruhnke, 1966).

Chandler (1962) observed that major structural changes, such as the introduction of the multidivisional form on which he focused, are often introduced by managers who are relatively young and new to their posts. Various possible explanations abound. The most optimistic one, and the one to which Chandler (1962) adheres, states that these new managers have a different training background, allowing them to understand and see things that those trained in a previous era did not notice. In Chandler's case, people like Alfred Sloan had a background in engineering, having graduated from the Massachusetts Institute of Technology. At MIT these engineers had learned to understand how to engineer organizations. Today's equivalent, in the context of outsourcing, might be managers with an M.B.A. education. These managers will have learned the latest business theories and techniques, including the focus on core activities and the potential value of supplier relations. According to this account, younger and more recently trained managers will show a tendency towards outsourcing because they know it is often a superior solution.

More generally, the training background of individuals can produce a set of behavioral patterns. In the study of the relative value of markets and organizations, it has been observed that sociologists and economists come from opposite assumptions (see, for instance, Baum and Dobbin's [2000] insightful book). For economists the market is the default mode of operations; hence the central question in transaction cost economics is "Why and when do markets fail?" In other words, the buy option (outsourcing) is presumed to be the preferred option, unless proven otherwise (Domberger, 1998; Williamson, 1975). For sociologists the opposite is true. They are focused on the benefits that organizations and networks thereof produce (Granovetter, 1985;

Knorr-Cetina and Preda, 2005; Kogut and Zander, 1992). Markets, in their minds, are the exception and not the rule. Anyone trained in either of these professions will carry along this set of preferences and may therefore be biased towards one type of solution. This bias is clearly a less optimistic explanation than Chandler's argument, which is based more around the technical superiority of professional managers trained in a more recent era. As far as I am aware there has not been any empirical research to investigate what effects professional backgrounds have on outsourcing decisions but there clearly is a research agenda to be tackled here.

A further explanation for the behavior of managers with a longer track record inside the organization and in their posts builds around their social and interpersonal relations. Since outsourcing often involves the transfer of people or even their firing, it could well be harder for those who have been around longer to make such decisions. By outsourcing they would be cutting off some existing ties and negatively affecting others. Even if they believe outsourcing is the best solution from the perspective of firm performance, they may need to trade off these gains against their social capital inside the organization. While that is also true for relative newcomers, they often have not built much capital to start with and thus stand to lose less of it. As alluded to earlier, in one case this seemed to allow the new management team of former consultants to outsource many activities that were previously conducted in-house. This mechanism can be one of the factors contributing to organizational inertia when it comes to outsourcing. Again, I do not know of anyone who has investigated this effect empirically.

## Understanding the outsourcing process

Relatively few research accounts have been published of how the outsourcing process takes place. How is it that outsourcing decisions take place in practice and how do organizations then execute such decisions and transfer activities, and possibly assets, including human resources, to outside suppliers? Is it possible to distinguish stages in the outsourcing process?

Clearly, like all organizational decisions, outsourcing decisions can be surrounded by a lot of "politicking." Power struggles or differences of opinion over what is the best outsourcing decision can generally occur in three different ways. They can occur along the lines of the organizational hierarchy, for instance between a firm's headquarters and one of its subsidiaries. A second type occurs between different functional areas, because different functional areas are generally interested in different outcomes. The third type is when certain individuals have private motives for supporting or rejecting outsourcing.

Hierarchical power struggles, between lower- and higher-level decision-makers, are usually resolved most swiftly, for obvious reasons. The higher level can use fiat to push through a decision. Yet that need not always be the case. One US manufacturing firm I investigated intended to outsource an important process, that was at the time performed inside its Dutch subsidiary, to a low labor cost location. Obviously local management and employees were less than thrilled with that prospect and opposed the decision. Rather than escalating the conflict by simply imposing its will, top management in the United States asked the subsidiary to present it with a rock solid case why this manufacturing process ought to be retained. Local management and employees then went out to gather as much information as possible and thought about further process improvements. Based on their analysis, top management eventually decided to retain the process. So in this case, information exchange helped to avoid the use of fiat.

Power struggles between functional areas and departments are generally harder to resolve. In table 4.2 I have summarized the effects outsourcing generally has on various functions. These effects can produce a set of predispositions. For instance, among purchasing managers it is hard to find true opponents of outsourcing as outsourcing in many ways forms their bread and butter. Accountants, as we have recently shown for business process outsourcing decisions (Mol, van Oosterhout, and Ritskes, 2005), are generally not very keen on outsourcing because it makes their job, of assessing firms' financial statements, more difficult. When these power struggles or mere differences of opinion between various functional specialists or departments come to the fore, decisions seem generally to be referred to higher organizational levels. In other words, inter-functional conflict may play a role before decisions are made primarily because conflicting advice is provided to the higher decision-making authority, but is perhaps not played out directly in the decision itself.

The third type of conflict, where a manager has some private agenda is harder to analyze because private agendas can take such a wide

**Table 4.2.** *Functional areas and outsourcing*

| Functional area | Effect of outsourcing | Attitude |
|---|---|---|
| Marketing | Outsourcing can either improve or deteriorate customer offerings. Prices of products may decrease but their uniqueness and the reliability of deliveries may decrease too. | Negative to positive |
| Purchasing | Outsourcing creates growth for the purchasing department, in the form of new relations to be managed and new contracts to be created. Managing outsourcing is the primary task of purchasing. | Positive |
| Operations | Outsourcing may undermine the quality of work but under some circumstances can actually improve it too. Outsourcing introduces the need to manage operations among multiple organizations. | Negative to positive |
| Finance | Outsourcing generally lowers cost levels. It invariably implies a shift from fixed to more manageable variable costs. | Positive |
| Information systems | Outsourcing may cause the need for a more complex information system, in which information from different suppliers is also integrated. At the same time this may pose an interesting technical challenge. | Negative to positive |
| Accounting | Outsourcing undermines the transparency of accounts because supplier-provided information will be less detailed. The predictability of numbers will decrease. | Negative |
| Human resources | Outsourcing potentially undermines social cohesiveness in the organization. It may also be harder to create a shared corporate culture among outsourced employees and suppliers. | Negative |
| Logistics | Outsourcing potentially complicates the supply chain because it increases the number of firms involved. But it allows for lower stock levels through just-in-time deliveries. | Negative to positive |

variety of forms. The individual concerned may either favor or oppose outsourcing and will attempt to influence the decision in order to further the private agenda. What drives that agenda is far less obvious though and a generalization is therefore hard to make, but various examples may serve as illustrations. Not outsourcing might provide a private benefit because it allows an individual to remain directly in charge of a bigger group of people thereby enhancing status and perhaps pay. Outsourcing to a certain supplier can help an individual with social or family ties to that supplier and might perhaps even lead to illegal payments. Successfully managing an outsourcing process could improve the career prospects of an individual. An individual may benefit from outsourcing a unit containing political opponents inside the organization. Another situation that could occur is where an individual knows a task is quite daunting or already headed for failure. Outsourcing could then produce a much needed scapegoat. This type of motive is, for instance, well known in the contracting of consultants (Kipping and Engwall, 2002).

A key factor that influences whether any of these conflicts takes place, what their magnitude is, and how they get resolved, is the social cost of outsourcing, which was discussed earlier, in chapter 2. Where such social costs are substantial, prolonged battles may emerge in which various groupings try to steer the decision in directions less harmful to their constituents. Whether or not outsourcing takes place then becomes a matter of the degree of success with which outsourcing can be "sold" to the organization. This selling process may require a lot of micro-management, possibly making the entire outsourcing operation less beneficial. In chapter 7 the theme of selling outsourcing, specifically selling outsourcing as experimentation, will be taken up again. A final note here is that who gets outsourced may also be a consequence of the outcomes of such political struggles.

Given all this discussion of the organizational and individual influences that are produced by social and psychological behavior, and that themselves produce less than economically optimal outsourcing decisions, what are we to conclude? A first possible route is to suggest that in the thick of things these factors matter very little. Outsourcing decisions are still by and large economizing events, one could argue, and deviations from the economizing approach that take place are best treated as part of the error term in a statistical analysis. In other words, some unexplained variance will always remain and we have to accept that our understanding of outsourcing will necessarily be limited by it. This is a highly problematic answer for various reasons. First, it is quite unclear whether it holds true empirically. Given the variance in outsourcing decisions that the economizing approach explains, a larger part of these decisions remains unexplained in most empirical analyses than is actually explained. Even if empirical evidence could be produced to support this argument, there is something fundamentally unsatisfactory about ignoring explanations which we know hold some ground. Such single-minded mono-disciplinary or mono-theoretical commitment has been equated by some to quasi-religious behavior (Ghoshal, 2005). It may also produce a self-fulfilling prophecy as deviations of the behavior that is prescribed are interpreted as anomalies that ought to be removed (Ghoshal, 2005).

A second route towards drawing a conclusion takes the other extreme position by arguing that the economizing explanation of outsourcing is errant because real organizational behavior is inherently more complex and economic rationality does not figure very prominently in it. Outsourcing decisions are the outcome of internal power struggles, and outcomes are partly driven by pressures from all kinds of outside institutions. Moreover, in the end, managers and employees alike seek to satisfy their private agendas rather than pursue organizational goals. In other words, there is not much that is economically rational about outsourcing decisions and it might be argued that the part that is economically rational is a byproduct of chance more than anything. Outsourcing, in this view, is a form of irrational managerial behavior. This to me is a rather sinister view of organizations and their inner workings. Organizations that really display a Dilbert-like dysfunctionality, and little more than that, are unlikely to survive under the pressures of customer demand and competition, although luck may at least temporarily help them through.

It is therefore the third route, which essentially is a synthesis of the first two, that I find most satisfying. It claims that outsourcing decisions are subject to multiple realities simultaneously. These include, but are probably not limited to, economic, social, psychological, and political rationalities. Although outsourcing fulfills the function of lowering cost levels or creating better products and services, it also fulfills other functions, like securing a manager's power-base, being seen to undertake actions that are in accordance with what other actors in the institutional environment expect, and satisfying individuals' various needs. If we want to understand outsourcing as a phenomenon better, we need to draw upon each of these rationalities and understand the various functions for which outsourcing may be used. While competition may be one of the factors forcing firms to outsource more, there are other factors in place too, if only because competition is never complete.

By stating that outsourcing decisions are best understood as being subject to multiple rationalities, I do not wish to imply that all outsourcing decisions are completely rational, though it would be my suspicion that all outsourcing decisions are at least largely rational on some criteria. As in any product of a social process there is always going to be some seemingly unexplainable part of outsourcing decisions. That unexplained part will contain behavior that apparently does not follow any of the rationalities and may indeed be produced by random, chance events. Thus there is some serendipity in place as well. Furthermore, as discussed before, decision-makers do not generally optimize their decisions along single or indeed multiple dimensions. Rather they seem content to follow various heuristics in order to come to satisfactory solutions.

## The motivation and identity of individuals in outsourcing

Since any outsourced activity has to be performed by people, there is some merit in looking at how the motivation and identity of the people who perform the outsourced activity are shaped. What happens to the motivation levels and identity of individuals who are transferred from the outsourcing organization to a supplier or become independent suppliers themselves? This is an area of growing interest in organizational behavior and organization theory. There are two empirical contexts where substantial changes have occurred that researchers have particularly studied.

First, there is the trend, especially strong in the United States, to use independent contractors for technical work (including IT). Barley and Kunda (2004) have recently published a very detailed account of the world of contractors. They provide some insightful conclusions into what becoming a contractor does to the individuals concerned. Contractors become contractors, so they argue, because they see themselves as experts but become increasingly disillusioned with the organizations for which they work, encounter events like downsizing or a change in working conditions, and engage in a new opportunity or anticipate higher rewards from going independent. Independent contractors generally seemed to earn more money, although they might lose some privileges along the way (Barley and Kunda, 2004). Also, being an independent contractor generally fits their work ethos, which is based around technical rationality and not organizational rationality or politicking. Still, many individuals need to be convinced to become independent contractors, which staffing agencies are very happy to do, as are some former colleagues.

The identity, and motivation, of contractors is different from that of regular employees (Barley and Kunda, 2004). Contractors sense a combination of respect and resentment from the employees of firms for which they work. On the one hand, their technical expertise is often appreciated. On the other hand, they continue to be treated as outsiders, or even invaders, by "regular" employees. Contractors also have a hard time choosing between trying to take initiative and put a lot of effort into their jobs and doing only what the job description requires. The former option makes regular employees feel threatened but the latter appears to signify a lack of commitment. As contractors become older and more experienced, they are also more resigned to their role of outsider (Barley and Kunda, 2004). To varying extents contractors also manage to develop a coherent identity, by disassociating themselves from the immediate technical context of their work. That is how they become what they will refer to as itinerant experts (Barley and Kunda, 2004).

The second context in which identity and motivation issues come to the fore is offshoring. Offshore outsourcing involves a transfer of activities across both geographical and organizational boundaries and hence is a relatively complex transaction. The large providers of offshore outsourcing services, like Wipro, Tata Consulting, and Infosys in India, have all built up separate delivery units for their key customers like major banks and airlines. Employees working in one of those units pledge a double allegiance. They may be Wipro employees but they perform work solely for Cisco, British Airways, or HSBC and represent that firm in dealing with its customers. It turns out such employees tend to become uprooted because they have trouble in clearly identifying which company it is they are working for. In some ways they feel superior to other Wipro employees because they work for a prestigious customer. On the other hand they are not truly treated as employees by that customer. Managing the identities and motivation levels of employees, therefore, is a major challenge for offshore outsourcing providers. Another potential issue that arises with outsourcing is whether safety standards can be maintained with outside contractors, who might be unfamiliar with working circumstances, for instance in the context of petrochemicals.

## Conclusion

In this chapter the issue of misalignment, too much or too little out-sourcing, was raised. One reason misalignment was said to occur is that firm-level outsourcing tends to follow a punctuated equilibrium model, involving longer periods of outsourcing inertia followed by shorter periods of rapid outsourcing. These periods of rapid outsourcing, and the outsourcing processes contained therein, can be explained by band-wagon models. Discussions of the outsourcing process further detailed how a variety of organizational and individual factors confound the relatively simple and neat micro-economic models discussed in earlier chapters. Thus outsourcing processes are complex and decision-makers attempt to satisfice multiple rationalities simultaneously.

# 5 | *Shifting the curve*

THUS far I have taken a rather static approach to the negative curvilinear argument, more or less neglecting whether shifts of the curve are feasible, horizontally, vertically, or in the steepness of the curve, and whether and how such shifts are firm-specific. This chapter deals with vertical shifts, while chapter 6 will tackle horizontal shifts and changes in the steepness of the curve. Here the focus is on differences between firms, especially why one firm's curve may be located higher than that of another firm. The central question is therefore how firms manage to achieve a transition as shown by arrow C in figure 3.2. So what is discussed here is how a firm may raise its constant $c$. This also implies that the performance aspects discussed in this chapter do not relate directly to the outsourcing level as such, unlike the previous or next chapters. Of course, firms only have some influence over constant $c$, as some part of a firm's performance will be predetermined by variables such as market conditions. Furthermore, only a part of the influence firms have over constant $c$ is discussed here. The first part of this chapter will read much like a standard strategic management treatise on performance differentials. Then the focus will be on more detail on how interorganizational relations, specifically buyer–supplier relations in the case of outsourcing, can be a source of sustained competitive advantage. Next this chapter will concentrate on firms' ability to manage outsourcing, by introducing the concept of external span of control. Various mechanisms are also described to improve this external span of control.

## Sources of performance heterogeneity

A vertical shift of the curve implies it moves either upwards or downwards. However, the focus here will be on upward shifts, for two reasons. First, most observers will be interested in how firms improve their performance, not how they make it deteriorate. The study of how firms improve their performance is a common description of the field of strategic management. Second, an analysis of the causes of above average performance will also implicitly address the causes of below average performance, as long as both forms of variance occur along the same dimensions, which seems to be a reasonable assumption to make. It implies, for instance, that if above average performance can result from superior management of supplier relations, as argued in more detail below, below average performance may result from inferior management of supplier relations. Outsourcing and supplier relations are argued to be strongly intertwined decisions (Takeishi, 2001).

A further observation is that performance heterogeneity can occur at both ends of the spectrum, through integrated activities and through outsourced activities. In other words, firms can enhance their performance by becoming better at the activities they undertake in-house but they can also enhance their performance by becoming better at managing those activities they have outsourced. Both of these will now be discussed in turn. Most attention will be paid to the latter issue though, because it fits the subject of this book.

## Internal operational effectiveness

Why and how firms get better performance out of their internal activities is perhaps the classic question in strategic management (Barney, 1991; Porter, 1985). Answers to that question can be found, therefore, in the two paradigms that have dominated the strategic management literature of the past twenty-five years. The positioning approach, developed primarily by Porter (1980; 1985), argues that a firm's competitive advantage results from the posture it takes in its final marketplace, which can involve a focus on costs, a focus on differentiation, or on a combination of the two. By analyzing its industry environment, Porter (1980) argued, a firm can find out how best to position itself in that industry. Porter's (1980) well-known five-forces model provides a practical tool for such an analysis. Porter (1985) also advanced the notion of a value chain that describes all of a firm's primary and support activities.

Barney (1991) and others (e.g. Amit and Schoemaker, 1993; Conner, 1991) criticized the positioning approach for being too focused on external analysis and not focused enough on the internal strengths and weaknesses of the firm and how these can contribute to its competitive advantage. Hence they proposed a resource-based view of the firm (Barney, 1991; Conner, 1991; Wernerfelt, 1984) that views firms as collections of resources. This collection of resources may, under certain circumstances, provide a source of competitive advantage. Barney and Hesterly (2006) discuss the VRIO framework as a tool for analyzing which of a firm's resources could provide it with competitive advantage. VRIO involves analyzing whether resources are Valuable, Rare, Inimitable, and controlled by the Organization. Valuable resources are those resources that contribute significantly to what customers perceive to be the value of a good or service produced by the firm. If resources contain no inherent value in the eyes of customers, they cannot help a firm improve its offerings. Rare resources are those resources that are not generally available and for which there is an imperfect market. Resources that are commonly available, like most natural resources, do not provide a source of differentiation. Inimitable resources are resources that cannot readily be copied by other firms, nor be substituted in their effects by other resources. If other firms manage to create a substitute resource or can easily imitate a firm's resources, the competitive advantage provided by those resources is temporary at best. And finally resources must be under the control of the organization because the ability to deploy them is what makes their value, rareness, and inimitability useful. Competences can be viewed as bundles of resources (Teece, Pisano, and Shuen, 1997). Such a bundle of resources is more likely to generate competitive advantage than a single resource because it is more complex. This complexity increases both the rareness and inimitability of resources and could possibly improve their value as well.

Examples of both positioning-based and resource-based competitive advantages are abundant in practice. In the airline industry, firms like Southwestern and Ryanair have clearly chosen to be the lowest-cost providers. Bugatti and its 400 km./h. Veyron model, on the other hand, is a clear example of a car manufacturer that seeks to differentiate itself from the competition based on its products. A well-known capability of General Electric is its nurturing of managerial talent inside the firm. This is how GE finds individuals who can take on the CEO role in future. Chelsea Football Club, on the other hand, acquired important resources externally through the transfer market, in the form of highly talented players and a coaching staff to help it compete for English and

European championships. Chelsea does not appear to possess that capability.

If firms manage to outperform their competitors based on such internal advantages, what consequences does this have for their out-sourcing–performance curve? The effect is twofold. First, it will raise the curve proportionate to the number of activities undertaken in-house. Only those activities on the left-hand side of the curve will be affected by internal advantages. Thus the more activities a firm has vertically integrated, the more it benefits from its internal advantages. In short, there is a leverage effect. But there is also a second effect, which follows theoretically from discussions on the resource-based view in chapter 2. For firms that have such internal advantages, the balance between make and buy will also shift towards the make option (integration) because the relative advantages of make become larger. Thus the optimal amount of outsourcing shifts towards make rather than buy. Recall that make activities are generally found to the left of the optimal point, as outsourceability is lowest there. Figure 5.1 demonstrates this outcome, as constant $c$ increases in value but the optimal of outsourcing also shifts somewhat to the left in this figure.

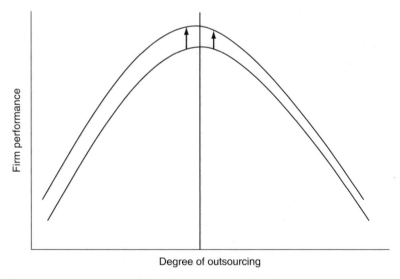

**Figure 5.1.** An upward shift of the curve produced by a higher internal operational effectiveness

## The external span of control

In this section the focus will shift from internal sources of advantage to advantage through outsourcing and from outsourcing design to implementation, through the management of relations with outside suppliers. As with internal operational effectiveness, it is possible in principle for some firms to be better than others in the management of external outsourcing relations. Of course, that will also hold for other external relations, but they will be treated here as a part of the constant $c$ that is a given. A sketch will now follow of what such differences consist of and what effect they have on the firm's overall performance.

There is some literature that discusses not only outsourcing design but also implementation or management (e.g. Bensaou, 1999; Butler, 2003). This work does not, however, provide a general conceptual framework for understanding inter-firm differences in the ability to implement designs. I propose to use the term "external span of control" as an indicator of such varying abilities. More precisely the external span of control is defined as the *firm's overall ability to manage multiple and varying relations with suppliers*. Henri Fayol (1949) first introduced the notion of a manager's span of control in 1916. He referred to it as the

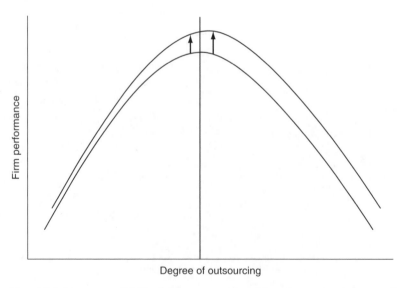

Figure 5.2. An upward shift of the curve produced by a large external span of control

number of workers a single manager can usefully manage. The observation that a single manager can control multiple but not an unlimited number of workers led to the classical, multiple-layered, pyramid-like organization structure, which we so commonly associate with the word "hierarchy." It is now recognized that diseconomies of scale prevent firms from adding unlimited levels to their hierarchies. Furthermore, technological changes allow managers to manage more employees effectively.

If one thinks of suppliers as workers and the firm as a manager of its suppliers, the metaphor is clear. Beyond the metaphoric though, it is equally true that firms cannot manage endless numbers of suppliers. Interestingly firms have also started structuring their supply relationships in a pyramid-like model in what is called tiering of suppliers, perhaps best exemplified by the *keiretsu* system. This raises the question of the extent to which sourcing managers face span-of-control problems in supplier relations. Practical experience shows that they make continuous trade-offs when implementing sourcing strategies (Hendry, 1995). A firm's managers do not have unlimited time and resources available to find and execute the best possible design. Thus they constantly need to distribute time and effort among supplier relations. Decision-making will be of a heuristic nature because (Simon, 1998: 119): "Administrators (and everyone else for that matter) take into account just a few of the factors of the situation regarded as most relevant and crucial. In particular, they deal with one or a few problems at a time, because the limits on attention simply don't permit everything to be attended to at once."

Bounded rationality not only affects whether the best possible designs can be found but also how these are effectuated. Firms cannot succeed in maximizing the transaction value of every relation. There is a transaction cost attached to each supplier relation a firm wishes to maintain and therefore adding suppliers increases overall transaction costs. As the complexity of the supplier network increases, coordination costs will increase exponentially and there are cognitive limits to the number of suppliers with which individual managers can deal. Thus there is a definite upper limit to the number of supply relations a firm can maintain. The literature, however, proposes a second limit that is related not to the quantity but rather to the quality of relations. It is found in the concepts of weak and strong ties (Uzzi, 1996). Firms and individuals alike are limited in their use of strong ties. Strong ties are distinguishable precisely because they are stronger than the average tie.

In other words, not every supplier relation can be of a cooperative kind. Rather, firms will maintain portfolios of relations of varying strength (Dyer, Cho, and Chu, 1998).

External span of control is a firm-level construct while Fayol's original notion involved individuals. Clearly an issue of the level of analysis arises here and concept-stretching must be avoided. In the area of outsourcing and supplier relations it is usually the firm to which relations are attributed and we speak of a firm "managing relations" (e.g. Dyer and Singh, 1998; Helper and Sako, 1995). In the literal sense of the word this may be incorrect since managers, not firms, manage but it is accepted practice and an abstraction which is required to analyze underlying problems usefully.[1] Surely there are important linkages between firm- and individual-level traits when it comes to dealing with outside parties (Zaheer, McEvily, and Perrone, 1998). Managers make a firm's decisions and execute those. A strong mutual understanding between key individuals at the buying and supplying firms can help in developing an inter-firm relation. In that sense it is important to realize the two levels of analysis operate conjointly. But provided that we accept that the firm manages relations, the concept of external span of control is also applicable to the firm, much like networks can be seen to exist both within organizations, at the level of individuals, and between them, at the level of organizations. A second issue is whether the type of supplier relations should be included. Discussions of Fayol's work have pointed at the influence of external circumstances on the size of the span of control. A manager's span of control depends among other factors on the task complexity of workers and their competence levels. Similarly there is much variation among supplier relations. This generates differences in management requirements since managing four partnership relations will be quite different from managing four arm's length relations. In effect, firms face a trade-off between the number of relations and the type of relations. Therefore it is appropriate to include the type of relation when defining external span of control. Box 5.1, illustrates in detail how a higher external span of control benefits Toyota.

[1] In management parlance many activities, actors, and structures are "managed" by firms. Firms, for instance, are seen to manage alliances, innovation, capital, and customer relations. For purists this may be something of an oddity, as a reviewer once pointed out to me, but for pragmatic purposes I propose to go along with this convention.

## Box 5.1. Toyota: supplier relations champion

The best-known example of creating value from supplier relations is probably Toyota. Like its lean production system (Womack, Jones, and Roos, 1990), its system of supplier relations is quite well understood, particularly the major contours of that system. But as is the case for its lean production system, understanding Toyota's system of supplier relations well does not by any means provide the ability to replicate it. Although other car manufacturers and firms from a wide variety of backgrounds have now copied parts of the system with varying degrees of success (Dyer, 1996), no one comes close to enjoying Toyota's overall success in practice. Therefore it is worth stressing its elements once more. Through intensive relations with suppliers Toyota creates new knowledge and distributes it throughout the supplier network, in which it operates as the central node (Dyer and Nobeoka, 2000). There are various micro-level mechanisms in place for joint learning (Dyer and Nobeoka, 2000). In addition the network is flexible and robust enough to deal with calamities when these arise (Nishiguchi and Beaudet, 1998).

There are various reasons why Toyota's supplier network is so hard to copy. First of all, it is highly complex, involving not only a multitude of relations but also extremely long-term relations, with a history, that involve combinations of interorganizational and interpersonal ties. Such long-term social ties and repeated interactions generate trust (Gulati, 1995) and cannot be replicated easily (Barney, 1991). Second, many suppliers are captive suppliers. Because of the *keiretsu* system, suppliers in Japan are historically tied to one of the automobile suppliers but none of the others. Nippondenso, for instance, is a Toyota supplier historically. These ties can also involve some ownership of the supplier firm by Toyota. In recent times there have been some changes but the system is quite robust. Other car-makers cannot simply come in and work with key Toyota suppliers. This lack of access means some supplier skills simply remain inaccessible for Toyota's competitors. Third, the system of relations is strongly linked to the Japanese system of doing business. While the catch-all phrase of "culture" should not be invoked to explain all cross-national differences, in-depth analyses of the Japanese system (Cusumano, 1985; Nishiguchi, 1994) have shown peculiarities not present elsewhere. Therefore it is hard for foreign rivals to construct an exact copy

(Dyer, 1996). Fourth, there is also a reputation mechanism at work. Because Toyota is known to cooperate and innovate more with suppliers than some other car-makers, especially GM and Ford (Nishiguchi and Beaudet, 1998), it can more easily attract suppliers with an interest in doing that. Ford and GM continue to carry a legacy of the past, when they were known to be interested mostly in getting the best short-term bargains, into their present supplier relations.

Yet other firms, many of them not automobile producers or even manufacturing firms themselves, want to replicate Toyota's successes with getting more out of suppliers, and rightly so. This example shows that supplier relations can provide an important and lasting form of competitive advantage, meaning they are unable to break with their past. A final thought around the importance of success: because Toyota is doing well, other firms want to be associated with it. There exists a Toyota bandwagon!

Nissan has unsuccessfully tried to emulate Toyota's outsourcing and supplier relations approach for decades. Media sources attribute some of the failure to differences in the background of Nissan top management, who were lawyers from top Tokyo schools, compared to Toyota executives who invariably had some engineering knowledge and were more practical and down-to-earth, a much-needed characteristic when it comes to day-to-day exchanges with suppliers. Thus Nissan was not well-equipped to copy the Toyota strategy. This shows that while firms may understand the best design and are willing to implement it, they may eventually not be equally effective in using it.

The Toyota example reveals that design by itself does not lead to success; implementation is equally important. Studies that focus on design only would use the header of coordination costs (Hendry, 1995; Nooteboom, 1999) to describe the investment of time and resources in control mechanisms for managing external relations. That, however, tells us little about how coordination costs occur and even less about how they may differ from one organization to the next. This is a problem more generally with the design focus: if there is a best design under a given set of circumstances, there is no way an organization can create competitive advantage based on that design, unless the implementation phase produces such advantages, or managers of competing firms decide to deviate from the best design. In terms of the discussion in chapter 4, deviation from the best design can again be seen as a form of misalignment, which can be explained by the heuristic nature of decision-making and the need to satisfice multiple objectives simultaneously. The concept of an external span of control is therefore a vehicle for discussing how implementation of designs contributes to competitive advantage.

In terms of the negative curvilinear framework, having a higher external span of control equally helps firms to shift their curve upwards, as do the internal production advantages that were discussed earlier. In addition, and again similarly to internal production advantages, a higher external span of control will as a byproduct imply a rightward shift of the curve as well, because it increases the comparative advantage of the buy option. Firms that are particularly good at exploiting supplier relations will outsource more in anticipation that their returns from outsourcing will be higher than those of competitors.

Of course, if a firm excels in both internal operations and external span of control, the two effects described here will tend to counterbalance each other, implying that for such a firm the optimal point will not shift leftwards or rightwards, but only upwards (compared to its competitors). Likewise a firm that is equally bad at both will not see a shift of its optimal degree of outsourcing towards either more outsourcing or more integration. It will, however, show a lower performance than its competitor firms. While successful firms are generally more publicized because of the higher appeal of success, there are as many unsuccessful firms when it comes to outsourcing. In this book some of the less successful firms include Railtrack, Abbey National, and British Airways. Such firms should expect their performance to drop as a consequence of being unsuccessful outsourcers and the £40 million cost of the Gate Gourmet debacle to British Airways, the takeover of Abbey National, and the bankruptcy of Railtrack seem to be indicators that this is indeed the case.

## Improving the external span of control

A logical question to ask next is what, if anything, firms can do to increase their external span of control. Put differently, what are the antecedents of the external span of control? There are some basic means for improving the span of control that need to be mentioned prior to discussing more elaborate mechanisms. Firms can improve the span of control by shifting more attention towards the outsourcing and supplier relations function through (a) assigning more people to this function or (b) improving the quality of the individuals assigned to it. Thus a relative shift of resources will lead to an improvement in the function. But, as for a manager's span of control, diseconomies of scale will arise when a firm aims to manage all tiers of its supplier network directly. Furthermore, talented individuals are scarce and usually deployable in alternative settings. For instance, they could also be used to improve the internal operational effectiveness. Therefore this type of growth is limited, in the same way it does not make sense to appoint five CEOs to a company. More generally, growth of the firm or an overall improvement of employees' competences will result in similar improvements in the external span of control but, of course, neither is achieved without effort. External span of control will further be co-determined by the industry and country in which a firm operates. Since, however, my interest is in differences between firms in similar industry and country contexts, these determinants will not be discussed extensively. Instead I will now discuss three generating mechanisms of external span of control: first the learning mechanism, which works in two distinct ways; then the competence mechanism; and finally the relational mechanism.

Through outsourcing, can firms learn how to outsource? There are indications this is indeed the case. Nike, as a classical example of outsourcing (Quinn and Hilmer, 1994), is attributed a learning curve in its dealings with suppliers that allowed it to outsource ever more manufacturing activities and to outsource more effectively.[2] But despite their obvious potential for learning, supplier networks have not been studied extensively in terms of their potential for learning (Lane, 2001). Lane discusses how firms can learn new technology, operational practices, or competences in supply chain constellations. Yet there is another side to learning, outsourcing, and supplier relations, which is how the firm can, over time, learn how to get more out of its outsourcing and supplier relations efforts. Previous experience allows a firm to make gradual adjustments to its outsourcing policies during implementation and produces foresight over the outcomes of supplier relations. Experience produces learning and learning produces better decision-making abilities. Kale, Dyer, and Singh (2002) have

---

[2] Interestingly an executive recently told me during a conversation that Nike, also having outsourced many logistics functions, was having severe troubles in guaranteeing its deliveries. As a consequences of these stockouts, Nike was forced to bring some of its logistics function back in-house.

pointed at the importance of prior alliance experience in shaping a firm's alliance capability. The distinction between content learning and process learning implies that there may be different mechanisms at work here. In the context of alliances, Reuer, Zollo, and Singh (2002) discussed how technology-specific experience and partner-specific experience can have differential effects on the need to amend alliance agreements during the implementation phase. While technology-specific experience leads to fewer amendments because of better initial agreements, partner-specific experience increases the need to amend agreements because initial agreements will be less detailed (Reuer, Zollo, and Singh, 2002).

More experience can produce increasing insight into when outsourcing is appropriate and under what conditions each particular type of supplier relation is most suitable. Organizations that have outsourced previously may be able to better their designs over time by learning from mistakes, as failure is an underutilized source of learning (Levinthal and March, 1993). Since governance mistakes tend to be costly there is an incentive to improve designs (Masten, 1993). Costly mistakes will eventually feed back into future decision-making, whether through an immediate response or because organizations are driven to the brink of extinction and activate their survival skills. As firms outsource more intensely, they encounter more learning opportunities, implying heavy outsourcers can become better outsourcers. Outsourcing can become the default mode of operations. Additionally there may be self-selection processes in place that cause firms that are particularly good at outsourcing to start outsourcing more, suggesting a possible reverse causality too. Where prior experience is concerned, such reverse causality will probably not exist. Previous experience gathered over time may be used to improve current decision-making. Managers who have erroneously outsourced in the past are less likely to promote future outsourcing as it will undermine organizational performance and their own positions within the organization. Thus the length and frequency of the firm's and the manager's experience in dealing with make-or-buy decisions and supplier relations will co-determine the firm's ability to implement designs in the future. Prior ties positively influence the likelihood of dealing with the same partner again (Gulati, 1995).

One form of speeding up learning is through knowledge spillovers between locations and units of an organization. By operating in multiple environments, firms can transfer outsourcing and supplier knowledge across borders, similar to knowledge transfer on marketing or product development. Japanese electronic firms have benefited from importing supplier models when building transplants in the United States. (Kenney and Florida, 1995). International knowledge exchange on the quality of suppliers can substantially reduce evaluation costs. A cross-functional exchange of knowledge can provide similar benefits. For instance, a firm could reduce the margin of error when making outsourcing decisions by exchanging experiences. The outsourcing of helpdesk and treasury functions provides some commonalities, for example in supplier selection procedures and negotiation processes. Cross-functional and cross-national knowledge exchange can increase the absorptive capacity of the firm when it comes to learning how to outsource. Yet it is precisely when firms want to learn from geographically and historically distant events that learning is most difficult (Levinthal and March, 1993) and therefore the effectiveness of knowledge transfer between locations and functions will co-determine how effectively firms can employ previous experience.

A second learning mechanism is concerned with learning how to make outsourcing and supplier relations decisions and implementing them. There are issues of timing involved in terms of how often to make decisions, what is an appropriate time to start sharing information with suppliers, when negative evaluations lead to termination of relations and a host of other possibilities to introduce formal mechanisms. Formal mechanisms may provide a means to improve the effectiveness of decision-making processes. As firms grow in size, so too does their supply base. Large manufacturing and service firms in particular are going to depend on a wide range of suppliers. It is now widely acknowledged (Donaldson, 2001) that with increasing size comes the need to formalize operations if a firm wishes to remain effective. Contingency theory states that sub-par performance results from an inability to fit the degree of formalization to the size of the firm (Donaldson, 2001). Firms wishing to use a wide range of suppliers will therefore need to formalize decision-making and feedback mechanisms in order to remain effective. In the literature on alliances the use of a dedicated alliance function has been shown to lead to more effective decision-making (Kale, Dyer, and Singh, 2002). These authors even maintain that a dedicated alliance function has more impact than alliance experience as such. In a similar vein some type of centralized sourcing center where decision-making is coordinated may help a firm improve its ability to deal with outsourcing. A centralized sourcing center can help create a collective memory but also provides a symbolic presence to demonstrate the importance of outsourcing. More generally, firms can use a variety of decision-making tools and structures to support their decision-making on outsourcing and supplier relations. One practical example is a decision-making tree for taking outsourcing decisions (Tayles and Drury, 2001). A regular review of both outsourcing decisions and the state of supplier relations may be another mechanism.

Beyond such learning and experience mechanisms there is also a competence mechanism in place, a second mechanism that distinguishes one firm from the next. In today's knowledge economy it becomes increasingly important to execute properly functions aimed at obtaining knowledge from dispersed external sources (Doz, Santos, and Williamson, 2000). Suppliers are an important source of external knowledge, especially for technical development (Lincoln, Ahmadjian, and Mason, 1998). However, the choice of which particular source to pursue is often a difficult one given the abundance of potential targets globally (Doz, Santos, and Williamson, 2000). In fact, it is often only as managers engage in relations with suppliers that they find out which suppliers are particularly useful for this purpose, implying trial-and-error is a necessary step. In addition a trust-building process must occur, which is unpredictable in nature (Ring and Van de Ven, 1994).

Sourcing managers need to be concerned with the question of whether to standardize communications with suppliers, with the disadvantage of missing richer communication opportunities, or to customize them, leading to more investment of resources like time. In addition, sourcing managers are the linking pins between the firm and its suppliers, which is an important link because knowledge is increasingly gathered from and distributed through the supply chain. Therefore their function, particularly in knowledge-intensive firms, is often not unlike that of account managers who act as linking pins to customers.

Furthermore the nature of the sourcing function is such that operational issues get tangled up with long-term interests. Since sourcing is directly concerned with the supply chain and thus with a firm's ability to deliver its products and services, any disruption must be dealt with immediately. A classic example of this is how Toyota used its long-term goodwill to cover short-term capacity problems caused by a calamity (Nishiguchi and Beaudet, 1998). Therefore it is often easy to draw up strategic plans and designs involving joint development and innovation but these may be crossed by operational concerns. As is well known from the literature on learning (Levinthal and March, 1993), there is an inherent tendency for exploitation activities to overgrow exploration activities. In other words, today's problems tend to be treated as more pregnant than tomorrow's issues.

Bensaou (1999) has argued that creating good designs to match internal and external conditions to appropriate supplier relations is one step of a competitive sourcing portfolio. The next step is to come up with managerial answers in terms of information-sharing, the role of boundary spanners, and the appropriate climate, in line with the design. Bensaou (1999) found large differences between organizations in their ability to handle the different types of design. Firms appear to be specialized in, or at least geared towards, certain designs and empirical research demonstrates there are differences between firms in the same industry and country with respect to their design specialization profile. In other words, not every firm performs equally well with a certain design. Bensaou (1999) coined such misalignment between ability and actual design "overdesign" and "underdesign."

In the 1980s and 1990s, the US automobile industry started to realize the potential benefits of buyer–supplier cooperation following the success of Japanese firms. Yet US car-makers have still not been completely successful in copying these designs (Dyer and Nobeoka, 2000) because of their inability to switch designs. Presumably, there is path dependence in building capabilities to manage certain types of designs. If industry-wide change stimulates the adoption of different designs, firms will be stuck with their old managerial abilities. What types of relation a firm best manages will be co-determined by the imprinting conditions (Stinchcombe, 1965) of its founding period and location. Nishiguchi (1994) has sketched in great detail how the Japanese subcontracting system arose and evolved in the early twentieth century and how elements of the original system are still present in today's practices. Sako (2004) has likewise stressed the importance of history in understanding current supplier capabilities. Thus a firm's historical base co-determines its current implementation ability.

In recent years a new relational perspective on interorganizational relations has emerged that explicitly recognizes that it is the joint activity of buyers and suppliers that leads to value-adding activities (Dyer and Singh, 1998), and this is used as a third mechanism here. This relational perspective also discusses competences but they are competences residing in the relation between firms and therefore different from an implementation capability inside the sourcing firm. Some of the internal learning from previous action may be induced by forces outside the firm though. In fact, complicated supply chain structures like the *keiretsu* and other firm-centered supply networks involve management at multiple levels (Lorenzoni and Baden-Fuller, 1995). The extent to which the focal firm and its first-tier supplier are able to develop joint understanding of the products and services they develop will translate into the effectiveness of the supply chain. For instance, when a first-tier supplier has, through building joint routines, developed a better understanding of the focal firm's requirements, it will be better able to manage its own (second-tier) suppliers. The development of joint routines between the firm and its suppliers allows for quicker and possibly more effective communications, freeing time for undertaking other activities with the same supplier or other suppliers. Inter-firm learning allows a firm to increase its external span of control and provides the opportunity to add to the number of suppliers or to increase average relation intensity. Yet in order to replicate a previous experience with other suppliers it is necessary to develop particularly strong examples. For Toyota, its relation with Nippondenso is a well-documented icon of a partnering relation that it can relate to when building relations with other suppliers.

Beyond dyadic relations, between the outsourcing firm and an individual supplier, one can also look at the collection of suppliers and the outsourcing firm as a supply network. In more tightly knit supply networks, more spillovers of knowledge and innovation occur. Embedded networks arise because of commonalities and associations between network members (Uzzi, 1996). Knowledge is bound to travel more freely and more swiftly in an embedded network (Uzzi, 1996). Where associations between network members are completely absent there is a need to set $n$ 1:1 communication channels, with $n$ being the number of network members. Where associations are complete, one 1:$n$ channel suffices. This implies there is room for economizing when some degree of association exists. In practice, almost by definition, there will be some intermediate degree of association. As firms seek to implement relational designs, it will be beneficial if at least some of that implementation takes on a repetitive character because repetition will increase implementation effectiveness. The associational character of embedded networks further promotes implementation ability, as information pertaining to one implementation will spill over to the next. Therefore embedded networks will promote the realization of numerous and cooperative supplier relations. The need to manage strong and embedded supplier ties will therefore co-evolve with the ability to do so.

To summarize, there are three mechanisms in place that firms can actively use to improve their external span of control. There is a learning mechanism. Firms that outsource a lot, or have done so in the past, will have used their experience to increase their external span of control. This will be more true if these firms can effectively transfer outsourcing knowledge between different geographical units and functions. The use of formal decision-making and feedback tools on outsourcing and supplier selection procedures and of specialized structures also increases the external span of control, particularly as firms grow larger in size. Then there is a competence mechanism, which argues that alignment between the firm's historically shaped management capability for various types of supplier relations and its current supplier relations portfolio increases the firm's external span of control. And finally there is a relational mechanism, which suggests that the strength of a firm's supplier ties and their embeddedness increase its external span of control.

## Conclusion

In this chapter the focus has been on how firms can obtain greater performance out of the same set of activities. I argued that there are two distinct mechanisms for shifting the curve upwards. First, it was shown how some firms excel in their internal productive operations, which causes them to outperform competitors and, as a byproduct, makes integration a more favorable alternative. Second, this chapter looked at how some firms are better at managing multiple and varying supplier relations, an ability that was termed "external span of control." Firms with higher external spans of control equally shift their curves upwards and, again as a byproduct, towards more outsourcing. Finally three different ways for improving the external span of control were discussed.

# 6 | *Shifts of the curve*

ALTHOUGH the previous chapter made clear that the outsourcing–performance curve is not entirely fixed, it focused particularly on inter-firm differences and how these affect constant $c$, in the formula underlying figure 3.2, and hence the top of the curve. There is, however, another parameter that determines at what level of outsourcing the optimum is found. This parameter, $b$, is more generic and driven by changes over time. It involves horizontal shifts of the curve, rather than vertical shifts. These shifts imply that the optimal outsourcing level can gradually become higher, or lower for that matter. The cause of such shifts is a change in the outsourceability of activities. Such a change is often caused by environmental factors over which firms have little or no control, although there are some instances where firms are active participants in shaping these factors. Initially the effect of these shifts will be considered in detail. This is followed by discussions of their causes and of how the effects of predictors of outsourcing levels can themselves change. Finally the steepness of the curve, as represented by parameter $a$ in the formula underlying figure 3.2, will be analyzed.

## Shifts in optimal outsourcing levels

In chapter 1 I described major changes in outsourcing levels over time. In recent times we have observed a shift towards more outsourcing by an overwhelming majority of firms; but there have also been times when vertical integration was in vogue, such as the middle part of the twentieth century. If we set off these two situations against the notion of an optimal level of outsourcing and a negative curvilinear effect of outsourcing on performance, three possible explanations for these changes emerge. First, it is possible that even though firms' outsourcing levels do not change, the population of firms changes over time, such that firms with high actual and optimal outsourcing levels get replaced by firms with low outsourcing levels, or vice versa. Second, it is possible that while the optimal level of outsourcing has remained constant, firms' level of misalignment has changed. Third, it is possible that the optimal level of outsourcing itself has changed because of exogenous factors, which in response has triggered (some) changes in actual out-sourcing levels. Also note that these possibilities are not necessarily mutually exclusive. In the face of a lack of direct empirical evidence to support or refute any of these three arguments, as no research has measured and compared optimal and actual outsourcing levels in any detail, the second-best option available to us is to investigate their plausibility.

Under the first option, firms may be well aligned in terms of their outsourcing predictors and outsourcing levels. But over time a specific subset of firms disappears while another emerges. This argument suggests that during the last twenty-five years, for instance, firms with low outsourcing levels have been disappearing while new entrants are characterized by high outsourcing levels. Leaving aside the particularly tricky question of why the appearance and disappearance of firms is related to their outsourcing levels if optimal outsourcing levels them-selves do not change, this explanation by itself is clearly insufficient to explain recent changes, because replacement levels are simply too low to explain the speed with which outsourcing levels have been chan-ging.[1] In addition, it is well documented how specific individual firms have changed their outsourcing levels.[2] This suggests the first option is at best a partial explanation.

The second option assumes no change in the optimal outsourcing level of an individual firm. It explains any changes in the actual

---

[1] As an empirical illustration, we (Mol, Schreuder, and Goedegebuure, 2001) showed that manufacturing firms in the Netherlands on average had increased their level of outsourcing, measured as external sourcing divided by turnover, by a full 4 percent between 1993 and 1998. Entry into and exit from Dutch manufac-turing did not even reach such levels in that five-year period, let alone that entry and exit by themselves could fully explain the change (even if we made the absurd assumption that exiting firms had a 1 percent outsourcing level while entering firms had a 99 percent outsourcing level).

[2] Unilever, for instance, vertically integrated everything from farms to rubber plantations in the mid twentieth century, but has been pursuing a "lean" policy more recently, for instance by completely outsourcing the production of some frozen food articles. Although our frozen spinach still looks like a Unilever brand, the firm is no longer its producer.

outsourcing levels of individual firms as increases or decreases in mis-alignment. This second option suggests not only that firms can remain misaligned for long periods of time but also that such misalignment can increase or decrease quite quickly and that it can grow in size almost limitlessly. This appears unlikely for several reasons. First, as we observed in chapter 3, misalignment in outsourcing is actually costly. Being severely misaligned for long time-periods can therefore produce failure of a firm, something which all of its stakeholders will presum-ably seek to prevent. Hence there are incentives to avoid too much misalignment. Second, when the outsourcing process was discussed, various factors emerged that made outsourcing decision-making look imperfect but not completely random. There is some core of rationality in what decision-makers do, although outsourcing appears to follow multiple objectives simultaneously. Finally, it appears likely that the predictor variables of outsourcing themselves change, as will be dis-cussed below when I elaborate on the third option. If they do, optimal outsourcing levels are not constant, which directly counters this second option.

Another way to look at these first two options would be to see the first option as being driven by a blind belief in the powers of the market and the second as being driven by a complete disbelief in those powers. But perhaps the truth lies in the middle. A variant of these first two possibilities, and one which builds upon population ecology accounts of change in the make-up of populations of organizations (Hannan and Freeman, 1977), would then be that over time heavily misaligned firms get replaced by less misaligned firms. Population ecology scholars maintain that non-adapted firms eventually become extinct. Firms that are heavily misaligned, because they outsource too much or too little, are not well adapted and underperform, and hence are likely victims for extinction. This is the "economizing" effect that Williamson (1991a) talked about, though the amount of misalignment required to produce bankruptcies is probably higher than transaction cost econom-ics would suggest. This combination of options 1 and 2 appears to be much more feasible. Yet it is helpful only in explaining changes in actual outsourcing levels, suggesting that actual outsourcing levels are changed to decrease misalignment somewhat, though not to elim-inate it altogether.

History suggests, however, that outsourcing levels can change in either direction. We have seen waves of vertical integration as well as waves of outsourcing. This does not sit well with the notion that firms seek to decrease misalignment, because such decreases surely ought to go in one direction if optimal outsourcing levels do not themselves change. This brings us to the third option: perhaps the optimal outsourcing level of an individual firm, as well as the average optimal outsourcing level for a population of firms, changes over time, as represented by an increase or decrease in parameter $b$. As I will discuss in a moment there is considerable evidence for believing that optimal outsourcing levels are indeed not constant over time. Therefore this third option is also a quite plausible answer to the question of why we observe so much change in outsourcing levels. It implies that the relative advantages of the make option and the relative advantages of the buy option change and that firms respond to such changes by (imperfectly) adapting their outsourcing levels to these changes.

As an example of this argument, consider developments in the outsourcing of software. While, in the early 1980s, it was seen as advantageous to develop software in-house, for instance in the banking sector, because good proprietary software could provide firms with a competitive advantage, standardization and the development of a strong set of specialized software suppliers makes this much less true today. Firms no longer create their own database programs and would not even dream of doing that. I will now elaborate on the causes for these changes.

## The causes of shifts

There are broadly two factors that cause the curve to shift from left to right or vice versa. One factor is technological change and the other is institutional change, in a very general sense of the word. Technology affects how transactions take place. Institutions affect the conditions under which transactions take place. There is much evidence that changes in either technology or institutions lead to changes in effective outsourcing levels.

### Technology

Technological change can alter the effectiveness of the make and/or buy options because it affects transaction and production costs, firm capabilities, and other determinants of outsourceability. For instance, new communications technology can enable instant contact with a supplier or electronic information-sharing between buyer and supplier. These types of information-sharing can facilitate coordination between various players in a supply chain and thus lower transaction costs. As Hamel (2002: 99) succinctly put it: "the fact remains that vertical integration, which was in the past a response to high transaction costs (which could be lowered by bringing key functions inside the corporate boundary), is becoming less critical in a world where real-time information allows for transparency and trust between business partners."

In the academic area of management information systems there is a long-standing debate around the possible effects of information technology on outsourcing levels. Malone, Yates, and Benjamin (1987) made a seminal contribution by arguing that IT reduces the transaction costs associated with operating in the market in various ways. Because of these lower transaction costs, markets become relatively more beneficial when compared to hierarchies and hence the increasing use of IT should lead to more outsourcing, and developments in IT indeed are a prime, if not *the* prime, driver of outsourcing. But later authors countered this notion. Clemons, Reddi, and Row (1993) spoke of the move towards the middle, by which they implied the formation of networks rather than either markets or hierarchies. Because information becomes so much easier to spread to many actors simultaneously through electronic means, for example by copying multiple recipients into an e-mail, IT supports electronic networks. Holland and Lockett (1997) described the formation of such networks in more detail by explaining how the introduction of EDI solidified existing cooperative relations rather than leading to more market-like conditions. These authors therefore believed that the introduction of information systems further promotes the formation of inter-firm networks of perhaps changing composition in which cooperative ties are formed between buyers and suppliers.

Regardless of the specific form that buyer–supplier relations takes on though, whether it be arm's length market-like relations or cooperative network relations, there appears to be broad agreement that the introduction of new information technology supports more outsourcing (or, put more negatively, makes vertical integration a less attractive alternative) although IT can also lower the internal costs of communication substantially.

As we have stressed elsewhere (Mol and Koppius, 2002), however, new information and communication technologies are not equally well equipped to handle all stages of the sourcing process. They are particularly effective in reducing the costs of search and in increasing the effectiveness of search by enabling buyers and suppliers to find potential partners beyond their traditional networks. Internet technology, for instance, can now be used to identify many component suppliers all over the globe, or to search for providers of offshore outsourcing services. But the costs of evaluating these suppliers and their product and service offerings are much harder to change through the use of information and communication technologies alone. Evaluation normally involves getting to know the other party in detail, finding out about the other party's history of relations with other buyers through personal connections, and establishing effective communications. Information and communication technologies now lend themselves somewhat for these purposes but virtual networks are, and will remain, at best an imperfect substitute for real networks. This is especially true in business-to-business transactions, where orders are normally specified.

Another way of thinking about this is to ask what kinds of "problems" IT helps to solve. All the evidence shows that firms are far more likely to outsource domestically than to rely on international suppliers (Mol, 2001; Mol and Koppius, 2002). Clearly there are some barriers in place that put a brake on international outsourcing. We discussed three categories of barriers to international outsourcing (Mol and Koppius, 2002), those related to the specific buyer–supplier relation, those related to geographical distance, and those related to cultural and institutional differences between the buyer's home country and that of the supplier. Among these three categories, IT is bound to have differential effects. IT has its most profound effect on physical distance, because it lowers transportation costs, makes it possible to track goods and people across the globe, and generally improves the accuracy of physically disconnected business processes. It will also have some impact on buyer–supplier relations because, for instance, it provides additional and instant communication tools, allows for low-cost intercontinental travel, and standardizes information flows. Where IT has a limited or even negligible impact is in the realm of institutional and cultural differences. IT does not change a government's import regulations, though liberalization may. IT does not do much to help overcome language differences. Nor does it help to deal with differences in cultural traits like power distance or the formality with which business dealings take place. In all then, IT definitely has a positive impact on the degree of international outsourcing as well as on the sophistication with which such outsourcing takes place. It does not, however, lead to the proclaimed "death of distance" (Cairncross, 1998). But because it increases the degree of international outsourcing, it makes the urgency of dealing with institutional and cultural distance all the greater.

Box 6.1 provides a vivid illustration of how intertwined the digital and real worlds are when it comes to the use of information technology in sourcing.

---

## Box 6.1. Electronic auctions in action

Stork Industrial Modules (SIM) from the Netherlands had been a supplier of storage cabinets for X-ray equipment to Philips Medical Systems (PMS) in Hamburg for some twenty years when it was confronted with the request to participate in an Internet-based electronic auction. Although PMS was generally satisfied with the product SIM supplied, it decided to try out the electronic auction, which it had learned about from a German university professor, to test the waters. Hans Büthker, general manager of SIM expressed his surprise in the following way: "Well, you can imagine that if you have been supplying a product for twenty years, and feel that you have a certain kind of relationship with your customer, this comes as a surprise. You're somewhat shocked. When we received these materials two weeks in advance, our first response was: If it's going to be like this, we best quit now."

Yet SIM decided to participate, along with nine other suppliers. It lost the auction badly, which from its perspective was disappointing. PMS, however, was very glad with the outcomes. The lowest bid, by a Romanian supplier, was almost 30 percent below the price it previously paid to SIM. SIM, meanwhile, had itself made a bid some 7 percent below its previous price. Since the lowest bidder was not certified, PMS decided to go with the next best bid, which was still 25 percent below what it had previously paid. This firm had a production facility in Hungary. The SIM–PMS relationship was terminated, though not without a small dispute about a final delivery, which both parties said was instigated by the other party.

In retrospect it appeared that while this outsourcing relationship was characterized by a lot of goodwill and trust prior to the auction, both parties had lost track of developing market conditions. PMS could probably have found a lower bidder long before electronic auctions became available, through a non-electronic bidding process, had it chosen not to remain with the same supplier. Of course, the execution of the auction helps to speed up the bidding process. Because of the real-time nature of the auction and the transparency of the bidding process, bidders might also be tempted to lower their bid beyond what they would do in an auction with just a single sealed bid.

At the same time SIM was perhaps needlessly extending the life-span of a product that was relatively low-tech in its product portfolio and which barely produced any innovation. The Netherlands was surely not very cost-competitive in the production of this item. The electronic auction, therefore, was more the carrier of change than its catalyst. At the same time this case illustrates how new technologies lower the costs of finding potential suppliers and selecting the best of these suppliers. Hence, as suggested before, IT lowers the costs of transacting with outside suppliers.

*Source:* Van Tulder and Mol (2002).

With all the focus on information technology in recent years, especially Internet-based technology, it is easy to forget about the range of other technologies that potentially affect make-or-buy decisions. An important technological area is production technology. Products and services become increasingly modularized. Modularization helps to separate production processes physically and organizationally. Furthermore, services have become more tradable in recent times, implying it is easier to transfer these services to outside parties and faraway locations (Araujo and Spring, forthcoming). Such tradability of services comes about through the ability to describe, quantify, and replicate services. Hence optimal outsourcing levels have increased through changes in production technology (Araujo and Spring, forthcoming).

Another important other set of technologies is transportation technology. The use of larger, more efficient, and more reliable vehicles, like container ships and modern trucks, has drastically reduced the costs of transporting goods, especially over long distances. The growth in air traffic also implies it is becoming increasingly common to transport people in order to perform a variety of services around the globe. Today's low transportation costs, while of course not being completely negligible, enable much more physical decoupling of activities.

As further technological innovations are introduced in transport, like the Airbus A380 airplane that can carry many more people, transportation costs continue to decline, making still more physical decoupling possible. This increases optimal outsourcing levels. The world's best suppliers are generally not located on a firm's doorstep. With lower transportation costs it may become an option to contract with such suppliers. More advanced transportation technology therefore leads to more outsourcing, and particularly more international outsourcing. In a long-term historical perspective, it can be argued (Lamoreaux, Raff, and Temin, 2003) that the very high transportation costs of the nineteenth century forced firms to use local supply sources, often in industry-specific districts, such as fashion (Marshall, 1919). As transportation, and communication, costs decreased, vertical integration and large-scale production became favorable because while it was feasible to use non-local sources, effective control over them could only be obtained though integration. As transportation costs have dropped even further, we have reached the stage where global inter-firm networks of production have emerged, where goods can be shipped at low costs and from outside supply sources that can be effectively controlled or replaced when necessary. Lower transportation costs therefore increase optimal outsourcing levels.

But there are yet more technologies at work. One is what might be called management technology. With the rise of M.B.A. education in various parts of the world, and the international flow of students through M.B.A. institutions, managers of firms are increasingly schooled along the same set of principles regardless of the country from which they originate or in which they work, or the industry in which they work.[3] There is, in other words, a language and set of beliefs emerging that is shared by decision-makers across a wide variety of firms. This management technology also allows buyers and suppliers

[3] This focus on relatively universal analytical skills is precisely what bothers the people who have criticized M.B.A. programs in recent times, such as Mintzberg (2004). These critics suggest more people skills, understanding of what is morally right and wrong, and sensitivization to context ought to be introduced into M.B.A. programs.

to interact more easily, even where they differ in other respects, for instance their country cultures. The convergence of management technologies across the world therefore allows for higher optimal levels of outsourcing (a shift of the curve towards the right), and especially for more international outsourcing.

## Institutions

The term "institution" has a long history in social science research. Scott (1995) distinguishes between various streams of research in institutionalism. Scott suggests the earliest contributions to institutional theory were produced in political science in the second half of the nineteenth century, in economics in the late nineteenth century, and in sociology from the turn of the twentieth century. More recently, neo-institutional theory has been developed, including its applications to the study of organization. Scott (1995: 33) defines institutions in a catch-all way: "Institutions consist of cognitive, normative, and regulative structures and activities that provide stability and meaning to social behavior. Institutions are transported by various carriers – cultures, structures, and routines – and they operate at multiple levels of jurisdiction." A more compact, although admittedly incomplete, understanding of institutions might be obtained by referring to them as the rules of the game, those rules that organizations have to obey in order to function effectively.

The role of institutions in outsourcing, then, refers to the rules of the game under which outsourcing decisions are made. The nature of the institutions a firm faces helps to determine its outsourcing policy. In chapters 2 and 3 I discussed this to some extent. Contract law, for instance, has an effect on the extent to which buying and supplying firms believe they can rely on agreements with their partners. In the absence of a strong contract, or of its enforcement, there is no mechanism in place for resolving conflicts, leading to much uncertainty about the value of contracts. Outsourcing is then less attractive because suppliers will not want to take on activities, or outsourcing firms may be unwilling to share intellectual property. Physical infrastructure and its reliability and safety can also play a role in outsourcing decisions. In the absence of a proper infrastructure, or when transportation is surrounded by fears of loss of resources, outsourcing becomes less viable, as physically sourcing components or even services becomes hazardous.

Institutional change can therefore produce change in optimal outsourcing levels. Box 6.2 gives an example of how a previously nonexisting outsourcing market, for technical contractors employed by or via agencies, could be created only after a series of institutional and technological changes.

---

## Box 6.2. The new world of technical contracting in the United States

In the United States an entire new industry has emerged. Firms now use what are called technical contractors for the provision of a range of services, many around information technology. Technological contractors are individuals who rent their services to outsourcing firms. They might be network specialists who help a firm to set up a new network. Or they could be Java specialists who help in the design of a firm's website. Prior to the late 1980s similar jobs also existed but they were performed inside firms. White-collar workers were not accustomed to being placed outside the organization, unlike blue-collar workers for whom lay-offs and downsizing were all too common terms. But several changes occurred that led to the outsourcing of these activities to technical contractors. Firms started firing their own employees and then rehired them to save on labor costs. They did not give them the rights of employees when it came to issues like pensions. They did not pay their taxes for them. Yet in managing them they often still treated them as if they were permanent employees of the firm. In response, the Internal Revenue Service (IRS) set up a test to determine who was or was not a permanent employee. The IRS then built a case against Microsoft, arguing it used many independent contractors as if they were employees. As a consequence many firms, or rather their lawyers, came to see the use of staffing agencies as the only option to solve this problem. If contractors became employees of the staffing agency, nobody could claim they were employees of the outsourcing firm.

As a consequence the same activities that used to be vertically integrated are now performed by a triumvirate. The contracting firm decides to outsource to lower its indirect labor costs, increase its flexibility, and improve its ability to bring in new knowledge developed elsewhere. The contractor has little option but to follow the contracting firm's wishes. One useful trade-off for the contractor, though, is that she or he gets to choose an area of specialization and is flexible in determining working hours and often working locations as well. And the agents introduced a mark-up on the contractors' basic wages that allows them to do their work, which is essentially the matching of demand and supply, along with the provision of some administrative services to contractors. Of course, each of the parties tries to negotiate the best possible deal and relations among the three parties can become strained.

So institutional changes, like new laws and tax regimes, have a direct impact on firm behavior. In this case, they produced a new market and simultaneously determined its structure. Interestingly, the outsourcing of technical contractors is not only now seen as a common phenomenon but also has become taken for granted. If a firm used no outside contractors, outside analysts would be likely to remark that it is not keeping up with new technological developments.

*Source:* Barley and Kunda (2004).

Possibly the most widely cited cause of increases in outsourcing levels in the popular press is globalization, or the internationalization of economic activities. Because of the increasing possibilities for engaging in international sourcing, firms should increase their reliance on best-in-world suppliers so the argument goes (Quinn and Hilmer, 1994). Globalization, of course, is something of a catch-all phrase these days. Hence in the context of institutional change and outsourcing I will attempt to treat it in a more focused manner. Specifically, I would like to suggest that increases in international economic activities, particularly international outsourcing, partly result from changes in the institutions that govern these economic activities.[4] These institutions can hinder or facilitate international outsourcing, and in recent years most institutional changes have been aimed at facilitation more than hindrance. Through complex multilateral negotiations in the World Trade Organization, formerly the GATT, tariff and non-tariff barriers to international trade have gradually been reduced. As a consequence it has become easier for, say, a manufacturing firm in the United States to access outside suppliers in China as the costs of doing so are much lower than before. But there

---

[4] There are, of course, parallel changes that also help to increase international economic activities, like new ways of organizing multinational firms, an increased willingness of managers to seek partners abroad, and technologies, as discussed earlier.

have also been fundamental transformations at the level of individual countries, in terms of how open they are to trade with outsiders. China again is a prime example of that but for many European firms, especially SMEs, Central and Eastern Europe is at least as important. Since 1989, countries like Poland, Hungary and now Romania have increasingly started to function as outsourcing destinations. These countries are trying actively to create the conditions that will make outsourcing firms in, say, Britain or France decide to outsource activities to local supplier firms. Clearly this also affects the costs of vertical integration, as many multi-national firms from Britain, France, and other countries have set up their own services and manufacturing operations in Central and Eastern Europe. But it influences the costs of outsourcing more, as it dispropor-tionately decreases production costs while simultaneously lowering the costs of transactions with international suppliers as well. In addition there is a multiplier effect because once the Romanian supplier engages in work for one Danish firm, others are likely to follow because of reputation effects and because the Romanian firm will be able to equip itself with the requisite skill-set to serve its Danish customers. The end-result is that firms, faced with a much richer choice of low-cost, or sometimes high-value, international suppliers, are able to increase their outsourcing levels. Globalization, in other words, produces a higher optimal level of outsourcing, implying the optimal level shifts to the right.

Economic liberalization is another trend that has been ongoing since at least the 1980s.[5] It involves the removal or loosening of existing regula-tions, the privatization of government activities, and the replacement of regulation by self-regulation or other market mechanisms. Liberalization of the economy tends to improve the likelihood of outsourcing over integration for several reasons. Privatization is the most clear-cut case, as it is in many ways little more than outsourcing by governments. When a government privatizes an activity it transfers that activity from within the bounds of the state to the outside, to a private supplier. Yet that private supplier still performs services that have some public character. Of course, there are all kinds of intermediate constructions, such as public–private partnerships, or the creation of independent legal entities that are still owned by the state. But even in these intermediate cases some outsourcing takes place. Liberalization of economies also promotes

---

[5] Note that economic liberalization and efforts to increase international economic activities in practice often, though not always, go together in government policies.

outsourcing in more subtle ways. The introduction of more market mechanisms into the economy means that markets, and thereby buy decisions, become the default option for transactions. And the removal of restrictions, for instance around labor laws, makes it more feasible to outsource as there is less of a need to monitor the obedience to these laws on-site. If buyers are held responsible for their suppliers' behavior this will tend to discourage outsourcing. Toulan's (2002) study of the levels of vertical integration in the Argentine economy during its liberalization wave clearly shows how liberalization promoted outsourcing in that country, because the associated larger market reduced asset specificity and hence made opportunism by suppliers less likely.

Legal change is another source of institutional change that affects outsourcing and that is often related to globalization and liberalization. Firms generally comply with laws so changes in laws can therefore enhance or restrict their ability to outsource. Swamidass and Kotabe (1993), for example, talk about the effect of the import rules in the US Harmonized Tariff Schedule on international sourcing. Tariff items 806.30 and 807.00 provided for the duty-free reentry to the United States of US-made components sent abroad for further processing or assembly. Between 1985 and 1988 imports under these provisions rose by 142 percent to $74 billion, compared to only a 27 percent rise in total imports (Swamidass and Kotabe, 1993). The new tariff rules therefore promoted international outsourcing.

A final note that applies to both technological and institutional changes is that they will impact on individual firms differently, depending on the context in which a firm operates and its strategy. As discussed earlier, institutional change is often nation-specific, so where a firm is located will determine which institutional changes it faces. But there are also industry-level effects. The manufacturing sector has been affected more than service sector by GATT and WTO negotiations. And IT has arguably had a more profound effect on financial services than on personal services. And some firms' strategies can more easily accommodate new technologies than others'.

## Changes in theoretical effects

Analytically speaking the above technological and institutional changes are the simple case. A technology gets replaced by a new one that perhaps allows for more effective communications with outside suppliers, and in response outsourcing becomes a more feasible option. But there is no change in how technologies and institutions relate to outsourcing, just a change in their sophistication or level of presence. The more complex case is when the nature of the effect of an outsourcing predictor variable changes. That is, what if a factor that previously discouraged outsourcing now promotes it? Or what if a factor that used to promote outsourcing no longer has an effect on outsourcing levels? In a recent article (Mol, 2005) I addressed an instance of such a change, in the form of R&D intensity.

Conventional industrial organization (IO) accounts of vertical integration (Stigler, 1951) tend to stress how it is used as a means to enhance the scale of operations and bargaining power. Technologically intensive industries normally favor a large operating scale because R&D investments are mostly fixed costs that can be recuperated more easily at high revenue levels. The marginal costs of production are relatively low in technologically intensive industries. Thus a technologically intensive industry can be expected to be dominated by one or a few firms that employ substantial amounts of backward vertical integration to maximize the scale of operations. More recent observers in the IO tradition (Harrigan, 1986; Porter, 1980) seem to concur that where R&D matters, vertical integration is preferred over outsourcing.

In transaction cost economics, Williamson's (1985: 141–144) discussion on the role of innovation in vertical integration decisions brings to light several arguments favoring integration under conditions of substantial innovation but also includes some discussion concerning hybrid agreements as a solution. The key advantage of integration is that it promotes cooperation between stages. On the other hand, it will compromise the high-powered incentives available in markets because costs and benefits will tend to be shared between the purchasing and supply stages in an integrated setting (Williamson, 1985). Additionally there may be instances of higher-level intrusion or accounting manipulation that can further distract from such incentives. The latter, however, will exist to a larger degree in markets where opportunistic behavior is more common. Williamson (1985) concludes that where innovation is of a proprietary rather than a generic type it will lead to integration or at the very least partial ownership (hybrid forms), particularly when combined with a need for specific assets. He further suggests that non-specific assets will normally only lead to generic innovation. Thus there appears to be a positive correlation between proprietary innovations and specific assets. This further suggests that if R&D is undertaken in-house it must be aimed at producing some type of proprietary innovation for the firm and should generally be associated with vertical integration according to Williamson. Teece (1986) has added that when the R&D intensity of a sector is high, it will be more prone to integrate activities into the firm rather than to outsource them in order to protect intellectual property rights. Pisano (1990) similarly argued that appropriation problems around knowledge, like that obtained from R&D, lead to vertical integration, as did Malerba and Orsenigo (1993).

Monteverde (1995) discussed the application of transaction cost economics in the exchange of technical engineering knowledge. He investigated empirically how unstructured technical dialog, one form of human asset specificity, affects outsourcing decisions. Because organizations can internally develop a specific dialect for exchanging unstructured and tacit knowledge, they are much more efficient at transferring this type of knowledge. Therefore the costs of transacting are substantially lower inside the organization and vertical integration is the preferred solution. Note that the latter observation, that organizations can be more efficient carriers of knowledge than markets, takes Monteverde's work closer to the knowledge-based explanation of Kogut and Zander (1992), which argues governance forms are less a result of market failure than one of organizational superiority in certain types of transaction. In sum, this conventional view suggests that innovation is created more efficiently inside firms than through markets. Outsourcing is not a means to innovate because outside suppliers lack incentives to innovate for the buying firm. Where they do innovate, it will be hard for the buying firm to appropriate the rents of innovations (Teece, 1986) as the supplier will seek to use it for a wide range of clients. Thus dedicated innovation is particularly hard to achieve under an outsourcing regime. All of this suggests that when R&D is an important part of an industry's value chain, firms in that industry will integrate more activities and outsource fewer, which best summarizes the conventional view on R&D and outsourcing.

But if R&D intensity and outsourcing are as incompatible as suggested above, how can we explain the rises in outsourcing in R&D-intensive environments that have been reported (Leiblein and Miller, 2003; Quinn, 2000)? The relational view (Dyer and Singh, 1998), argues that much of a firm's innovation now occurs in conjunction with outside suppliers rather than inside the firm. Because developments in non-core technology areas have become very rapid, it is no longer feasible to keep up with all of these technologies in as much detail as needed (Brusoni, Prencipe, and Pavitt, 2001; Quinn, 2000). Therefore, outside technology sources are in many instances the only option for firms that wish to stay up-to-date (Hagedoorn, 1993). Barney (1999) has suggested that firms need not necessarily own all relevant capabilities, including those related to the production of innovation, as long as they have sufficient access to them. Such access may well be obtained through relations with outside suppliers.

Brusoni, Prencipe, and Pavitt (2001) have noted that among manufacturing firms knowledge is now becoming more extensive than is necessary for the activities performed inside the firm. In other words, firms must know more than they make in order to be able to integrate the inputs of various specialist outside suppliers. The more uneven rates of technological change in underlying components and the more often the interdependencies between components change, the more slack knowledge the buying firm needs to maintain (Brusoni, Prencipe, and Pavitt, 2001). Nishiguchi (1994) has argued that the use of outside suppliers creates the option to access a much larger productive network and knowledge pool. This network provides much-needed flexibility to cope with changes in demand and helps to lower time-to-market substantially. Afuah (2001) further suggested that over the life-cycle of a technology firms are best off by gradually increasing their extent of outsourcing. Only when a radical, competence-destroying technological change occurs does it make sense to revert to vertical integration into this new technology (Afuah, 2001).

In the context of innovation, Langlois and Robertson (1992) have developed the notion that it is feasible to develop initial innovation through outsourcing in a decentralized network, especially if substantial network externalities are present. If outsourcing is to make sense in the context of R&D-intensive businesses though, relations with suppliers ought to replicate some of the characteristics of firms. For if relations are of a strict arm's length type, there is no incentive for external suppliers to undertake innovative activities on behalf of the buying firm. Dyer and Singh (1998) have developed a relational view of rent attainment, which argues that interorganizational relations, including buyer–supplier relations, can provide benefits similar to hierarchies without the production cost disadvantages associated with hierarchies. Dyer and Nobeoka (2000) detail through their case study of Toyota how new technology is developed through dedicated buyer–supplier relations. This new model of interorganizational relations as a means to innovation is superseding traditional in-house development so it is argued (Dyer and Singh, 1998; Kinder 2003; Quinn, 2000). This trend ought to be reflected in the outsourcing levels of R&D-intensive industries, which should rise as a consequence.

In the article (Mol, 2005) I demonstrated this shift from R&D intensity being a negative predictor of outsourcing levels to becoming a positive predictor for fifty-one manufacturing industries. Thus where outsourcing used to be negatively predicted by R&D intensity, it now appears to be a positive predictor. This is reflective of new ways of organizing buyer–supplier relations for maximizing value (Dyer and Singh, 1998; Zajac and Olsen, 1993), as discussed in chapter 5.

R&D intensity is, of course, just one example and for other variables a similar story may apply. Another point of relevance here is that outsourcing or integration may produce what economists call "externalities". Externalities in outsourcing are best described as side-effects that occur as a firm outsources or integrates an activity. For instance, if a firm outsources a particular service, and is the first to do so, it is effectively creating a new market for that service with a new supplier. Once this first firm has outsourced the activity, others can follow and build upon that supplier's experience with its first customer. For the supplier there may be learning effects that can be transferred to other customers. And as the supplier increases its own operations, scale economies will start to become effective as well.

As a consequence of these supplier learning processes, and increasing outsourcing by buyers, a supply market may become more mature over time. This maturity can be driven by technological developments as well. The PC industry provides a case in point. As it moved out of the early entrepreneurial stages, standards were being developed for software and hardware, and specialized component suppliers emerged for components like hard disks and memory units. As a consequence, PCs became more alike and technologies more interchangeable between firms, further increasing the attractiveness of the buy option for PC manufacturers like IBM and Digital. In conclusion, outsourcing externalities arise as a consequence of the interplay between buyers and suppliers, within the context of technological change. These externalities further complicate outsourcing decision-making, which serves the points made about uncertainty and causal ambiguity in chapter 4, and also reaffirm the need for a dynamic analysis of outsourcing levels and processes.

## The consequences of horizontal shifts

The analyzed technological, institutional, and organizational changes, a large majority of which have been promoting shifts towards more outsourcing over recent years, have very substantial consequences for the optimal and actual behavior of firms and firms' resulting performance. What was a highly successful outsourcing policy in the 1960s, lots of vertical integration with some outsourcing of completely standardized goods and services, would be met wearily and perhaps with some laughter by today's managers. And if it were to be implemented in say a medium-sized manufacturing firm in Wales, it could easily lead to disaster. Similarly, and as Chandler (1977) observed, the many small manufacturing firms operating in industrial districts in the late nineteenth and early twentieth century were replaced by large vertically integrated firms that could overcome the transaction costs associated with imperfectly functioning markets and produce at a much larger scale. So a first consequence of these shifts towards more outsourcing is that they put a "best before" date on any outsourcing strategy. In outsourcing there are no time-invariant successful strategies.

A more indirect effect of technological and institutional changes is that they increase the uncertainty surrounding outsourcing decision-making. Under such conditions making outsourcing decisions becomes like shooting at a moving target. By the time a decision is implemented, it is no longer the "right" decision. This further increases the need for heuristically driven decision-making, as discussed in chapter 4. In addition the quicker these changes occur, the more the need for heuristics grows. Hence, the quicker the changes, the more sizeable misalignment will be as well. Since many observers suggest that the pace of change, including technological and institutional change, facing organizations is increasing, this implies there is an increasing need for heuristics in outsourcing decision-making, unless the decision-making technologies available to managers improve even faster than technologies and institutions change. Since it is not obvious that good empirical measures exist of either changes affecting outsourcing or of outsourcing decision-making technologies, one can only speculate as to which force is stronger.

The consequences of a shift like that around R&D intensity described above are even more complex. Such a shift changes not only optimal outsourcing levels themselves but also the very model that underlies these optimal outsourcing levels. Thus not only are decision-makers shooting at a moving target but they are doing so with a gun that is moving too. Clearly that only increases the likelihood of inaccurate decisions further. It also raises the question whether outsourcing decision-making procedures and rules, such as "if a component is technologically innovative it ought not be outsourced," can actually be set in stone. They probably ought not to be too fixed truths. But then how can scholars help firms to make better decisions? In the next chapter I will look into dynamic and interactive ways of experimenting with outsourcing as a possible solution to this problem. The type of shift as witnessed for R&D intensity also poses some problems for how academic research on outsourcing takes place. Some of these will be detailed in chapter 8.

## Steepness of the curve

Thus far two of the three parameters from the formula presented in chapter 3, which underlies figure 3.2, have been discussed in some detail. In chapter 5, parameter $c$, the constant determining the height of a performance optimum, was discussed. Earlier in this chapter, parameter $b$, which determines the optimal amount of outsourcing, was analyzed as well. That still leaves the third parameter, parameter $a$, to be scrutinized further. Parameter $a$ determines the steepness of the curve. Another way of looking at parameter $a$ is to say that it determines what price a firm will pay for a non-optimal amount of outsourcing. In other words, what is the cost of a given amount of misalignment for a particular firm? If the steepness of the curve increases, i.e. if parameter $a$ becomes more negative, the costs of misalignment will rise accordingly. This begs three key questions. What determines the steepness of the curve (the magnitude of parameter $a$)? Is it good, bad, or neither good nor bad if a firm has a relatively steep curve? To what extent can this steepness be managed or altered?

The steepness of the curve is determined by how activities are distributed on the outsourceability dimension. When all activities are more or less equal in outsourceability, such that the performance loss attached to making a wrong outsourcing decision is relatively limited, the curve will not be steep. When there are large differences in outsourceability, such that some activities should clearly be outsourced while others should clearly be integrated, a much steeper curve results. Perhaps the best way to describe how activities are distributed on the outsourceability dimension is to refer to specialized versus general assets, where assets can be anything from physical equipment to knowledge or human effort. Recall from chapter 3 that a wide range of activities needs to be undertaken to satisfy customer demand. Suppose there are two firms that differ in their degree of asset specialization. A firm with general assets is relatively well equipped to deal with the full range of activities itself. A firm with specialized assets, on the other hand, is very well equipped to deal with a smaller range of activities but poorly equipped to deal with other activities. For the firm with general assets the performance gap between integrating or outsourcing a given activity will be much smaller than for the firm with specialized assets. This works on both sides of the outsourcing optimum, as the specialist firm's advantage of integrating an activity with low outsourceability is larger than the advantage of the generalist firm but the specialist firm's advantage of outsourcing an activity with high outsourceability is equally larger than the advantage of the generalist firm. Because of that larger advantage, the cost of making a wrong decision is also larger for the specialized firm.

Figures 6.1 and 6.2 jointly illustrate this argument. In figure 6.1 the specialist and generalist firms are displayed and it can be seen that for specialist firms there is a much bigger difference in the outsourceability of activities between the left and right sides of the graph than is the case for the generalist firms. Figure 6.2 provides curves for specialist and generalist firms. Figure 6.2, which follows from figure 6.1, shows that the specialist firm has a much steeper curve than the generalist firm. The steepness of the curve, in other words, is determined by the degree to which a firm's production assets are specialized.

The second question is whether a steeper curve is good, bad, or neither, from a performance perspective. The answer is somewhat complex and can be found in figure 6.2. A more specialized firm will produce a higher performance optimum, as its asset base is better geared towards the activities it undertakes in-house. Yet at the same time the more specialized firm will face a steeper fall if it is misaligned, either by outsourcing or by integrating too much. Therefore the performance difference between the specialist and generalist firms will

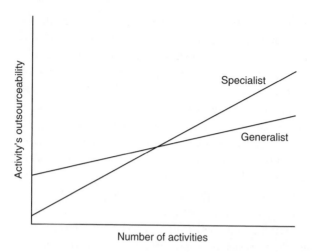

**Figure 6.1.** The distribution of outsourceability across activities for specialist and generalist firms

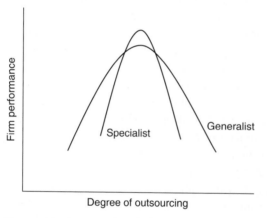

**Figure 6.2.** Degree of outsourcing and firm performance for specialist and generalist firms

become smaller further away from the optimum until the point is reached where the generalist firm actually starts to outperform the specialist firm.

This analysis produces an important conclusion in the context of firms' outsourcing strategies. Firms have been advised to concentrate on core competences, and judging by the statements that accompany outsourcing decisions many firms have decided to follow that advice by becoming more nimble. The advice in one sense seems sound, firms that specialize are able to increase their performance potential. At the same time, being more specialized also increases a firm's vulnerability to mistakes. Since I concluded earlier that firms are almost by definition misaligned, such vulnerability cannot be discarded. As firms become ever more specialized their vulnerability to mistakes (in the form of misalignment) will increase. Thus there will also be an optimal degree of asset specialization, depending on the trade-off firms want to make between risks and returns.

The answer to the second question thus directly sets up the answer to the third question. Within bounds, firms can change the steepness of their outsourcing curves by altering their degree of asset specialization. This degree of asset specialization is a high-level decision in the firm's overall strategy, as it revolves around what the productive structure of the firm looks like. Thus the degree of asset specialization will probably be decided upon with not just outsourcing levels in mind, which may be a reason why the chosen degree of asset specialization in practice will often be suboptimal from the outsourcing point of view. Furthermore, any changes in the degree of asset specialization are likely to take time, implying that alterations will be limited in extent as well.

## Conclusion

In this chapter it was discussed why optimal outsourcing levels are not constant over time and space. Especially over the last twenty to thirty years, there have been profound changes, primarily in the form of the introduction of new (information) technologies and changes in the institutional arrangements that underlie (inter-firm) transactions, which have caused the optimal as well as the actual level of outsourcing to increase rather dramatically. Then the changing nature of the pre-dictor variables of outsourcing was discussed. It was shown that the same factors that once hindered outsourcing may now be promoting it, though the form in which outsourcing occurs may be a different one. Finally, inter-firm differences in the steepness of the outsourcing–performance curve were discussed, in particular their causes and effects.

# 7 | *Managing outsourcing*

E ARLIER chapters have focused entirely on the academic perspective of outsourcing, with a view to describing the phenomenon. In this chapter the question that will be addressed is what further advice can be given to managers who deal with outsourcing, to generate some prescription as well. In previous chapters various building blocks for a firm's outsourcing policy have been provided. Here two popular prescriptive notions are first dispelled, around core competences and outsourcing and around strategic outsourcing, by laying out their premises and debating those, and this leads to a much more refined understanding of both ideas. The chapter then moves on to discuss the role of managerial intent in outsourcing before offering a perspective on outsourcing as experimentation. Next is the treatment of the relation between outsourcing and corporate strategy, and this is followed by a discussion of what is tentatively called the optimal outsourcing tool. In the process, I try to identify a number of practical guidelines.

## Core competences and outsourcing

In chapters 1 and 2 the writings of James Brian Quinn were referred to many times. Quinn (1992; 1999; 2000; Quinn, Baruch, and Zien, 1997; Quinn, Doorley, and Pacquette, 1990; Quinn and Hilmer, 1994) is the best-known representative of the school of thought that argues both that "if an activity is not core, it is best outsourced" and that "if you are not the best in the world in an activity, find a supplier who is and outsource to that supplier." Quinn's views are both highly cited and somewhat influential among practitioners, having been published in the *Sloan Management Review* and online by the Outsourcing Institute on multiple occasions. Even practitioners who are not aware of Quinn himself seem to repeat his ideas in order to build a case for outsourcing. Unfortunately these ideas are also completely wrong and even damaging. Quinn arrives at his flawed conclusions because he operates from a number of assumptions that are fundamentally incorrect.[1] These include the following.

## 1. A core competence resides in an activity, i.e. it is something firms do

Quinn's approach builds upon the notion that there are core and non-core activities and that non-core activities do not use a firm's core competences whereas core activities do. In Prahalad and Hamel's original (1990: 82) definition, however, core competences are "the collective learning in the organization, especially how to coordinate diverse production skills and integrate multiple streams of technologies." More recently, Hamel (2002) has stressed that core competences are based around knowledge and do not simply equate to a series of activities firms undertake. Core competences and activities thus reside at different levels of analysis and since it is activities that firms can outsource, outsourcing also operates at a different level from core competences. Therefore it is not clear why a firm's definition of its core competences should have straightforward implications for its outsourcing policy or its decision to outsource a given activity. This is not to say that its definition ought not to have any impact on outsourcing policies and decisions, just that there is no direct one-to-one relation.

## 2. There is a dichotomous distinction between core and non-core

A second characteristic of Quinn's approach is his belief there are essentially just two categories of activities, core and non-core, and that it is rather straightforward to establish to which category a given activity belongs. But practitioners are now finding that the distinction between core and non-core activities is often hard to draw (*Financial Times*, 2005a). Customers do not care whether a firm believes an

---

[1] To clarify: this is not an academic discussion, in the sense of irrelevant or hypothetical, aimed at proving someone else's ideas are wrong. This discussion is needed because these ideas seem to have a profound influence on the practice of management.

activity is core or non-core. If a non-performing activity that was deemed non-core by the firm, such as catering in the case of British Airways, seriously impacts the customer's perception of a product or service, the firm had better come up with a better answer than a plea with its supplier to solve the problem. What is more though, and as I have demonstrated in chapter 3, there are all kinds of degree when it comes to categorizing the role of specific activities. Thus catering may not be the most central activity for a firm like BA but it is a lot more central to BA's success than it is to that of HSBC. Core and non-core are therefore probably best seen as two ends of a continuum where the vast majority of activities lie somewhere in between those extremes.

### 3. Every firm is best-in-world in some activity and needs to be best-in-world in something in order to compete effectively

In order to decide whether to outsource an activity, Quinn argues, a firm first needs to identify where it is best-in-world. Then, it can proceed to outsource its other activities to an external supplier that is best-in-world in a particular activity. This obviously presupposes that firms operate in global markets and can make use of international suppliers without too much cost. Almost all firms, however, compete for customers in rather local markets, though they may operate in a multiplicity of local markets at the same time. There is no need to be the best-in-world at anything in order to be successful as long as a firm is better than its direct competitors (Hamel, 2002). In reality, very few firms are best-in-world at anything, if only because only one or just a few firms can really be the best, yet they survive and are profitable. Competition may be a strong mechanism for allocating success but it is not an all-encompassing mechanism. Furthermore the likelihood of a best-in-world supplier being located locally or domestically is fairly low. Since there are additional transaction costs associated with international outsourcing (Mol, van Tulder, and Beije, 2005), the use of a best-in-world supplier located abroad can be either a good or a bad idea. This presupposes that a firm is capable of tracing and relating to that best supplier in the first place, something social network analysts (Burt, 1992; Uzzi, 1997) and those with an interest in the costs of search and evaluation (March, 1991; Rangan, 2000) would rate as unlikely. So the notion of best-in-world appears at least to be somewhat overblown.

### 4. An activity designated as non-core has a negligible effect on a firm's competitive advantage and can be separated from other activities at (almost) no cost

Quinn takes it as a given that the fact an activity can be described as non-core implies the activity has a limited, or no, effect on performance and that therefore there is no reason to try and perform the activity in-house. By doing so, Quinn largely ignores connections or interfaces between activities. Yet these interfaces have been described as value-creating intersections (Kotabe, 1992; Porter, 1985). By outsourcing an activity, it will become much harder or quite impossible to manage the interfaces well. Hamel (2002: 99) has suggested that "something that is outsourced usually ceases to provide a competitive advantage, unless a company has a unique and proprietary relationship with its partners. While being 'virtual' may bring flexibility, the capacity to earn above-average profits still depends on having a defensible competitive advantage." Kotabe (1998) presented a similar argument in his comparison of US and Japanese manufacturing firms. In short, there are costs associated with splitting up the set of activities among multiple players.

### The notion of "strategic" outsourcing

There is a second prominent stream of practice-based explanations, one that partly overlaps with the work of Quinn, who also uses the term strategic outsourcing (Quinn, 1992; Quinn and Hilmer, 1994), but which also can be found in the writings of a range of other authors (Gottfredson, Puryear, and Phillips, 2005; Willcocks and Kern, 1998). The core contention of this second stream is that outsourcing is becoming more strategic in nature over time, and less focused on mere cost reductions. What seems to be implied by the the term "strategic" is that outsourcing somehow helps to add value to services and products. The idea of strategic sourcing is not particularly new; it has been around for at least some fifteen years now (Venkatesan, 1992). Like Quinn's work, the strategic sourcing argument rests on a number of important yet potentially flawed assumptions. It is also somewhat subject to circular reasoning.

## 1. *Outsourcing is becoming more strategic*

Venkatesan (1992) and others (Quinn, 1999) have talked about the increasing importance and changing nature of outsourcing. Outsourcing, so it is argued, is having an ever larger impact on the competitive advantage of firms because it is occurring more frequently and because its nature is changing. Because outsourcing relationships are becoming partnerships, joint value can be created. The formal version of this latter argument is the relational rent thesis (Dyer and Singh, 1998). While there is some truth to these arguments, there is both a lack of empirical substantiation for them and much confusion surrounding them. Let us first consider the extent to which outsourcing relationships are indeed becoming partnerships. In the early 1990s it was believed that IT outsourcing was going to start producing many partnerships (Loh and Venkatraman, 1992). Today few outsourcing firms seem to regard the majority of their IT outsourcing deals, or even any of them, as strategic partnerships. Strategic outsourcing in many instances is rhetoric rather than reality. In a sample of Dutch manufacturers I found that their key relationships mostly did not display partnership traits (Mol, 2001). While academic research has established that clear benefits can be associated with partnership outsourcing, especially under circumstances of high uncertainty and when partners' capabilities are complementary, it has not actually established that such partnerships are very common at present. In the current wave of business process outsourcing something similar is occurring at the moment. There is talk of "transformational outsourcing" (Linder, 2004), which appears to refer to leveraging outsourcing to change the nature of activities in the firm, and of the coming of strategic offshore outsourcing relations (Feeny, Lacity, and Willcocks, 2005) but not much evidence to back up such statements. Much of the rhetoric around strategic outsourcing seems to be driven by suppliers, such as Accenture, EDS, and IBM, wishing to improve their bargaining situation. If these suppliers can position their services as being strategic or even transformational this has obvious merits for their ability to sell these services. Consultants likewise appear to benefit from giving advice on how to create outsourcing partnerships or to make outsourcing transformational. The number of outsourcing relations that should be called strategic is therefore inherently limited.

## 2. Because outsourcing is becoming more strategic, firms ought to outsource more

A second underlying claim is that because outsourcing is becoming more strategic, firms can benefit from outsourcing more. At the surface that appears to make sense, since something good is always desirable. A first obvious objection to this statement though is that, as we have seen above, it is not quite clear whether outsourcing is indeed becoming more strategic. If it is not but we are made to believe that it is, the advice to outsource more makes no sense and is in fact harmful. But even if the existing set of outsourcing relations is causing a positive performance impact, and thus appears of strategic value, there are two good reasons why one should not automatically assume that it therefore makes sense to start building more, similar outsourcing relations. First, there surely is some selection bias in those activities that have already been turned into outsourcing partnerships. These activities were chosen because outsourcing partnerships provided some obvious perceived benefits and because it was deemed feasible to create an outsourcing partnership. That implies that for those activities that were not initially chosen it may be much harder or much less valuable to establish an outsourcing partnership. *In extremis* firms would be trying to create an outsourcing partnership in order to procure pure commodities. This really does not seem to make sense. Second, as argued in chapter 5, there is a limit to the number of relations managers and the firms they work for can usefully manage. That limit, which was referred to as external span of control, is more likely to be exceeded when a firm attempts to add additional outsourcing partnerships. In other words, there are limits upon the maximum number of outsourcing partnerships that make it less beneficial to add further partnerships even if existing partnerships perform particularly well. Such diminishing returns again do not imply that firms should not seek additional outsourcing partnerships but they do imply that doing so is costly and perhaps not very effective.

## 3. By outsourcing more, outsourcing will become more strategic

There is also a claim that outsourcing decisions are becoming more strategic because more decisions to outsource are being made. In other words, the strategic value of outsourcing increases with the frequency of outsourcing decisions. As we have seen in previous chapters, that is

entirely untrue. If firms outsource more, this simply means that the costs
and benefits of outsourcing will have a relatively larger weight in determining overall performance compared to the costs and benefits of integration. In other words, if more outsourcing takes place, this increases
the overall performance from outsourcing (for those firms that have not
outsourced to their optimal point yet) or decreases the overall performance from outsourcing (for those firms that have outsourced beyond
their optimal point). More outsourcing does not by definition make
outsourcing more strategic. Whether outsourcing adds to a strategy
depends on how much has been outsourced compared to how much
ought to be outsourced. Making the right outsourcing decisions has
always been important, and barring completely unforeseeable circumstances, will remain important. All of this does not mean that outsourcing has not and will not become more strategic, but it implies that
evidence to support that claim is shaky at best and that we ought to
observe this empirically in order to believe it. Perhaps there is indeed a
shift towards more outsourcing relations in which joint value is created,
but even so we need to establish its magnitude.

Another part of the argument runs more or less like this: by outsourcing
firms create new supplier relationships that they can then nurture and turn
into something beautiful. Doing so will allow them to capture "relational
rent," in the sense that these relationships start to produce some unique,
innovative outcomes. But in effect, for the types of activities firms are now
outsourcing, like business processes, there may not yet be any good
suppliers and even if there are it could take years for these relationships
to start paying off. Most CEOs and middle managers today do not have
years to sit and wait for these outcomes to materialize. What may therefore
well happen is that firms outsource activities that are better kept in-house.[2]

If we again take up the earlier argument that increased outsourcing
leads to outsourcing becoming more strategic, it is easy to see that circular
reasoning has been established. Outsourcing is becoming more strategic;

---

[2] I recently saw a practitioner presentation of a process that Dell had outsourced a
few years ago but had just recently integrated back into the firm in a manner
somewhat reflective of an internal market (some might call this insourcing). This
latter move apparently paid dividends as it allowed for a combination of market-
based and hierarchy-based traits. The impression that emerged, however, was
that Dell had wanted this solution all along but could not realize it initially
because of the hazards of organizational change processes. By first outsourcing,
Dell managed to circumvent these difficult internal change processes.

because it is becoming more strategic firms ought to outsource more; and by outsourcing more they actually make outsourcing more strategic. If one buys into this circular argument, there is no mechanism to hold firms back from outsourcing all of their activities because doing so appears to lead to the best results. Practical experience and research findings tell us otherwise, however. The conclusion has to be that strategic outsourcing is possible but only for a relatively small range of activities. Most outsourcing is not strategic in nature and never will be. Some part of outsourcing is strategic and should be exploited as well as possible.

Based on this discussion it is obvious that neither Quinn's core activities prescription for outsourcing nor the idea of strategic outsourcing, which together largely mirror the current rationale in defense of outsourcing that companies present to the outside world as well as discussions of outsourcing in much of the popular press, provides a sound basis for managerial decision-making, especially not if followed religiously. I will therefore devote the remainder of this chapter to building some complementary managerial prescriptions.

## Managerial intent

Almost all of the literature, and admittedly much of the discussion in this book thus far, takes it for granted that once it has been established that there is a best way of outsourcing in an industry, managers will actually follow that trajectory. In other words, the discretion of managers to design idiosyncratic outsourcing strategies is limited, or in the accounts of some economists or sociologists even non-existent. What managers appear to be doing according to the economists is to choose an appropriate governance structure, i.e. the right outsourcing level, to fit various antecedent variables. If we are to believe the sociologists, managers choose outsourcing levels and supplier relations on the basis of the web of relations in which they and their firms are enmeshed. Neither account leaves much room for choices that deviate from these predictions. In fact if managers do deviate from these predictions, their behavior is described as "non-optimal."[3]

---

[3] The entire field of strategic management seems to be going through a stage where economic and sociological approaches were first contrasted (Baum and Dobbin, 2000) and now become increasingly integrated. That may well be a necessary step in the formation of some unifying paradigm for the field. Yet it also produces the unfortunate and worrisome side-effect that other approaches, like managerial or psychological perspectives, are gradually pasted away.

But what if firms and managers could actually redesign the rules of the game? What if they could turn their industries on their head or at least challenge received wisdom on outsourcing? What if environments could be shaped and were not given? In Box 7.1, an example is provided of a firm that did just that by choosing to disobey generally accepted industry practices on outsourcing and benefited from doing so.

---

## Box 7.1. Zara: Spanish stubbornness

In the European retailing business it is received wisdom that products ought to (a) be outsourced and (b) be sourced in large quantities from low-wage countries, China in particular. It takes some courage to start tinkering with that formula, especially when it has proven to be successful in the past. Inditex, the owner of over 2,000 Zara fashion stores, seems to have that courage. Its practices run counter to received wisdom. For instance, Zara does not participate much in fashion shows or even view these as important sources of information. Instead it tries to respond very rapidly to changes in customer demand that it observes in its stores. As a consequence Zara does not change its collection four times a year as is customary in most fashion houses but on a more or less continuous basis and is able to bring a new design into its stores within five weeks.

Its outsourcing strategy reflects that philosophy. Zara vertically integrates design, just-in-time production, logistics and sales and has continued to base most of its manufacturing activities at La Coruña in Galicia, a region in Spain otherwise mostly known for its dwindling fishing fleet. Store managers and designers communicate on a daily basis. Because the information technology in use is not particularly complex, and in fact somewhat old, cost savings are obtained in this area. Store managers can look at new designs every day and order whatever they believe is going to sell well. New designs are immediately put into production, mostly by a range of local Galician cooperatives. China accounts for only 12.5 percent of the production volume of Inditex. Products are prepared for transportation locally as well and then shipped, by plane, to faraway destinations. In its production activities Inditex does not seek to maximize scale but instead opts for small batches to avoid having to mark down too many products in its stores and to have the flexibility to change its products quickly. By doing so its customers keep coming back to

Zara stores because they know that if they do not buy something this week, it may be gone forever the week after. Because Zara's customers know they are going to see new things whenever they come into the store, there is also a reduced need for advertising spending.

So Zara is successful despite, or perhaps because of, its denial of established industry rules that dictate much outsourcing, and especially from faraway low-cost locations, is a necessity. This shows that deviation from what appear to be optimal strategies can be a good thing, as long as it is done for the right reasons.

*Source:* Inditex: the future of fast fashion. *The Economist*, June 18, 2005, pp. 63–64.

More generally, then, outsourcing strategies need not be derived in a deterministic manner. Of course, and as I have argued throughout this book, everything else being equal, there is an optimal outsourcing level and deviations from that optimum are costly and become costlier as they become larger. But there is no reason to assume that everything else has to be equal. Zara, by coming up with a radically different business model, could design an outsourcing strategy that appeared less than optimal when compared against the industry standard. For Zara, however, it turned out to be a great outsourcing strategy, because it fitted its business model particularly well. When properly undertaken, business model innovation can be a key source of competitive advantage because it rewrites an industry's rules (Hamel, 1998; Markides, 1999).

Business model innovators in the airline industry, like Ryanair and Southwestern, came up with outsourcing strategies that involved much less integration than hitherto seen in flagship carriers like British Airways and Lufthansa. This contributed to their lower cost base. Decision-makers in these firms, primarily their CEOs, have likewise rewritten the rules of the airline industry. So it seems that if a manager finds a new value proposition, along the lines of Zara, she or he can create competitive advantage by internalizing and possibly co-locating the relevant set of activities. If, on the other hand, the manager has found a formula that greatly reduces cost levels, like the low-cost airlines, a firm may benefit from outsourcing more activities than industry conventions would suggest. This shows how managerial intent, in the form of rethinking of the rules of the game by an individual, can influence outsourcing decision-making. But managerial intent can also come to the fore in other ways, for instance because individuals are motivated to spend their time and efforts in certain ways. In this manner, vertical integration may perhaps provide a tool for motivating people.

## A guide to outsourcing as experimentation

When in late 2005 Abbey National, after being taken over by Spain's Grupo Santander, decided to bring back in-house its call center activities it reversed an earlier decision. Just two years before, the previous management of Abbey National had decided to outsource these activities to third-party suppliers in India. An Abbey insider was quoted as saying "[g]iven the risk to our reputation of moving the jobs offshore, you want the service to be top notch. If it isn't top notch, then why are you there?"[4] What Abbey had engaged in was, in effect, an *outsourcing experiment*.

But few firms are willing to think of their outsourcing decisions as experiments. Instead they prefer to see and explain them as correct decisions that came about after some analysis and thinking. This at least partially explains the popularity of the core activities and strategic outsourcing arguments, which provide for such rationalization, similar to the use of the word "synergies" in mergers and acquisitions. This tendency to rationalize outsourcing decisions, once taken, is usually even stronger in retrospect. But as we have seen throughout this book, many outsourcing decisions are surrounded by substantial uncertainty and causal ambiguity, an inability to link outsourcing decisions to performance outcomes. Therefore most outsourcing decision-making, like it or not, is actually experimental in nature. This raises the question of what can be done to improve the odds of running successful experiments. The answer might include the following.

## 1. Run the right number of experiments

An instinctive response might be to suggest that the right number of experiments is the largest possible number because more experiments will produce more information and, with more information in hand, better decision-making can be obtained. This obviously neglects the costs of experimenting. If we recall the Cisco example cited earlier in

---

[4] http://www.thisismoney.co.uk/news/article.html?in_article_id=404606&in_page_id=2 (accessed on December 15, 2005).

the book (Abrahamson, 2004) where Cisco outsourced, then integrated, and then outsourced the same activity within a two-year time-span, it is obvious that frequent switches can be harmful. Abbey National's experiments probably also involved such switching costs. Hence, as for any form of organizational change, a balance must be struck between complete inertia and total chaos (Abrahamson, 2000) or between what Schein (in Coutu, 2002) calls the anxiety of learning and the anxiety of survival. In Schein's view, learning can only take place when participants are afraid that their very survival, or that of the organization for which they work, is at stake. This is why poorly performing firms have had a relatively easy time selling outsourcing while it is hard to undertake outsourcing when things are going particularly well. There is something truly dysfunctional about this because outsourcing (or integrating) an activity now might better prepare firms for the future. If pain and a crisis can be avoided by acting now, then why not act? The answer is that firms suffer from outsourcing inertia, which needs to be overcome.

By selling outsourcing as an experiment, and executing it as such, managers can go out and demonstrate whether there is real value in outsourcing. Generally it is also better to run many smaller experiments than a few very large ones that could have disastrous consequences. So rather than outsourcing many accounts activities at once, perhaps firms should start by just outsourcing payrolls. This way, a firm does not risk undermining essential systems but can potentially benefit from the advantages of outsourcing. An additional advantage of running a large number of smaller experiments is that it is easier to retract a few without losing face. They were, after all, experiments!

## 2. Run some experiments in ways that deviate from industry competitors

In chapter 4 I discussed how outsourcing of major activities often tends to come in industry-wide waves. But various examples from interviews also showed that many managers are unaware of their competitors' outsourcing policies or at least of their intricacies. Both of these observations lead to the conclusion that it is hard for firms to use outsourcing experimentation as a source of competitive advantage. If all a firm does is mimic its competitors' behaviors, and there is no room for differentiation or deviation from what others do, outsourcing as such cannot be the source of competitive advantage, although it is of course possible that superior performance resides elsewhere, for instance in how supplier relations are managed (recall the discussion in chapter 5).

Likewise, a lack of awareness of what competitors actually do makes it hard to see how outsourcing contributes to the competitive advantage of firms *vis-à-vis* their industry competitors. Although the performance of a competitor's product may be tested and compared against an internal benchmark, it will remain unclear whether outsourcing has an impact on a competitor's product performance. Likewise, overall corporate or SBU performance numbers may be compared but if all one can find out is that they are different, without being able to trace the source of these differences, these numbers are not very insightful.[5]

In order to benefit most from outsourcing experimentation, two steps are therefore needed. First, firms should know what it is that their competitors outsource or integrate, and how this influences their performance. Obviously such information is not easy to obtain but at least an effort must be made. Customers and suppliers are often good sources of information as are all kinds of industry and trade events or reverse engineering of products and even services. Second, rather than assuming that outsourcing (or integration) is the right decision because it is what competitors do, firms should deliberately deviate in small ways from the competition, for instance by outsourcing items that competitors are still keeping in-house. The information these outsourcing experiments produce can generate real value after a while if it is used to inform future decision-making.

## 3. Install feedback loops within and between experiments

This book is centered on the notion of an optimal level of outsourcing at which maximum performance results. And I have shown that deviations from the optimum, implying too much or too little outsourcing, are costly and increasingly so (as evidenced by the notion of a negative curvilinear effect of outsourcing on performance). But there is, of

---

[5] Such a lack of insight into the outsourcing behavior of competitors not only ruins the value of outsourcing experimentation but also constitutes a major failure in competitive intelligence. Many firms seem content to pay a lot of attention to what their competitors do in the marketplace but are not investing much effort into how competitors' offerings come about. Given the importance assigned to outsourcing and other external relations in recent years, and all the discussion around their performance-improving effects, this is inconsistent to say the least.

course, a practical problem with this notion, that I have thus far neglected entirely: *How does a firm know whether it is outsourcing as much as it should be outsourcing or perhaps outsourcing too much or too little?* In other words, how does cognition about optimal outsourcing levels come about?

Earlier we have explored the *theoretically correct answer* to this question. Given the asset specificity levels of activities, the uncertainty surrounding them, the firm's own competences in comparison to those of potential suppliers, the institutional environment the firm operates in including such things as property rights laws and international trade regimes, the level of communication technologies available to the firm, and a host of other factors, we can predict how much the firm ought to outsource (through the outsourceability of its activities).

The problem with such broadly constructed concepts is that they are imperfectly measurable. In fact, all the scholarly work on outsourcing uses measures that are anywhere between somewhat satisfactory and poor. For a non-academic to take and understand the theoretical work and then also apply it to a practical context is presumably asking too much. Any attempt by a firm to translate these broad theories into practical outsourcing predictors is doomed, therefore, to run into measurability problems. This does not mean a return to the simplistic prescriptions discussed earlier is needed. Firms can make some efforts to measure outsourcing better. In all too many firms the overall degree of outsourcing is treated as an accounting measure, often recorded to keep regulators and shareholders at ease. But there is no reason why it should not also be used as a decision-making variable. And firms can equally easy track their own performance. Thus some outsourcing–performance link can be established over time.

There is, of course, a second *more practical and deductive route* to finding out what is an optimal level of outsourcing for an individual firm. That route uses the knowledge obtained from a continuous stream of many small outsourcing experiments to inform outsourcing decision-making. But what is needed in order to make these experiments pay off? I would like to suggest firms ought to install two feedback mechanisms if they want to benefit from experimentation. These mechanisms are feedback within experiments and feedback between experiments, respectively.

The first feedback mechanism is already in place in most firms, albeit generally in an intuitive rather than a structured sense, because while the outsourcing process is still occurring, firms tend to monitor the effects of outsourcing. Because outsourcing (and insourcing) processes receive so much more attention than activities that have been out-sourced (or integrated) some time ago, firms also receive and process many more signals on the performance of the activities that are going through an outsourcing process. When an activity is first outsourced, this is viewed as a project and hence people are assigned to the manage-ment of this project. At a later stage the fact that an activity is out-sourced becomes something that is taken for granted. In the case of Abbey National, outsourcing of call centers had clearly not achieved this status yet and that, combined with a changing of the guard at the level of top management, led Abbey to reconsider its decision.

This example raises an important issue though. In the Abbey case it was not just the effects of outsourcing that produced a reversal of the decision but it was also the pressure from higher authorities. As dis-cussed in chapter 4, the decision to outsource (or integrate) an activity, produces an escalating commitment on the part of the decision-maker. Because that decision-maker has committed to a course of action, in the form of outsourcing, he or she will identify with and be identified with the success of the action. Even when outsourcing does not work out as well as expected, the decision-maker will attempt to hide that from others. There will also be a reluctance to change course since that implies admitting the initial decision was wrong.

By formalizing the outsourcing decision as an experiment and mak-ing transparent the conditions under which the experiment takes place, this problem can at least partly be overcome. Such formalization of outsourcing experimentation entails the recognition that it is accepta-ble to fail since running an experiment, by definition, is an uncertain course of action. Everyone will acknowledge that some experiments turn out to be successful while others fail. The manager who proposed and executed the experiment cannot be held liable for its failure, unless that manager of course knowingly made mistakes by engaging in an experiment which was doomed to fail. Obviously not everything is open to experimentation. As should be clear by now, it is generally a bad idea to outsource a company's CEO in the same way that integrat-ing the production of electricity into the firm does not work well for the overwhelming majority of firms.

Acknowledging that outsourcing is experimentation also implies that successes and failures open up avenues for learning. A much-discussed example of experimentation in recent years is Harrah's Entertainment, which runs its experiments according to guidelines devised by its CEO and former Harvard Business School professor Gary Loveman (Loveman, 2003). In the casinos that Harrah's owns, literally thousands of small experiments take place every year. These experiments generate a wealth of data that allows Harrah's continuously to make changes to its formula. Outsourcing experiments should take on a similar character. By gradually outsourcing some business processes, firms can find out what works and what does not work for them. For instance, firms may initially underestimate the amount of effort they need to put into a supplier relation when they outsource a specific activity. At that point they can decide whether to increase the effort or to insource the activity instead.

The Harrah's example also shows that learning need not be restricted to a single experiment. In other words, feedback loops can be installed between experiments. Harrah's uses knowledge it gained from previous experiments to inform future experiments (Loveman, 2003). Likewise, the outcomes of one outsourcing experiment can be used to inform the next experiment. Of course, the outsourcing of business processes differs from the outsourcing of components. But there are similarities between them too. For instance, outsourcing decision-making procedures may be replicated from one decision to the next. Or the metrics used to measure the success of experiments can be reapplied in different circumstances. But because of the compartmentalization of outsourcing decisions this seldom happens in practice. Thus successful experimentation also requires some "central brain" that registers and processes the results of previous experiments and from which decision-makers can draw to gain knowledge. The responsibility for setting up and organizing the outsourcing experimentation process therefore has to be situated in the highest echelons of the organization for it to work.

### Selling experimentation

But the hardest part of outsourcing as experimentation might not be running the experiments or disseminating knowledge obtained from the experiments. It could well be the difficulty of selling the notion of outsourcing experimentation to the organization and its stakeholders. Because outsourcing often carries social costs and organizational upheaval, it is not a decision that ought to be taken lightly. Outsourcing involves people and the notion of experimenting with outsourcing therefore suggests an organization is happy to experiment with its people. That is unlikely to be a popular message for the average employee. What might be successful selling strategies for outsourcing experimentation to be acceptable to employees and others?

One strategy may be to simply present the benefits of outsourcing as experimentation, in order to lower learning anxiety. Because outsourcing experimentation leads to better outsourcing decisions, it will improve the performance of the firm. This is obviously a rather indirect and abstract argument to make. But when outsourcing experimentation improves the chances of making the right decision it also reduces the likelihood that decisions need to be reversed in future. In other words, the organizational upheaval and social costs associated with the decision to outsource, and to a lesser extent with the decision to integrate as well, will be lower. Thus the kinds of excesses Abrahamson (2004) observed in Cisco are less likely to take place. This ought to be of clear benefit to employees as well.

A second sensible strategy is to engage in outsourcing as experimentation without calling it that. It might instead be called something like an "outsourcing decision-making system" or an "outsourcing knowledge system." Such systems are perfectly normal and acceptable when it comes to the management of employees or suppliers (vendor rating). The system, as noted before, registers previous outsourcing experiences and current outsourcing efforts. Therefore, it is also relatively easier for employees and others to recognize the benefits of such a system because they can draw parallels with these other systems.

A third strategy involves stressing the costs of not engaging in outsourcing experimentation, in order to increase survival anxiety. The argument could be that if outsourcing is not undertaken, the odds of firm survival decrease. Because employees want to be guaranteed a job now and in the future, they might be willing to comply with outsourcing decisions. A milder variant would be that to outsource some part of the firm's activities now, it may not be necessary to go through major restructuring, for instance through massive outsourcing, in the future.

## Outsourcing and firm strategy

Another important issue is how outsourcing strategy can be aligned with a firm's general strategy. By treating outsourcing in isolation from strategy, the risk of subsystem optimization exists. At a very broad level outsourcing can be linked to Michael Porter's (1985) generic strategies. Outsourcing is a strategy that fits less well with a differentiation strategy than it does with a cost leadership strategy, because it is hard to differentiate a firm from its competitors if many of its inputs are supplied by external suppliers who might also be supplying competing firms. Outsourcing does, on the other hand, lend itself quite well to cost leadership as firms can pick the lowest-cost suppliers of various activities from the marketplace. Porter himself (1998), by the way, has expressed skepticism over the effects of outsourcing because it tends to take away from the firm's uniqueness and ability to differentiate itself from other firms. This competitive leveling tends to lower profitability levels in industries, so Porter argues.

The other big school of strategic management is the resource-based view of the firm (Barney, 1991) which takes a firm's internal resource endowments, and not its industry and environmental conditions, as the point of departure in strategy-making. This is the line of thought closest to Quinn's point of view, so it is unsurprising to see that outsourcing is here primarily seen as a consequence of the firm's present resource base. The stronger the firm's resource base for a given activity, the less likely it is to outsource that activity, although the firm's resource base ought correctly to be seen in comparison with those of its potential suppliers.

Thus we have two different prescriptions on the outsourcing policy a firm ought to follow given its overall strategy. One, following Porter's generic strategies, suggests that outsourcing levels ought to correspond with the extent to which the firm follows a differentiation strategy. The other, following the resource-based view, suggests that outsourcing levels follow from the resource set a firm has created in order to compete in its markets. Both are useful and applicable ideas on how to unite corporate strategy and outsourcing. But both suggest that outsourcing strategy follows corporate or generic strategy. What I would like to suggest, though, is that outsourcing strategy and corporate/generic strategy can also occur in parallel, or even that corporate/generic strategy can follow outsourcing strategy.

Box 7.2 details how one Dutch manufacturing firm was able to use its difficulties with outsourcing to its advantage. More generally it is interesting to ask under what conditions outsourcing plays a role in shaping corporate/generic strategy. Research has shown (Afuah, 2001) that when new, disruptive technologies are introduced in an

## Box 7.2. The bike that requires no pedaling

In Britain, bicycles for some people do not go under the name "bike," which they use to refer to motor cycles, but instead are referred to as pedal bikes. Yet not all of today's bicycles require much pedaling anymore. In the Netherlands, one of the local producers, Sparta, produced its original "Spartamet" (Sparta bicycle with ancillary engine) in the 1980s. Some 20,000 of these were sold, although young people did not want to be seen anywhere near the vehicle. When, in the late 1990s, Sparta introduced a new bicycle with an ancillary engine, the ION, the challenge was therefore to widen its market appeal.

The ancillary engine for the Spartamet was developed in conjunction with a fairly large German supplier of components to the bicycle industry. When Sparta came calling for its ION model and explained its needs, the supplier thought them to be absurd. The development of the new engine required a detailed understanding of electronics. Sparta therefore found itself without a supplier for the most crucial component of its new bicycle. It decided to develop the capability in-house and hired new people to do so.

As a consequence of successfully mastering that step, it can now offer additional services to dealers that were previously non-existent. For instance, dealers are provided with access to some of the software so they can run all kinds of checks on a bicycle that needs servicing through their own PCs. The bicycle sold well and in retrospect the supplier thought it had missed an interesting opportunity. This type of bicycle has now acquired its own name: E-Bike.

Hence Sparta managed to turn what looked like a bad situation, a technical problem with no supplier being present, into a money-making situation. It developed its own intellectual property, instead of relying exclusively on suppliers to do that. As a consequence it now has a differentiated product which seems to be well liked by consumers. When markets do not offer a ready-made product, creativity can be a good alternative.

*Source:* Interview; http://www.sparta.nl/.

industry, there is substantially more room for gaining competitive advantage through outsourcing strategy. Firms that have developed these new technologies in-house or have exclusive access to them through key suppliers are in a better position to exploit them and hence to gain important first-mover advantages. Previous outsourcing strategies will therefore dictate the corporate response to new technologies. More generally, when any sort of non-linear change occurs in an industry, outsourcing strategy will help to shape corporate/generic strategy.

Insinga and Werle (2000) warn against the difficulty of implementing an outsourcing strategy at the operational level. As outsourcing is operationalized, its original strategic intentions can get lost in the day-to-day concerns typical of operations. Conversely, outsourcing decisions taken at the operational level may produce unintended and often unwanted side-effects. Thus another point to take into account when incorporating outsourcing into a firm strategy is whether the outsourcing strategy can actually be operationalized and implemented.

## The optimal outsourcing tool

Where academics seem to be dealing with "why" questions for much (perhaps too much) of their time, practitioners are generally more focused on "how to" questions. Whenever I confront them with some of the ideas discussed in this book, they do not ask why one would observe a negative curvilinear effect associated with outsourcing. Instead they are interested in how to turn that piece of knowledge into practicable action. Perhaps the best way to do that would be through what one might call an "optimal outsourcing tool." Such a tool would determine the optimal outsourcing levels for a specific firm.

Of course there are all kinds of advice available to managers who are contemplating outsourcing. One practitioner-cum-author I spoke to about my research said "I can't see how what you're saying is beneficial. I've already written up a checklist of twenty items in this little booklet published through this organization. If managers just follow my list they will be OK." As discussed earlier in this book, there are also plenty of consultants and other advisers available who are willing to shed their light on an outsourcing decision. And there are more applied journal articles that provide decision-makers with flow charts and the like (Tayles and Drury, 2001; Venkatesan, 1992).

Each of these methods suffers from some limitations though. Some of the checklists concentrate on only one sector or industry, or one type of activity, like manufacturing, thus lacking the generalizability practitioners are seeking. Furthermore, the focus on single activities takes away from firm-level considerations about how much to outsource and from the very real consequences of a firm's overall outsourcing level on its overall performance. Many of the flow charts lead to single factors determining the outcome. If the box "not strategic" is ticked for an activity, the outcome of the chart will simply never be vertical integration. This is not to say that the fact that an activity bears no obvious relation to the firm's strategy is unimportant, just that it is unclear why it should be of overriding importance.

Another limitation is in how the advice is derived. This is usually through one of two routes. One route is to use a few practical examples, sometimes through academic research and sometimes through mere anecdotes, to draw up the factors underlying the model. This severely compromises the generalizability of the advice. The other route is to draw upon one or two conceptual frameworks, with the core competence approach coming to mind as an obvious framework, and only include factors from those frameworks. This leads to the advice being very limited and one-dimensional in scope.

A better solution would therefore be to draw upon a variety of systematic scholarly accounts of the factors that influence optimal outsourcing levels. The notion of outsourceability, discussed in chapter 3, springs to mind as a means of capturing this. Given the firm's portfolio of activities, its own characteristics, and environmental characteristics, an average outsourceability of activities would emerge. With this in hand, a multivariate prediction could be made of the optimal outsourcing levels of a given firm. The advice that follows would be an overall prediction of how much a firm ought to outsource, say 65 percent of its turnover.

Next a decision-maker could rank the entire portfolio of the firm's individual activities by their outsourceability. This would lead to the identification of the specific activities that lie to the left and to the right of the optimum. Thus it would contain specific outsourcing advice on all activities. Furthermore, it would allow for the identification of the activities that fall just right, or just left, of the optimum. These activities are likely candidates for a form of outsourcing that involves close cooperation (partnerships) with suppliers. At that stage, firms have an idea of their overall optimal degree of outsourcing, of which specific activities to outsource, and of which outsourcing relations to turn into partnerships. An optimal outsourcing tool, in other words, could have real value for practitioners dealing with outsourcing decisions.[6]

## Conclusion

This chapter focused on what further pieces of practical advice on outsourcing can be given. The chapter started by correcting two popular notions, that firms ought to outsource non-core activities, and that outsourcing is becoming ever more strategic. It then discussed the role of managerial intent, especially how firms need not see the outsourcing–performance curve purely as a given but can create idiosyncratic outsourcing strategies. Next, attention turned to the notion of outsourcing as experimentation and how to effectuate that. Then, the link between outsourcing strategy and firm strategy was discussed in detail, leading to some further recommendations. Finally, the creation of an optimal outsourcing tool was discussed.

[6] This raises the question why the tool has not been created yet. The answer is that people in both worlds, the world of practice and the academic world, are discouraged from doing so through incentive systems and because of gaps in their knowledge-bases. Practitioners have to deal with the day-to-day demands of their jobs and generally do not have the wider vision to analyze outsourcing outside their specific firm and industry context; and they seldom have the scholarly research background needed. Academics, who are not judged upon criteria other than (journal) publications and to some extent teaching performance, are not incentivized to do this type of work, and generally also lack the marketing clout to turn this kind of output into a success. As a consequence the co-production of knowledge between practitioners and academics stalls (Van de Ven and Johnson, forthcoming).

# 8 | Outsourcing research agenda

H AVING studied key outsourcing trends and outsourcing research, proposed a new perspective on outsourcing and firm performance, elaborated on that perspective in various ways, and sketched some practical guidelines for dealing with outsourcing, we now need to consider the agenda for academic research on outsourcing. This chapter will do just that by looking first at theoretical challenges. Based on the discussion of outsourcing in this book, a number of theoretical challenges have arisen. Each of these will be discussed in turn and then an attempt will be made at providing an integrated answer. Next, some possible extensions will be discussed. Finally, various methodological, methodical, and empirical challenges will be discussed as well.

## Theoretical challenges

### Economizing and socializing perspectives

As discussed earlier, outsourcing has mostly been viewed as an economizing (Williamson, 1991a) phenomenon in the management literature, whether it is through a transaction cost, resource-based, or other economizing lens. The economizing perspective proposes a set of antecedent variables, primarily transaction and firm conditions, which are supposed to predict governance structures (outsourcing levels). Deviation from these predictions, also called misalignment, is a costly affair. The substantial explanatory power of the economizing perspective for understanding levels of outsourcing was discussed. Yet sole reliance on using this perspective as the holy grail of outsourcing was also critiqued.

A number of specific complements to economizing were proposed that might broadly be categorized under the heading of "socializing." These included concepts and theories such as organizational inertia, increasing commitment, bandwagoning, and organizational politics.

These socializing factors were argued to affect outsourcing as well, primarily outsourcing processes but also outsourcing levels. The mechanism by which socializing factors helped to explain outsourcing was through the provision of a context within which decision-makers took their decisions. The socializing factors helped decision-makers deal with the complexity and uncertainty surrounding outsourcing decisions and helped them relate these decisions to the environments in which they operated. Some empirical evidence in support of the socializing perspective was provided. A key theoretical challenge in the area of outsourcing is to bring the socializing and economizing perspectives together in a fruitful manner, one which does not deny the usefulness of one or the other perspective, but rather builds upon their complementarities. This is a struggle in which the entire field of strategic management has been engaged for some time now (Baum and Dobbin, 2000; Martinez and Dacin, 1999; Oliver, 1999).[1]

To overcome it, what needs to happen is the creation of more theoretical accounts that involve both perspectives, for instance along the lines of the work of Martinez and Dacin (1997). Various relevant questions come to mind. When is outsourcing more of a response to the need to maintain or increase financial performance and when is it more of a response to the pressures exerted by inside and outside institutions? Is there some alternating sequence in the long run between the socializing and economizing explanations in the same way Abrahamson and Fairchild (1999) suggest that rational and emotional factors alternate in the creation of management fashions? To what extent are the antecedent variables of outsourcing themselves socially shaped or an imprint of the environment in which they are shaped (Nishiguchi, 1994)? And is there some inherent economic disadvantage associated with the extensive use of socializing mechanisms in outsourcing decision-making? This provides for an interesting and underexplored research agenda.

In a sense, however, even this is only a first step in the process of moving towards a truly multidisciplinary approach to outsourcing. Such a multidisciplinary approach surely ought to take into account more than just the socializing and economizing perspectives. In this book, I have attempted to make a contribution towards such a

---

[1] The founding of the journal *Strategic Organization* was also partly stimulated by this struggle.

multidisciplinary approach not only by including discussion of economizing and socializing but also by drawing upon managerialism, history, psychology, political science, and at times other subjects. But
admittedly there is much more work to be done to come to a true
multidisciplinary understanding of outsourcing.

## Outsourcing levels (designs) versus outsourcing processes

Another issue addressed here in some depth is the relative dearth of
research on the outsourcing process. Most extant literature focuses on
outsourcing level or outsourcing design, a variable that is more easily
measured and can be explained in a less messy way than outsourcing
process. Process, in general, has not received the attention it deserves in
strategy research, so it has been argued (Mintzberg, Quinn, and
Ghoshal, 1995). A better understanding of outsourcing processes
increases the practical relevance of academic research because practitioners spend much more of their time managing outsourcing processes, in the form of projects, than they do analyzing outsourcing
levels, although they do of course spend considerable time managing
relations with outside suppliers after outsourcing processes have been
rounded off.

There is, in other words, room for improved understanding by an
increased focus on the outsourcing process. This raises a variety of
research questions. When do managers (firms) initiate outsourcing
processes? Which actors inside and outside a firm are involved in outsourcing processes and how do these actors interact? What determines
the length of outsourcing processes? Are there differences in success
among outsourcing processes and what explains such differences? Are
some outsourcing processes terminated and if so for what reason?

In this book some possible answers were provided as well. I showed
that organizational inertia may produce misalignment in outsourcing
levels, especially when the underlying antecedent conditions of outsourcing, as sketched by economizing approaches, change. When such
misalignment occurs, the need for realignment is one possible reason
for the initiation of outsourcing processes, especially when severe misalignment leads to a crisis. But socializing factors featured very heavily
as well, particularly bandwagon factors. These bandwagon factors
help to determine the timing, frequency, and amplitude of outsourcing
processes. Other factors discussed include personal preferences and

organizational politics. Organizational politics also play an important role in the further development of outsourcing processes.

One can speculate that the length and success of outsourcing processes depends on a number of factors. Obviously the complexity and the requirements for knowledge transfer of what is being outsourced are key considerations, as complexity will add to the length of the process and increase its likelihood of failure. The extent to which outsourcing was the right decision will facilitate the outsourcing process. Furthermore, the political struggles around outsourcing discussed in chapter 4 will come into play. Finally, the length, success, and termination of outsourcing processes will be closely related to one another. Less successful processes will likely take more time to be completed, unless of course they are terminated prematurely. Termination of outsourcing processes, and the associated reversion to integration, may be the consequence of inferior performance but may equally well result from a change of the guard, as described in several examples in this book, or of changed circumstances that make the initial outsourcing decision look less favorable in retrospect.

In future research, it would be useful to see more theoretical and empirical work on the outsourcing process. Such work could shed more light on the questions raised above. It could also look in more detail at the interaction between outsourcing levels and outsourcing processes. While one obvious conclusion is that outsourcing processes change outsourcing levels between time $t$ and time $t + 1$, other, more detailed findings are required as well. For instance, do firms at very low or very high outsourcing levels tend to engage in more and more extensive outsourcing processes? This also ties into the experimentation agenda discussed in chapter 7. A final point is that it would be useful to see formal testing of the notion put forward earlier that outsourcing follows a punctuated equilibrium model, where long periods of outsourcing inertia are followed by shorter periods featuring many simultaneous outsourcing processes.

## Static versus dynamic explanations

Related to the previous observation that most research has looked at outsourcing levels, and not processes, it is also true that research has mostly taken a static, not a dynamic, view of outsourcing. A focus on processes naturally introduces a more dynamic look at outsourcing, as tracking a process involves looking at changes over time. Yet that is not the only way to look at outsourcing in a more dynamic way. In chapter 6 it was argued that there is also merit in looking at the antecedent variables of outsourcing levels in a more dynamic way.

This involves both changes in the levels of antecedent variables, like a reduction in asset specificity levels through the commoditization of components, and changes in how these antecedents impact outsourcing, as discussed through the example of R&D intensity. Hence it would be beneficial to add some further questions to the outsourcing research agenda. Which antecedent variables of outsourcing change over time and under what conditions do such changes take place? What does it take for the effect (direction) of an antecedent variable to change? How sensitive are optimal outsourcing levels to changes over time of antecedent variables or the effect of these variables? How can these changes be detected? What are appropriate firm-level responses to such changes? What is the relationship between these changes, outsourcing inertia, and the formation of competitive and institutional outsourcing bandwagons?

These questions show, along with all the historical evidence (Lamoreaux, Raff, and Temin, 2003), that outsourcing strategies, and as a consequence any relation outsourcing may have to performance, are context-dependent. Specifically, the dimensions of time and space have to be invoked in order to make sense of outsourcing. Most outsourcing research does not explicitly do that though, presumably because there are reputational pay-offs associated with being able to present research findings as universally valid or because of the perceived need to tie into well-known concepts or theories. The appeal to outsiders of a finding on outsourcing in the Latvian dairy industry will be much more limited than the appeal of a finding on outsourcing in general. Thus it makes sense to present a finding as broadly as is acceptable to the outside world, which is represented by academic reviewers. Those who present findings on US firms or the car industry additionally have the benefit of being able to present their findings as the baseline against which all other studies need to be compared. More focus on interpreting empirical findings within the time and space of measurement would, however, enrich the outsourcing literature. But theory formation can also benefit by incorporating changes over time. For instance, if firms are organizing supplier relations in new ways, theories on outsourcing ought to reflect such changes.

## Integration

From these three challenges, economizing versus socializing, design versus process, and static versus dynamic explanations, one overall grand challenge emerges. That grand challenge is how the various perspectives and issues presented here can be integrated into a single outsourcing and performance framework. I will now try to build such a framework, both verbally and graphically. In doing so, some broad generalizations are unfortunately unavoidable.

Both outsourcing designs and outsourcing processes can be a source of competitive advantage. Outsourcing designs can broadly be described through an economizing perspective, particularly if one takes a static point of view. This economizing perspective contains a range of economic organization frameworks, of which transaction cost economics and the resource-based view are the two primary ones. To move from one outsourcing design to the next, firms go through outsourcing processes, however. The timing and magnitude of these outsourcing processes are best explained through a socializing perspective, including but not limited to bandwagoning and contagion models.

A more dynamic picture of outsourcing is therefore obtained by understanding how outsourcing designs and outsourcing processes alternate among each other, almost in the sense of Lewin's (1951) model of unfreezing–changing–refreezing. An existing outsourcing design is first unfrozen, when a make-or-buy decision is taken. That design is then changed, through an outsourcing process. Finally it is frozen again, once the outsourcing process has taken place. As critics of Lewin's model have argued though, the constant pressures to change that are present in today's (large) corporation ensure the freezing stage is not fully reached anymore. In large corporations there is always some ongoing outsourcing or insourcing process such that the overall level of outsourcing is never stable. Firms may be changing too much (Abrahamson, 2004).

The economizing perspective helps us to identify an optimal level of outsourcing. Deviations from that optimum are costly, and increasingly so the further from the optimum a firm is. This produces a negative curvilinear effect of the level of outsourcing on firm performance. When a non-optimal level of outsourcing occurs, we speak of misalignment. By realigning itself a firm can lower the gap between optimal and actual performance. In order to explain realignment, the socializing perspective is much more relevant than the economizing perspective. The socializing mechanism, however, does not generally produce perfect alignment (full realignment). Instead, it often produces what is best called overshooting, i.e. too much outsourcing where there was too little before. The reason is that the socializing mechanism involves heuristic, and not exact, decision-making. Heuristics are applied in the face of uncertainty and causal ambiguity.

Then there are three further dynamic effects that influence optimal outsourcing levels and performance outcomes. First, individual firms differ in the extent to which they are able to exploit outsourcing and vertical integration for performance purposes. Some firms are better at using outsourcing, as they have what I referred to as a larger span of external control. Similarly, others manage to exploit internal activities better, thereby similarly enhancing their performance. Second, firms go through a variety of technological and institutional changes that impact their optimal outsourcing levels. These changes make it more, or less, feasible to outsource than was the case before. Third, the distribution of activities in terms of their outsourceability may change, which alters the steepness of the curve. Firms face a trade-off between optimal performance (returns) and predictable performance (risks). As a consequence, firms are faced with a continuous need to realign themselves. In chapter 7 it was described how outsourcing experimentation might be one practical way to do that as would the development of an optimal outsourcing tool. Figure 8.1 shows a graphical overview of this discussion.

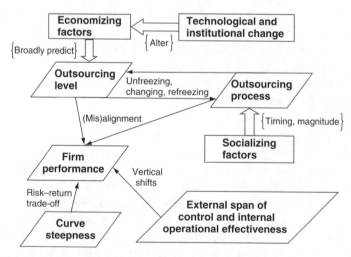

**Figure 8.1.** An integrated perspective of outsourcing: design, process, and performance

## Possible extensions

### International sourcing

One extension of the argument that the extent of outsourcing has a negative curvilinear effect on a firm's performance is to apply a similar logic to the location dimension of sourcing. In other words, perhaps firms equally need to strike a balance between domestic and international, or global, supplier locations.[2] Is there a natural limit to how much offshoring and international outsourcing firms can profitably undertake? The number of tests of the effect of international sourcing on firm performance is currently extremely limited (Mol, van Tulder, and Beije, 2005; Quintens, 2006).

It is widely suggested that international sourcing occurs in order to improve firms' performance, particularly their cost effectiveness (e.g. Trent and Monczka, 2003). Firms located in OECD countries often find that the costs of labor are excessive compared to the value that is added to their products. While faraway locations such as China lag in productivity, they make up for this lower productivity by providing much lower labor costs, sometimes even culminating in de-automation of tasks when they are transferred to these locations. Indeed, I have observed some cases, such as a range of bicycle components procured by Dutch producers, where the production cost differences are so large that it makes no sense even to consider domestic sourcing. This labor cost advantage is of course most significant when labor costs actually make up a substantial part of overall production costs. Otherwise, the production cost advantages may not be large enough.

At the other extreme we find some international sourcing that is motivated by knowledge or innovation concerns.[3] For some inputs, such as aircraft parts, technical expertise may be required that is only available in other countries and hence makes international sourcing not so much a choice as an imperative. The source countries in these instances would mostly be other OECD countries. Where raw

---

[2] This argument is developed fully in Kotabe and Mol (forthcoming).

[3] Quintens (2006) makes a similar distinction between cost-driven and innovation-driven international sourcing. He also discusses more incidental, capacity-driven international sourcing. The latter can arguably be reduced to one of the other two forms though.

materials are concerned, a choice may not even be available to source them domestically. Similarly, for certain intermediate products, it makes much sense to source them from locations near the raw materials source. Another argument in favor of international sourcing is that it may allow a firm to produce closer to consumer markets, thereby increasing access to these markets. Japanese manufacturing firms have, for instance, over time replicated supply chains in North America and Europe to operate closer to these markets (Kenney and Florida, 1995). Production and sourcing experience in these regions has also allowed them to improve their product offerings. Another reason to opt for international sourcing is that demand from various regions can be pooled and hence maximum scale and bargaining power is achieved through single sourcing from a foreign supplier.

On the other hand, there are also some disadvantages associated with international sourcing. Typically the first type of problem many managers and the popular press put forward is "cultural differences" between buyers and their foreign suppliers. Indeed, such differences may affect relationships negatively but institutional and language problems pose other potential sources of problems in these relations. One Dutch manufacturer, for instance, mentioned during an interview how its Spanish supplier never appeared to respond to its faxes, which were written in English. When, however, the company had one of its employees translate the fax into Spanish, an almost immediate response emerged. Cultural misunderstandings and other communication problems can lie at the heart of quality problems, although these can also be caused by differences in technical standards or even merely different expectation patterns of the actors involved. Another source of discontent over international sourcing is the long lead times and supply chain uncertainty it often produces. Levy (1995) takes up this issue in much more detail. Then there are international trade rules that help determine the feasibility of international sourcing (Swamidass and Kotabe, 1993). Finally there is the possibility that foreign suppliers integrate forward into the buyer's market, sometimes by inventing around patents or ignoring them altogether. Intellectual property may not be guaranteed in other countries. For instance, stories abound of intellectual property violations in China, like reverse engineering and copying of components or entire products by Chinese suppliers and competitors, although evolution in China's legal system may change that.

These advantages and disadvantages suggest that there may also be limits to how much, and how little, international sourcing a firm ought to apply if it wishes to reach optimal performance. As a firm engages in more international sourcing, the disadvantages become larger to the point where they severely impede performance. If firms do no international sourcing at all, they cannot access any of the advantages of international sourcing such as a wider supply base from which to choose suppliers. This line of reasoning is consistent with research in the international business and neo-institutional economics traditions (Williamson, 1985). When firms use foreign suppliers, production costs are potentially lowered. In some instances, of course, production costs of a local supplier are indeed lower than those of any foreign supplier but this is the exception and not the rule. Transaction costs, on the other hand, are invariably higher for international sourcing, as there are all kinds of institutional, cultural, and language barriers that must be overcome.

Rangan (2000) has discussed this in terms of the costs of "search and evaluation." Searching for supply sources abroad, whether internal or external sources, is more expensive than searching for local supply sources because it involves the need for additional information. Evaluating those foreign supply sources is much more expensive, as the costs of evaluation are strongly related to the familiarity that decision-makers have with the other party. Since foreign firms are likely to be less familiar and decision-makers cannot draw on their networks so much to help them evaluate these sources, substantial evaluation costs are induced. Rangan (2000) uses this argument to explain why buying firms are much more likely to choose a domestic supplier than a foreign supplier, even when the physical distance between the buyer and each of these suppliers is the same.

International sourcing is therefore a balancing act between production and transaction costs (see also Mol, van Tulder, and Beije, 2005) and a negative curvilinear relationship could be in place between the degree of international sourcing and firm performance. Firms need to find the proper balance between domestic and foreign supply sources if they wish to locate on the top of the curve and obtain the highest possible performance. They do this by using foreign sources for part, but not all of their sourcing. Sourcing everything from abroad produces poor performance results because the disadvantages of international sourcing, like the hollowing-out argument (Bettis, Bradley, and Hamel,

1992; Markides and Berg, 1988), become too large. Focusing all efforts on domestic supply sources, however, is a serious form of myopia with equally disastrous effects for firm performance, primarily because important opportunities to improve competitiveness are missed. Hence, as is the case for outsourcing, activities may vary in their suitability for international sourcing, such that a negative curvilinear relationship between the extent of international sourcing and firm performance is obtained. It would be interesting to see some empirical tests of this hypothesis.

It is worth noting that the optimal degree of international sourcing is likely to vary much more among firms than the optimal degree of outsourcing because the degree of international sourcing depends more heavily on firm-specific factors like firm size, whether a firm is a multinational, and how it is organized internally (see, for instance, Mol, Pauwels, Matthyssens, and Quintens, 2004; Mol, van Tulder, and Beije, 2005). The standard deviation of the degree of international sourcing is therefore bound to be much higher than that of outsourcing. Furthermore, the performance impact of the degree of international sourcing, the location dimension, is lower than that of outsourcing, the ownership dimension (Mol, 2001), an effect exacerbated by the existence of location bandwagons, implying firms choose suppliers from the same cluster or country.

## Privatization

Another possible extension, along similar lines to those suggested above for offshoring and international outsourcing, is to look at the performance consequences of the privatization of government activities. The rest of this book deals with private firms and therefore no clear evidence base has been presented for public activities. But in many ways the privatization decision is to a government what the outsourcing decision is to a private firm. It raises the question of where the boundaries of the organization ought to lie. Should the running of the railways be part of a government's mandate, as it is in many continental European and Asian countries? Or is privatization of railway operators, as has been tried in the United Kingdom from the 1990s and elsewhere before (Domberger, 1998), a better option? And privatization equally can affect the performance of the underlying activities, as debates around the present state of the UK railway system make all too clear.

There are, though, some obvious problems of context and measurement if one wants to test the hypothesis that the performance of government is a negative curvilinear function of the extent to which it has privatized activities. It is less clear what would be a suitable unit of analysis. A country's entire governmental system is possibly too complex and diverse to consider. A single agency or local government may not take enough privatization decisions to present a useful measurement unit. And looking at a single decision only, such as railway privatization, has the drawback that any performance finding is likely an effect of the activity's characteristics, as discussed at length in chapter 3. A further problem is the lack of an objective overall performance measure, or at least of an overall financial performance measure. How does one measure and compare the performance of a government unit? What is its competitor or benchmark? Hence the notion of a negative curvilinear relation between a governmental unit's level of privatization and its performance seems primarily useful as a metaphor or a thought exercise. But perhaps specialists in the study of government would disagree.

More generally, curvilinearity between a behavior and its (performance) outcomes may be expected in many management decisions involving trade-offs. Recent management research seems therefore to be more prone to looking at curvilinear relations, possibly aided by the existence of more powerful and more versatile statistics packages. For instance, why should one expect the benefits of investments in training and development of employees to be larger than the costs indefinitely? And why should increases in R&D spending continue to lead to a higher performance? All such types of investment suffer from diminishing returns and at some points the costs start to outweigh the benefits. Perhaps linearity is the exception and not the rule.

## Outsourcing and management innovation

Management innovation is an area of increasing practitioner and academic interest (Birkinshaw and Mol, 2006; Hamel, 2006). Management innovation may be formally defined as "the invention and implementation of a new management practice, process or structure that represents a significant and novel departure from generally accepted or standard management practices, and is intended to further organizational goals" (Birkinshaw, Hamel, and Mol, 2005). Outsourcing can be seen as one important historical management innovation. Indeed, authors have taken this perspective on outsourcing, specifically on the landmark Kodak & IBM/Digital IT outsourcing deal of 1989 (Loh and Venkatraman, 1992).

Since "new" in the above definition of management innovation refers to new to the state of the art, it is reasonable to assume that firms other than Kodak have engaged in management innovation while taking and implementing outsourcing decisions. In the realm of business process outsourcing, the notion of coordination without co-location (Puranam and Srikanth, 2006) is a possible management innovation. It refers to firms that outsource some of their business processes to suppliers that are both external and remotely located (for instance in India). To effectively do that, these firms need to develop an entirely new set of operating routines (Puranam and Srikanth, 2006). The notion of "outsourcing as a management innovation" raises various questions. How prominent is outsourcing among other management innovations, historically or today? Under what conditions does outsourcing become a management innovation? What, if any, is the performance bonus attached to firms that turn outsourcing into a management innovation? And how can outsourcing be turned into a management innovation? The exploration of the link between outsourcing and management innovation thus provides another important research angle. Investigating that angle first requires a better understanding of the management innovation phenomenon, what causes management innovation, how it takes place, and what performance effects it has. Thus the emerging management innovation agenda may need some further development prior to a deeper understanding of outsourcing as a management innovation.

## Methodological, methodical, and empirical challenges

Following these theoretical puzzles and earlier discussion in this book, it is also possible to develop a set of methodological, methodical, and empirical guidelines for future outsourcing research.

### Replication

Obviously it would be highly desirable to see additional empirical replications of the main model discussed here. Can a negative curvilinear relationship between outsourcing and performance also be uncovered among services firms? Does this relationship hold in other countries, including countries where major institutional voids (Khanna and Palepu, 2000) are present? By replicating this finding in different industries, like services, or different countries, like India, more light can be shed on the universality of this core relationship.

Such replications ought ideally to control more for the antecedent variables of outsourcing, to establish whether a direct outsourcing–performance relationship still holds, even after these other factors have been controlled. This effectively implies a replication with some extensions. Replication could be based on large samples of firms but it might also take the form of a long-term experiment inside a single firm. By varying that firm's outsourcing levels and observing the consequences of that variation, academics can learn more about the effects of outsourcing on performance. It may be difficult, however, to find a firm that would willingly engage in such an experiment.

## Time

Time is a notion that deserves more attention in outsourcing research than it has hitherto been given. In this book, time emerged in several ways. First, it was observed that the costs and benefits of outsourcing may accrue at different points in time. Outsourcing can sometimes be seen as a short-term fix, producing short- to medium-term cost advantages. Its long-term effects can be less beneficial, particularly for activities in which learning and innovation are crucial (Hendry, 1995), though such problems can sometimes be overcome by cooperation with key suppliers. In general, one might hypothesize, a temporal trade-off exists between the short-term benefits of outsourcing and its longer-term costs. This hypothesis has not been put to the test though. Even in the empirical studies to which I referred in order to build the negative curvilinear model, no direct tests took place of the decreasing benefits and increasing costs of outsourcing. None of the studies in the transaction costs literature tests this either. What we did observe (Kotabe and Mol, 2005), however, was that the link between outsourcing and performance, in our sample, was strongest when a three-year lag between behavior, outsourcing, and its consequences, in the form of performance, was applied. That suggests that not all of the effects of outsourcing are immediate.

In a recent study (Kotabe, Mol, and Ketkar, 2006) we have begun to address such long-run effects of outsourcing by building a stage model. It explains how firms start by offshoring production activities to low-cost destinations, next outsource these activities to local suppliers, but then find this gradually erodes their own competences. As a consequence, they find themselves forced to reintegrate the activities. We refer to this as a "vicious outsourcing cycle." This vicious outsourcing cycle will not always occur, of course, but where it does, it demonstrates that time matters in outsourcing. Additional studies that incorporate time-lags are therefore needed and such studies might also want to address more directly whether the temporal trade-off of costs and benefits indeed takes place, for instance by following a single outsourcing process for some time. Most published studies, especially those relying on the survey methodology, have not been particularly successful in introducing such time-lags.

A second way in which time plays a role in outsourcing is through changes in the optimal degree of outsourcing over time, as discussed at length in chapter 6. Behavior that was seen as clearly unwise, or even unthinkable, in the past has now become part and parcel of how firms operate. The case example around technical contractors (Box 6.2) showed that entirely new supply markets may emerge in areas that firms previously thought of as important to their competitive advantage and which they felt a need to integrate. Since we find ourselves in a wave towards more outsourcing at present, most of the changes that occur in the optimal degree of outsourcing ought to point towards more outsourcing. But that is a supposition, not an evidence-based statement. Hence it would be of interest to see how the optimal degree of outsourcing changes over time. A research design drawing on data covering more than a decade might shed some light on this question.

In chapter 7, I discussed the claim that outsourcing is becoming more strategic. One of the conclusions of that discussion was that we have almost no empirical evidence to assess that claim. It too involves supposed changes over time. For outsourcing to become more strategic means it must start playing a larger role in firms' efforts to obtain sustainable competitive advantage. So far, we appear not to have seen materialize earlier claims that outsourcing is becoming more strategic. For instance, IT outsourcing, if anything, now appears more driven by cost considerations than it did ten years ago, in spite of claims around strategic IT outsourcing. An empirical design that could shed some more light on this matter would be a longitudinal case study, or series thereof, that tracks a firm's outsourcing efforts in various areas. Such a case study would look at all of the firm's outsourcing relationships as a portfolio and then, for each of the elements of that portfolio, assess to what extent it contributes to competitive advantage. By measuring this several times, perhaps yearly over a ten-year time-period, a picture ought to emerge of how strategic outsourcing can be and whether that changes over time. The problem at the moment appears to be that as the type of outsourcing that receives most attention – manufacturing, IT, or business processes – changes so do the tastes of academics and other writers. That relieves claimants that a particular type of outsourcing is strategic of responsibility for the truth of their claims because attention has shifted to the next type of outsourcing. One might perhaps argue that outsourcing is faddish (Kunda and Ailon-Souday, 2005) but that is surely also a proper description for the behavior of those studying it.

## Performance

The measurement of performance, or effectiveness, is a constant concern in management research (Venkatraman and Ramanujam, 1986). As noted in chapter 3, measurement of how outsourcing influences performance poses an additional dilemma, because outsourcing is inherently related to some performance measures, like "return on sales." There are two strategies for dealing with this problem. One strategy is to find a single measure that is more balanced, such as the "return on value added" measure employed in our study (Kotabe and Mol, 2005). The other strategy is to use a basket of measures. This could allow for a balancing of negative and positive effects. The problem with the latter approach, of course, is that a basket of measures is simply not available in most cases, desirable as it is.

## Data sources

A majority of studies on outsourcing in the management area are based on survey methods. Economists, on the other hand, tend mostly to use secondary data. Another key research method, but one not much explored in outsourcing research, is the use of qualitative data, for instance through case studies or ethnography. The findings presented in this book draw on all three of these methods. To some extent this is caused by convenience arguments, such as availability of data, and the rules of scholarly publishing. But it also prompts two other important observations.

First, different questions require different means for answering them. Qualitative work plays an important role in the construction of new theory. The whole notion of bandwagoning in outsourcing is fueled by anecdotal observations of how Kodak's decision impacted other firms (Loh and Venkatraman, 1992) or, in the case of some of the band-wagon research described here, on how firms take up outsourcing advice from consultants and suppliers. Qualitative research can also point to unexplored areas of study. Some of the interview quotes presented in this book, for instance, generate new research questions. One of the things these interviews showed is that few firms seem to have formal procedures in place for make-or-buy decisions. This raises the question of why this is the case. Do formal procedures perhaps not lead to better decisions? Are there no clear leads from which decision-makers can draw to construct formal procedures? Or is outsourcing simply not important enough to invest much time in? These questions may even-tually lend themselves to quantitative testing.

Second, there is complementarity in the use of different data sources as it allows for triangulation among these sources. While conversations with managers broadly pointed to the existence of an optimal level of outsourcing, through examples of good and bad outsourcing decisions, the use of archival data can help to establish statistical significance and generalizability. Alternatively, archival or survey data may generate patterns that are not easily explained by existing theory. Under those circumstances it makes sense to try and understand the causation in these patterns through further qualitative work. The field of outsour-cing, like that of strategy and organization theory as a whole (Heugens and Mol, 2005), would benefit from a rebalancing between quantita-tive and qualitative research methods.

To summarize this discussion, the following "good practice" criteria for outsourcing research are recommended:
- replication of research findings across different contexts
- a weighing of the costs and benefits of outsourcing in the short and long term
- an investigation of whether the antecedents and consequences of outsourcing hold over time – a longitudinal perspective

- the use of a variety of performance measures
- a proper balance of quantitative and qualitative research where both types of research inform each other.

## Conclusion

In this chapter, the future outsourcing research agenda has been addressed, especially how it is informed by the ideas and findings discussed in this book. The chapter started by looking at some of the unresolved theoretical challenges, especially what a multidisciplinary understanding of outsourcing and performance could look like. It then proposed some possible extensions, either using the negative curvilinear perspective or looking at the outsourcing phenomenon from a very different angle. Finally, some of the methodological, methodical, and empirical challenges in outsourcing research were discussed.

# 9 | *Future trends and conclusions*

O NE of the observations with which this book started was that outsourcing is by no means a new phenomenon. Rather, it was argued that outsourcing is almost "as old as the hills." Several older examples of outsourcing were also discussed. Outsourcing is an inherent feature of the way we organize ourselves. The question whether we will continue to see outsourcing is, therefore, a nonsensical one. There has been, is, and will continue to be outsourcing as long as firms and markets are around, regardless of whether markets are islands in a sea of firms (Simon, 1991) or firms are the anomaly to be explained (Coase, 1937; Williamson, 1975). Outsourcing, in many ways, is an artifact of the economy at large, and certainly of any economy that progresses beyond the hunter-gatherer stage.

But this does not imply there is anything like an actual or optimal outsourcing level that is stable across time or space. Nor does it mean that managerial mindsets on outsourcing are an *idée fixe* or that it is inevitable that we should see more outsourcing processes than insourcing processes in the future. If anything, we ought to believe that we do not know and cannot predict what will happen to each of these variables. Yet it is possible to outline some of the causes of trend shifts and therefore to come up with a few "what if" scenarios.

In the short to medium term, say the next ten to fifteen years, key indicators point to further increases in outsourcing levels. Information technology, which has already been one of the key drivers of the outsourcing trend as discussed in chapter 6, looks likely to continue to have a positive effect on outsourcing levels. IT transforms the ease with which firms deal with outside suppliers. IT itself continues to develop at a rapid pace, by increases in hardware and software capability and the wired and wireless capacities of electronic networks. Better IT ought to make even more outsourcing feasible. And it can be argued that in many country and industry settings, especially in emerging and developing countries, IT has not yet been deployed or used to the fullest extent possible. There is therefore potential for further increases in outsourcing.

When it comes to the institutional drivers of outsourcing, the bag is perhaps a little more mixed yet still broadly favorable towards outsourcing, as argued in chapter 6. Key Asian economies, notably China and India, continue to be opened up for international trade and investment opportunities. As a consequence, many Western firms grab those opportunities and increasingly outsource to those destinations. The same holds true for other emerging countries around the world, like Pakistan, South Africa, and Chile. European Union countries are still engaged, though perhaps in a haphazard fashion, in the restructuring of their economies that partly involves such things as privatization and the rearrangement of contract law. At the same time there are voices that are becoming increasingly critical of outsourcing, a word that has now taken on more than a neutral tone and a subject that has become an ideological battleground as witnessed by discussions in politics. And the international political and security situation is unpredictable. Perhaps terrorism will at long last have undesirable effects on international trade flows. Or maybe the United States, China, or both will seek to use large-scale economic isolationism as the means to wage some new Cold War. These scenarios are not looming large at present, yet it would be foolish to discount them as completely unrealistic. Geopolitical affairs have historically been difficult to predict and there is no reason to believe that is about to change.[1]

Outsourcing is further determined by managerial mindsets that, as discussed in chapter 4 especially, also strongly support outsourcing. That is another effect that is likely to carry over into high outsourcing levels in the short to medium term. Unlike fifteen to twenty years ago, most managers have now come to the conclusion that outsourcing is not a panacea for all problems. Yet in business circles, and among many academics, outsourcing is still seen as not only an inevitable but also a beneficial solution towards the improvement of firm performance. Business schools teach about outsourcing, often focusing on how to outsource, while assuming that outsourcing itself holds many

---

[1] The Fukuyama (1992) thesis, which argued that we had come to the "end of history," and the domination of a single political system over all the others, after the Cold War ended, is now greeted with broad skepticism, or mostly ignored altogether.

desirable properties. Newspapers and other media write about out-sourcing, sometimes doubting its socially disruptive effects but seldom putting into doubt how it helps firms to improve their performance. Consultants have talked about outsourcing extensively, often hopping from one wave of outsourcing to the next. Quite a few specialized consulting firms have emerged that consider advising on outsourcing decisions to be their core competence.[2] This managerial mindset is likely to further increase actual outsourcing levels, and, through externalities, perhaps also optimal outsourcing levels.

In the longer term it is much less clear whether the managerial mindset continues to favor outsourcing. As discussed in chapter 1, over time there have been alternations in the way outsourcing has been seen, with the middle of the previous century being a time when vertical integration, not outsourcing, was judged to be the firm's route towards competitive success. Kunda and Ailon-Souday (2005) argue that outsourcing is only the latest rhetoric or discourse in a long line. They see outsourcing, in an extension of the work of Barley and Kunda (1992) and Abrahamson (1997), as being part of a rational wave of thinking. Historically, rational waves have been followed, according to the swing of the pendulum, by normative waves during which some of what happened during the rational waves became undone (Abrahamson, 1997; Barley and Kunda, 1992). One cannot assume, in other words, that managerial mindsets will support outsourcing indefinitely, but any change in these mindsets is likely to be a relatively long-term process.

An overall increase in outsourcing levels carries implications for outsourcing and insourcing processes. First, it implies that outsourcing processes will continue to be more frequent and more substantial than insourcing processes. In a large majority of organizations, more activities will be placed outside organizational boundaries than will be taken (back) inside. And by reason of the togetherness of outsourcing and inward internationalization (international sourcing) this also implies most organizations will continue to shift activities to foreign suppliers, many of them in countries with lower production costs. Second, this implies that knowledge and ability around outsourcing processes will continue to come at a premium relative to knowledge and ability around insourcing processes. Individuals who are skilled at

---

[2] Note that there is considerable irony, and a range of question marks, around the fact that some firms choose to outsource their outsourcing decisions.

outsourcing processes, organizations which master these processes, and their advisors like consultants or academics, can benefit from that ability. And since they stand to benefit they will try to find ways to promote outsourcing further. Before the outsourcing tide really turns then, we may expect to see some "irrational exuberance" (Abrahamson and Rosenkopf, 1997).

Also of continuing interest in the short to medium term will be the development of buyer–supplier relations. Will we actually see more of the acclaimed cooperative relations that add value and help firms improve their competitiveness? Or are these relations the exception rather than the rule and are attempts to create them futile? If they are not futile, then how should firms go about creating them? This is an area where academic research has come up with some answers but by no means enough to be conclusive or, indeed, be able to provide practicing managers with much in the way of useful advice. At present there is a broad trend towards more cooperative relations, which is supported by several environmental factors. There is no immediate reason to believe this trend will end soon.

## Conclusions

In this book an attempt has been made to propose a new perspective on outsourcing and performance. This perspective studies all of the activities a firm needs to perform to satisfy its suppliers, though it recognizes these activities differ greatly in important respects. The perspective looks both at outsourcing designs or levels and at outsourcing processes. It also incorporates, and to some extent integrates, insights from a variety of disciplinary perspectives, including economics, sociology, psychology, and history while using management as the overriding discipline. It contains both static and dynamic components. The perspective acknowledges the influence of technological and institutional change drivers on outsourcing. And it helps to interpret important changes in recent times in how outsourcing takes place, notably the design of buyer–supplier relations. Finally, it potentially holds implications for organizations in many industry and national contexts.

The following may serve as a final attempt at summarizing the perspective presented in this book. Firms serve their customers through a bundle of activities, some of which are performed internally while others are outsourced to suppliers. Each of these activities can be characterized on the dimension outsourceability, defined as the amenability of that activity to outsourcing from a performance perspective. Outsourceability is determined by many factors, which are broadly found at the transaction, firm, industry, and country levels. Given the variance in outsourceability, some activities are better outsourced while others ought to be integrated (from a performance perspective). Optimal performance is reached when all activities are correctly outsourced or integrated. Deviations from the optimum are costly, and in such a way that the further from the optimum, the more costly these deviations become. The pattern this produces is a negative curvilinear relationship between outsourcing and performance, with the top of the curve presenting the performance optimum. In reality, firms do not normally locate at the top of their curves and are misaligned. The timing and magnitude of their outsourcing and insourcing processes are co-determined by various heuristics other than outsourceability, notably the presence of outsourcing bandwagons. These factors produce the misalignment and resulting suboptimal performance that is characteristic of the real world. Firms can raise their performance curve, relative to that of their competitors, not only through realignment but also through a superior operational performance or by being better outsourcers, captured through their external span of control. External span of control refers to the ability of a firm to manage multiple and varying relationships with outside suppliers and is influenced by learning, competences, and relations and networks. The optimal point is not static over time. Rather, it changes as a consequence of shifts in environmental factors, the two most important being technological change and institutional change. These factors have been the drivers of the higher outsourcing levels we have witnessed over the past twenty years. Changes may also be observed in the steepness of the curve, with a steeper curve making misalignment more costly. Steeper curves come about when the distribution of activities along the outsourceability dimension changes, as specialist means-of-production assets replace generalist means. The key guidance provided to managers in recent years has been that firms should outsource non-core activities and that outsourcing is becoming more strategic. Both notions were proven to be false simplifications. Instead the notion of experimenting with outsourcing was put forward as a managerial guideline. Finally, the perspective presented here produces a range of interesting future research issues.

There are few, if any, invariant laws in the study of organizations. Instead hypotheses and empirical observations in this area are better seen in light of the context of measurement, such as the country in which they are generated or observed (Cheng, 1994; Rosenzweig, 1994). With that in mind, I have chosen to present a perspective on outsourcing designs and processes and the resulting performance that is deliberately dependent on such contextual variables as time, geographical and network location, and competitive context. Outsourcing is a complex phenomenon that ought to stretch academics beyond a singular perspective, which is what I have attempted to do here. It is ultimately up to the reader, of course, to assess the extent to which this has been a successful attempt. But I hope it can be agreed that outsourcing is a topic that ought to remain of considerable interest to the worlds of practice and theory alike. To start where we began, if torture can be outsourced, then surely outsourcing deserves to be tortured – in the analytical sense that is.

# *Appendix*

## Research methods

This book is based on various research methods and data sources that were obtained over the last twelve or so years. These are listed below. Most of these research methods are described in more detail in other publications and I therefore refrain from doing so here. The book also contains a number of short case studies drawn from publicly available materials, with appropriate citations provided in the text.

1. A series of thirty-four interviews across nine different industries in the Greater Rotterdam area in 1995 and 1996. These nine industries included four on the buyer side (petrochemicals, shipbuilding & ship repair, transshipment, and distribution & storage) and five on the supplier side (computer services, consulting, engineering services, leasing, and temporary labor agencies). The interviews were supported by secondary data, including company reports and publicly available sources. This study focused on three questions: Why is it that we see so much more outsourcing? What are current trends in outsourcing? What are the effects of outsourcing (partly in terms of regional employment levels)? This research was reported in de Wit, Mol, and van Drunen (1998) and de Wit and Mol (1999).

2. An input–output analysis of various sectors of the Dutch economy, which showed the level of interconnection among sectors between 1977 and 1992. This research was reported in de Wit, Mol, and van Drunen (1998). By showing a growing interconnection between sectors, we found support for increased outsourcing across these sectors.

3. A series of eleven interviews with large multinational firms with headquarters or regional headquarters in the Netherlands in 1997 and 1998. The interviews were accompanied by secondary

data, including company reports and publicly available sources. This study focused on describing the international sourcing strategies of large multinational firms. This research was reported in Tecson (1998) and Mol (2001).

4. A series of three interviews and a panel discussion with Philips, Stork, and the supplier association NEVAT in Germany and the Netherlands in 2000. The interviews were supported by other primary and secondary data. The aim of this study was to discover how the introduction of an electronic auction for medical cabinets had impacted both the buyer and the former supplier. This research was reported in a case study by van Tulder and Mol (2002).

5. A series of five interviews with Novartis, DSM, and Dow in Switzerland and the Netherlands in 1999. The interviews were supported by other secondary data. The focus of this study was on how firms used electronic means, like auctions and catalogs, to support their sourcing strategies. This research was reported in Mol (2001).

6. A case study on the production and sourcing network of Ford's Mondeo model based on publicly available data in 2000. This case study attempted to document the network and explained what strategic choices Ford had made. This research was reported briefly in Mol and Koppius (2002) and fully in Mol (2002).

7. A large database with secondary data gathered by Statistics Netherlands (Centraal Bureau voor de Statistiek) between 1993 and 1998. The industry-level variant of this database was reported in Mol (2005). The firm-level variant was reported in Mol (2001), Kotabe and Mol (2005), and Mol and Kotabe (2005). Because both the outsourcing variable (external purchasing divided by total sales) and the performance variable (return on value added, measured as net profits divided by sales minus external purchasing) are more-or-less normally distributed, ordinary least squares (OLS) regression provides for the best statistical technique. In our analyses we control for other factors, like firm size, industry, export intensity, and uncertainty.

8. A survey with a response of 204 manufacturing firms in the Netherlands in 2000 and 2001. The survey covered three areas of

sourcing strategy and related these to firm performance: outsourcing; international sourcing; buyer–supplier relations. This research was reported extensively in Mol (2001) and also in Mol, Pauwels, Matthyssens, and Quintens (2004) and Mol, van Tulder, and Beije (2005).

9. A series of twenty-three interviews with manufacturing firms in the Netherlands in 2003. These firms competed in four different industries: (1) pumps and compressors; (2) instruments and appliances; (3) bicycles; (4) electric motors, generators, and transformers. This research has not been completely reported in detail before (some of it is reported in Mol and Kotabe, 2006). We selected four industries which had gone through large swings towards outsourcing in the 1990s. We approached firms in these industries through Chamber of Commerce registers. Interviews were tape-recorded, transcribed in full, and executed by two interviewers. The interviews focused on changes in these firms' outsourcing levels, what had triggered such changes, and how they affected (performance) outcomes. Interview outcomes were shared with respondents for approval.

# References

Abrahamson, E. (1996). Management fashion. *Academy of Management Review* 21: 254–285.

(1997). The emergence and prevalence of employee management rhetorics: the effects of long waves, labor unions, and turnover, 1875 to 1992. *Academy of Management Journal* 40(3): 491–533.

(2000). Change WITHOUT pain. *Harvard Business Review* 78(4): 75–79.

(2004). *Change Without Pain*. Boston: Harvard Business School Press.

Abrahamson, E., and G. Fairchild (1999). Management fashion: lifecycles, trigger, and collective learning processes. *Administrative Science Quarterly* 44: 708–740.

Abrahamson, E., and L. Rosenkopf (1993). Institutional and competitive bandwagons: using mathematical modeling as a tool to explore innovation diffusion. *Academy of Management Review* 18(3): 487–517.

(1997). Social network effects on the extent of innovation diffusion: a computer simulation. *Organization Science* 8(3): 289–309.

Afuah, A. (2001). Dynamic boundaries of the firm: are firms better off being vertically integrated in the face of a technological change? *Academy of Management Journal* 44(6): 1211–1228.

Alchian, A. A., and H. Demsetz (1972). Production, information costs, and economic organization. *American Economic Review* 62: 777–795.

Amit, R., and P. J. H. Schoemaker (1993). Strategic assets and organizational rent. *Strategic Management Journal* 14(1): 33–46.

Aoki, M., B. Gustafsson, and O. E. Williamson (1990). *The Firm as a Nexus of Treaties*. London: Sage.

Araujo, L., and S. Spring (forthcoming). Services, products, and the institutional structure of production. *Industrial Marketing Management*.

Arrow, K. J. (1974). *The Limits of Organization*. New York: John Brockman Associates.

Balakrishnan, S., and B. Wernerfelt (1986). Technical change, competition and vertical integration. *Strategic Management Journal* 7(4): 347–359.

Barley, S. R., and G. Kunda (1992). Design and devotion: surges of rational and normative ideologies of control in managerial discourse. *Administrative Science Quarterly* 37: 363–399.

(2004). *Gurus, Hired Guns, and Warm Bodies: Itinerant Experts in a Knowledge Economy*. Princeton: Princeton University Press.

Barney, J. (1991). Firm resources and sustained competitive advantage. *Journal of Management* 17(1): 99–120.

Barney, J. B. (1999). How a firm's capabilities affect boundary decisions. *Sloan Management Review* 40(3): 137–145.

Barney, J. B., and W. S. Hesterly (2006). *Strategic Management and Competitive Advantage: Concepts and Cases*. Upper Saddle River, N.J.: Pearson/Prentice Hall.

Barringer, B. R., and J. S. Harrison (2000). Walking a tightrope: creating value through interorganizational relationships. *Journal of Management* 26(3): 367–403.

Barthelemy, J., and D. Geyer (2001). IT outsourcing: evidence from France and Germany. *European Management Journal* 19(2): 195–202.

Barzel, Y. (1982). Measurement cost and the organization of markets. *Journal of Law and Economics* 25: 27–48.

Baum, J. A. C., and F. Dobbin (2000). *Economics Meets Sociology in Strategic Management*. Stamford, Conn.: JAI Press.

Baum, J. A. C., and C. Oliver (1991). Institutional linkages and organizational mortality. *Administrative Science Quarterly* 36: 187–218.

Baumol, W. J. (2002). *The Free-Market Innovation Machine: Analyzing the Growth Miracle of Capitalism*. Princeton: Princeton University Press.

Bensaou, M. (1999). Portfolios of buyer–supplier relationships. *Sloan Management Review* 40: 35–44.

Bettis, R., S. Bradley, and G. Hamel (1992). Outsourcing and industrial decline. *Academy of Management Executive* 6(1): 7–16.

Birkinshaw, J. (1997). Entrepreneurship in multinational corporations: the characteristics of subsidiary initiatives. *Strategic Management Journal* 18: 207–229.

Birkinshaw, J., G. Hamel, and M. J. Mol (2005). Management innovation. Working Paper, AIM, London.

Birkinshaw, J., and M. J. Mol (2006) How management innovation happens. *Sloan Management Review* 47(4): 81–88.

Bonazzi, G., and C. Antonelli (2003). To make or to sell? The case of in-house outsourcing at Fiat Auto. *Organization Studies* 24(4): 575–594.

Brown, D., and S. Wilson (2005). *The Black Book of Outsourcing: How to Manage the Changes, Challenges, and Opportunities*. Hoboken, N. J.: John Wiley and Sons.

Brück, F. (1995). Make versus buy: the wrong decision cost. *McKinsey Quarterly*, no. 1: 28–47.

Brusoni, S., A. Prencipe, and K. Pavitt (2001). Knowledge specialization, organizational coupling, and the boundaries of the firm: why do firms know more than they make? *Administrative Science Quarterly* 46(4): 597–621.

Buckley, P. J., and M. Casson (1976). *The Future of the Multinational Enterprise*. London: Macmillan.

Budros, A. (1999). A conceptual framework for analyzing why organizations downsize. *Organization Science* 10(1): 69–82.

Burt, R. S. (1992). *Structural Holes: The Social Structure of Competition*. Cambridge, Mass.: Harvard University Press.

Butler, M. J. R. (2003). Managing from the inside out: drawing on "receptivity" to explain variation in strategy implementation. *British Journal of Management* 14: S47–S60.

Cachon, G. P., and P. T. Harker (2002). Competition and outsourcing with scale economies. *Management Science* 48(10): 1314–1333.

Cairncross, F. (1998). *The Death of Distance*. Boston: Harvard Business School Press.

Capon, N., J. U. Farley, and S. Hoenig (1990). Determinants of financial performance: a meta-analysis. *Management Science* 36(10): 1143–1160.

Casadeus-Masanell, R., and D. F. Spulber (2000). The fable of Fisher Body. *Journal of Law and Economics* 43(1): 67–104.

Chandler, A. D. (1962). *Strategy and Structure: Chapters in the History of American Enterprise*. Cambridge, Mass.: MIT Press.

(1977). *The Visible Hand: The Managerial Revolution in American Business*. Cambridge, Mass.: Belknap Press.

Cheng, J. L. (1994). On the concept of universal knowledge in organizational science: implications for cross-national research. *Management Science* 40(1): 162–168.

Cheon, M. J., V. Grover, and J. T. C. Teng (1995). Theoretical perspectives on the outsourcing of information systems. *Journal of Information Technology* 10: 209–219.

Chesbrough, H. W., and D. J. Teece (1996). When is virtual virtuous? Organizing for innovation. *Harvard Business Review* 74(1): 65–72.

Christensen, C. M. (1997). *The Innovator's Dilemma: When New Technologies Cause Great Firms to Fail*. Boston: Harvard Business School Press.

Clegg, S., C. Hardy, and W. R. Nord (1996). *Handbook of Organization Studies*. Thousand Oaks, Calif.: Sage Publications.

Clemons, E., S. P. Reddi, and M. Row (1993). The impact of information technology on the organisation of economic activities: the "move to the middle" hypothesis. *Journal of Management Information Systems* 10(2): 9–33.

Coase, R. (1937). The nature of the firm. *Economica, new series*. 4: 386–405.

Coase, R. H. (2000). The acquisitions of Fisher Body by General Motors. *Journal of Law and Economics* 43(1): 15–31.

Cohen, M. D., J. G. March, and J. P. Olsen (1972). A garbage can model of organizational choice. *Administrative Science Quarterly* 17(1): 1–25.

Conner, K. R. (1991). A historical comparison of resource-based theory and five schools of thought within industrial organization economics: do we have a new theory of the firm? *Journal of Management* 17(1): 121–154.

Coutu, D. L. (2002). The anxiety of learning. *Harvard Business Review* 80: 100–106.

Cronk, J., and J. Sharp (1995). A framework for deciding what to outsource in information technology. *Journal of Information Technology* 10: 259–267.

Cross, J. (1995). IT outsourcing: British Petroleum's competitive approach. *Harvard Business Review* 73(3): 94–102.

Cusumano, M. A. (1985). *The Japanese Automobile Industry: Technology and Management at Nissan and Toyota*. Cambridge, Mass.: Council on East Asian Studies, Harvard University. (Distributed by the Harvard University Press.)

Cyert, R. M., and J. G. March (1963). *A Behavioral Theory of the Firm*. Englewood Cliffs, N.J.: Prentice Hall.

D'Aveni, R. A., and D. J. Ravenscraft (1994). Economies of integration versus bureaucracy costs: does vertical integration improve performance? *Academy of Management Journal* 37(5): 1167–1206.

David, P. A. (1985). Clio and the economics of QWERTY. *American Economic Review* 75(2): 332–337.

David, R. J., and S.-K. Han (2004). A systematic assessment of the empirical support for transaction cost economics. *Strategic Management Journal* 25: 39–58.

De Looff, L. A. (1995). Information systems outsourcing decision making: a framework, organizational theories and case studies. *Journal of Information Technology* 10: 281–297.

De Wit, B., and M. J. Mol (1999). Uitbesteden, topprioriteit en valkuil. *Holland Management Review* 16 (August): 46–57.

De Wit, B., M. J. Mol, and E. C. Van Drunen (1998). *Uitbesteden en Toeleveren: Motieven, Trends en Effecten*. Utrecht: Lemma.

Delios, A., and W. J. Henisz (2003). Political hazards, experience, and sequential entry strategies: the international expansion of Japanese firms, 1980–1998. *Strategic Management Journal* 24(11): 1153–1164.

DiMaggio, P. J., and W. W. Powell (1983). The iron cage revisited: institutional isomorphism and collective rationality in organizational fields. *American Sociological Review* 48: 147–160.

Doig, S. J., R. C. Ritter, K. Speckhals, and D. Woolson (2001). Has outsourcing gone too far? *McKinsey Quarterly*, no. 4: 26–37.

Domberger, S. (1998). *The Contracting Organization: A Strategic Guide to Outsourcing*. Oxford: Oxford University Press.

Donaldson, L. (2001). *The Contingency Theory of Organizations*. Thousand Oaks, Calif.: Sage Publications.

Doz, Y., and G. Hamel (1998). *Alliance Advantage: The Art of Creating Value through Partnering*. Boston: Harvard Business School Press.

Doz, Y., J. Santos, and P. Williamson (2000). *From Global to Metanational: How Companies Win in the Knowledge Economy*. Boston: Harvard Business School Press.

Dragonetti, N. C., F. Dalsace, and K. Cool (2003). A comparative test of the efficiency, focus and learning perspectives of outsourcing. Cahier de Recherche du Groupe HEC, no. 776/2003, Paris.

Dyer, J. H. (1996). How Chrysler created an American Keiretsu. *Harvard Business Review* 74(4): 42–56.

Dyer, J. H., D. S. Cho, and W. Chu (1998). Strategic supplier segmentation: the next best practice in supply chain management. *California Management Review* 40(2): 57–77.

Dyer, J. H., and K. Nobeoka (2000). Creating and managing a high-performance knowledge-sharing network: the Toyota case. *Strategic Management Journal* 21(3): 345–368.

Dyer, J. H., and H. Singh (1998). The relational view: cooperative strategy and sources of interorganizational competitive advantage. *Academy of Management Review* 23(4): 660–679.

*Economist* (2005). Parked. April 9.

Ettlie, J. E. (1988). *Taking Charge of Manufacturing: How Companies are Combining Technological and Organizational Innovations to Compete Successfully*. San Francisco: Jossey-Bass.

Fayol, H. (1949). *General and Industrial Management*. London: Pitman.

Feeny, D., M. Lacity, and L. P. Willcocks (2005). Taking the measure of outsourcing providers. *MIT Sloan Management Review* 46(3): 41–48.

*Financial Times* (2005a). A web that requires constant attention. August 25, p. 14.

(2005b). Outsourcing does work but must be done correctly, say experts. August 24, p. 3.

(2005c). Life beyond outsourcing: customer service comes home. December 12, p. 14.

(2005d). Staff dispute over, says Gate Gourmet. December 17/18, p. 3.

Foss, N. J. (1999). Research in the strategic theory of the firm: "isolationism" and "integrationism." *Journal of Management Studies* 36(6): 725–755.

Freeland, R. F. (2000). Creating holdup through vertical integration: Fisher Body revisited. *Journal of Law and Economics* 43(1): 33–66.

Friedberg, A. H., and W. A. Yarberry (1991). Audit rights in an outsource environment. *The Internal Auditor* 48(4): 53–59.

Fukuyama, F. (1992). *The End of History and the Last Man*. New York: Free Press.

Geyskens, I., J.-B. E. M. Steenkamp, and N. Kumar (forthcoming). Make, buy, or ally: a meta-analysis of transaction cost theory. *Academy of Management Journal*.

Ghoshal, S. (2005) Bad management theories are destroying good management practices. *Academy of Management Learning and Education* 4: 75–91.

Ghoshal, S., and P. Moran (1996). Bad for practice: a critique of the transaction cost theory. *Academy of Management Review* 21(1): 13–47.

Gilley, K. M., and A. Rasheed (2000). Making more by doing less: an analysis of outsourcing and its effect on firm performance. *Journal of Management* 26(4): 763–790.

Gottfredson, M., R. Puryear, and S. Phillips (2005). Strategic sourcing from periphery to the core. *Harvard Business Review* 83(2): 132–139.

Granovetter, M. (1985). Economic action and social structure: the problem of embeddedness. *American Journal of Sociology* 91(3): 481–510.

Grossman, G. M., and E. Helpman (2002). Integration versus outsourcing in industry equilibrium. *Quarterly Journal of Economics* 117(1): 85–120.

Grossman, S. J., and O. D. Hart (1986). The costs and benefits of ownership: a theory of vertical and lateral integration. *Journal of Political Economy* 94(4): 691–719.

Gulati, R. (1995). Does familiarity breed trust? The implications of repeated ties for contractual choice in alliances. *Academy of Management Journal* 38(1): 85–112.

Guler, I., M. F. Guillén, and J. M. Macpherson (2002). Global competition, institutions, and the diffusion of organizational practices: the international spread of ISO 9000 quality certificates. *Administrative Science Quarterly* 47(2): 207–232.

Hagedoorn, J. (1993). Understanding the rationale of strategic technology partnering: interorganizational modes of cooperation and sectoral differences. *Strategic Management Journal* 14(5): 371–385.

Hamel, G. (1998). Strategy innovation and the quest for value. *Sloan Management Review* 39: 7–14.

(2000). *Leading the Revolution*. Boston: Harvard Business School Press.

(2002). *Leading the Revolution: How to Thrive in Turbulent Times by Making Innovation a Way of Life*. New York: Plume.

(2006). The why, what and how of management innovation. *Harvard Business Review* 84(2): 72–84.

Hamel, G., and C. K. Prahalad (1994). *Competing for the Future*. Boston: Harvard Business School Press.

Hannan, M., and J. Freeman (1977). The population ecology of organizations. *American Journal of Sociology* 82: 929–964.

Hargadon, A. B. (2002). Brokering knowledge: linking learning and innovation. *Research in Organizational Behavior* 24: 41–85.

Harrigan, K. R. (1986). Matching vertical integration strategies to competitive conditions. *Strategic Management Journal* 7: 535–555.

Haunschild, P. R., and A. S. Miner (1999). Modes of interorganizational imitation: the effects of outcome salience and uncertainty. *Administrative Science Quarterly* 42: 472–500.

Helper, S. R., and M. Sako (1995). Supplier relations in Japan and the United States: are they converging? *Sloan Management Review* 36(3): 77–84.

Henderson, J., and N. Venkatraman (1989). Strategic alignment: leveraging information technology for transforming organizations. *IBM Systems Journal* 32(1): 4–16.

Hendry, J. (1995). Culture, community and networks: the hidden cost of outsourcing. *European Management Journal* 13(2): 218–229.

Hennart, J.-F. (1993). Explaining the swollen middle: why most transactions are a mix of "market" and "hierarchy." *Organization Science* 4(4): 529–547.

Heugens, P. P. M. A. R., and M. J. Mol (2005). So you call that research? Mending methodological biases in strategy and organization departments of top business schools. *Strategic Organization* 3(1): 117–128.

Holland, C. P., and A. G. Lockett (1997). Mixed mode network structures: the strategic use of electronic communication by organizations. *Organization Science* 8(5): 475–488.

Holmström, B., and J. Roberts (1998). The boundaries of the firm revisited. *Journal of Economic Perspectives* 12(4): 73–94.

Huber, R. (1993). How Continental Bank outsourced its crown jewels. *Harvard Business Review* 68(3): 121–129.

Insinga, R. C., and M. J. Werle (2000). Linking outsourcing to business strategy. *Academy of Management Executive* 14(4): 58–70.

Jacobides, M. G. (2005). Industry change through vertical disintegration: how and why markets emerged in mortgage banking. *Academy of Management Journal* 48: 465–498.

Jensen, M. C., and W. H. Meckling (1976). Theory of the firm: managerial behavior, agency costs and ownership structure. *Journal of Financial Economics* 3: 305–360.

Jenster, P. V., H. S. Pedersen, P. Plackett, and D. Hussey (2005). *Outsourcing – Insourcing: Can Vendors Make Money from the New Relationship opportunities?* Chichester: John Wiley and Sons.

Jurison, J. (1995). The role of risk and return in information technology outsourcing decisions. *Journal of Information Technology* 10: 239–247.

Kale, P., J. H. Dyer, and H. Singh (2002). Alliance capability, stock market response, and long term alliance success: the role of the alliance function. *Strategic Management Journal* 23(8): 747–767.

Kenney, M., and R. Florida (1995). The transfer of Japanese management styles in two US transplant industries: autos and electronics. *Journal of Management Studies* 32(6): 789–802.

Kern, T., L. P. Willcocks, and E. van Heck (2002). The winner's curse in IT outsourcing: strategies for avoiding relational trauma. *California Management Review* 44(2): 47–69.

Khanna, T., and K. Palepu (2000). The future of business groups in emerging markets: long-run evidence from Chile. *Academy of Management Journal* 43(3): 268–285.

Kinder, T. (2003). Go with the flow – a conceptual framework for supply relations in the era of the extended enterprise. *Research Policy* 32(3): 503–523.

Kinkel, S., and G. Lay (2003) *Fertigungstiefe: Ballast oder Kapital?* Karlsruhe: Fraunhofer Institut Systems- und Innovationsforschung. Mitteilunge aus der Produktionsinnovationserhebung, no. 30.

Kipping, M., and L. Engwall (2002). *Management Consulting: Emergence and Dynamics of a Knowledge Industry*. New York: Oxford University Press.

Klein, B. (2000). Fisher–General Motors and the nature of the firm. *Journal of Law and Economics* 43(1): 105–141.

Klein, B., R. A. Crawford, and A. A. Alchian (1978). Vertical integration, appropriable rents, and the competitive contracting process. *Journal of Law and Economics* 21: 297–326.

Knickerbocker, F. T. (1973). Oligopolistic reaction and multinational enterprise. Division of Research, Graduate School of Business Administration, Harvard University.

Knorr-Cetina, K., and A. Preda (2005). *The Sociology of Financial Markets*. New York: Oxford University Press.

Kogut, B., and N. Kulatilaka (1994). Operating flexibility, global manufacturing and the option value of a multinational network. *Management Science* 40(1): 123–139.

Kogut, B., and U. Zander (1992). Knowledge of the firm, combinative capabilities, and the replication of technology. *Organization Science* 3: 383–397.

Kotabe, M. (1992). *Global Sourcing Strategy: R&D, Manufacturing, and Marketing Interfaces*. New York: Quorum Books.

(1998). Efficiency vs. effectiveness orientation of global sourcing strategy: a comparison of US and Japanese multinational companies. *Academy of Management Executive* 12(4): 107–119.

Kotabe, M., and M. J. Mol (2004). A new perspective on outsourcing and the performance of the firm. In *Global Corporate Evolution: Looking Inward or Looking Outward*, ed. M. Trick. Pittsburgh: Carnegie Mellon University Press.

(2005). Outsourcing and financial performance: a negative curvilinear relationship. Working Paper, London Business School.

(forthcoming). International sourcing strategies: redressing the balance. In *Handbook of Global Logistics and Supply Chain Management*, ed. J. T. Mentzer, M. B. Myers, and T. P. Stank. London: Sage.

Kotabe, M., M. J. Mol, and S. Ketkar (2006). An evolutionary stage theory of outsourcing and competence destruction: a triad comparison of the consumer electronics industry. Working Paper, London Business School.

Kotabe, M., and G. S. Omura (1989). Sourcing strategies of European and Japanese multinationals: a comparison. *Journal of International Business Studies* 20(1): 113–130.

Kunda, G., and G. Ailon-Souday (2005). New designs: design and devotion revisited. In *The Oxford Handbook of Work and Organization*, ed. S. Ackroyd, R. Batt, P. Thompson, and P. S. Tolbert. Oxford: Oxford University Press.

Lacity, M., and R. Hirschheim (1993). *Information Systems Outsourcing: Myths, Metaphors and Realities*. Chichester: John Wiley and Sons.

(1995). *Beyond the Information Systems Outsourcing Bandwagon*. Chichester: John Wiley and Sons.

Lamoreaux, N. R., D. M. G. Raff, and P. Temin (2003). Beyond markets and hierarchies: toward a new synthesis of American business history. *American Historical Review* 108(2): 404–433.

Lane, C. (2001). Organizational learning in supplier networks. In *Handbook of Organizational Learning and Knowledge*, ed. M. Dierkes, A. Bertoine Anthal, J. Child, and I. Nonaka. Oxford: Oxford University Press.

Langlois, R. N. (2004). Chandler in a larger frame: markets, transaction costs, and organizational form in history. *Enterprise and Society* 5(3): 355–375.

Langlois, R. N., and P. L. Robertson (1992). Networks and innovation in a modular system: lessons from the microcomputer and stereo component industries. *Research Policy* 21(4): 297–313.

Lei, D., and M. A. Hitt (1995). Strategic restructuring and outsourcing: the effect of mergers and acquisitions and LBOs on building firm skills and capabilities. *Journal of Management* 21(5): 835–859.

Leiblein, M. J. (2003). The choice of organizational governance form and performance: predictions from transaction cost, resource-based, and real options theories. *Journal of Management* 29(6): 937–961.

Leiblein, M. J., and D. J. Miller (2003). An empirical examination of transaction- and firm-level influences on the vertical boundaries of the firm. *Strategic Management Journal* 24(9): 839–859.

Leiblein, M. J., J. J. Reuer, and F. Dalsace (2002). Do make or buy decisions matter? The influence of organizational governance on technological performance. *Strategic Management Journal* 23(9): 817–833.

Levinthal, D. A., and J. G. March (1993). The myopia of learning. *Strategic Management Journal* 14(8): 95–112.

Levy, D. L. (1995). International sourcing and supply chain stability. *Journal of International Business Studies* 26(2): 343–360.

Lewin, K. (1951). *Field Theory in Social Science: Selected Theoretical Papers.* New York: Harper.

Lincoln, J. R., C. L. Ahmadjian, and E. Mason (1998). Organizational learn- ing and purchase–supply relations in Japan. *California Management Review* 40(3): 241–264.

Linder, J. C. (2004). Transformational outsourcing. *Sloan Management Review* 45(2): 52–58.

Loh, L., and N. Venkatraman (1992). Determinants of information technol- ogy outsourcing: a cross-sectional analysis. *Journal of Management Information Systems* 9(1): 7–24.

Lorenzoni, G., and C. Baden-Fuller (1995). Creating a strategic center to manage a web of partners. *California Management Review* 37(3): 146–163.

Lorenzoni, G., and A. Lipparini (1999). The leveraging of interfirm relation- ships as a distinctive organizational capability: a longitudinal study. *Strategic Management Journal* 20(4): 317–338.

Loveman, G. (2003). Diamonds in the data mine. *Harvard Business Review* 81(5): 109–113.

Lynch, C. F. (2004). Why outsource? *Supply Chain Management Review* 8(7): 44–48.

Malerba, F., and L. Orsenigo (1993). Technological regimes and firm behavior. *Industrial and Corporate Change* 2(1): 45–72.

Malone, T. W., and R. J. Laubacher (1998). The dawn of the E-lance economy. *Harvard Business Review* 76(5): 144–152.

Malone, T. W., J. Yates, and R. I. Benjamin (1987). Electronic markets and electronic hierarchies. *Communications of the ACM* 30(6): 484–497.

March, J. G. (1991). Exploration and exploitation in organizational learn- ing. *Organization Science* 2(1): 71–78.

    (2006). Rationality, foolishness, and adaptive intelligence. *Strategic Management Journal* 27(3): 201–214.

Markides, C. (1995). *Diversification, Refocusing, and Economic Performance.* Cambridge, Mass.: MIT Press.

(1999). A dynamic view of strategy. *Sloan Management Review* 40(3): 55–63.

Markides, C. C., and N. Berg (1988). Manufacturing offshore is bad business. *Harvard Business Review* 66(5): 113–120.

Marshall, A. (1919). *Industry and Trade: A Study of Industrial Technique and Business Organization*. London: Macmillan.

Martinez, R. J., and M. T. Dacin (1999). Efficiency motives and normative forces: combining transactions costs and institutional logic. *Journal of Management* 25(1): 75–96.

Masten, S. E. (1993). Transaction costs, mistakes, and performance: assessing the importance of governance. *Managerial and Decision Economics* 14: 119–129.

McCarthy, I., and A. Anagnostou (2004). The impact of outsourcing on the transaction costs and boundaries of manufacturing. *International Journal of Production Economics* 88(1), 61–71.

McLaren, J. (2000). "Globalization" and vertical structure. *American Economic Review* 90(5): 1239–1254.

Milgrom, P., and J. Roberts (1987). Informational asymmetries, strategic behavior, and industrial organization. *American Economic Review* 77(2): 184–193.

(1992). *Economics, Organization and Management*. Englewood Cliffs, N.J.: Prentice Hall.

Mintzberg, H. (2004). *Managers not MBAs: A Hard Look at the Soft Practice of Managing and Management Development*. San Francisco: Berrett-Koehler.

Mintzberg, H., B. W. Ahlstrand, and J. Lampel (1998). *Strategy Safari: A Guided Tour through the Wilds of Strategic Management*. New York: Free Press.

Mintzberg, H., J. B. Quinn, and S. Ghoshal (1995). *The Strategy Process*. New York: Prentice Hall.

Mol, M. J. (2001). *Outsourcing, Supplier Relations and Internationalisation: Global Sourcing Strategy as a Chinese Puzzle*. Ph.D. series, number 10. Rotterdam: ERIM.

(2002). Ford Mondeo: a Model T world car? In *Cases on Global IT Applications and Managment: Successes and Pitfalls*, ed. F. B. Tan. Hershey, Penn.: Idea Group.

(2004). Offshoring: an international approach. *European Business Forum* 19(Autumn): 47–49.

(2005). Does being R&D intensive still discourage outsourcing? Evidence from Dutch manufacturing. *Research Policy* 34(4): 571–582.

Mol, M. J., and O. R. Koppius (2002). Information technology and the internationalization of the firm. *Journal of Global Information Management* 10(4): 44–60.

Mol, M. J., and M. Kotabe (2006) Economized at the core but socialized around it: bandwagoning in outsourcing decisions. Working Paper, London Business School.

Mol, M. J., J. van Oosterhout, and A. Ritskes (2005). Bandwagoning in business process outsourcing. Working Paper, London Business School.

Mol, M. J., P. Pauwels, P. Matthyssens, and L. Quintens (2004). A technological contingency perspective on the depth and scope of international outsourcing. *Journal of International Management* 10(2): 287–305.

Mol, M. J., J. Schreuder, and R. Goedegebuure (2001). Het belang van inkoop in de Nederlandse industrie en de veranderende rol van de inkoper. *Inkoop & Logistiek*, November: 21–25.

Mol, M. J., R. J. M. van Tulder, and P. R. Beije (2005). Antecedents and performance consequences of international outsourcing. *International Business Review* 14(5): 599–617.

Mol, M. J., and D. Vermeulen (2003). The economic implications of outsourcing. Working paper *METEOR RM/03/027*, University of Maastricht.

Monczka, R., and R. J. Trent (1991). Global sourcing: a development approach. *International Journal of Purchasing and Materials Management* 27(2): 2–8.

Monteverde, K. (1995). Technical dialog as an incentive for vertical integration in the semiconductor industry. *Management Science* 41(10): 1624–1638.

Monteverde, K., and D. J. Teece (1982). Supplier switching costs and vertical integration in the automobile industry. *Bell Journal of Economics* 13(2): 206–213.

Moran, P., and S. Ghoshal (1996). Theories of economic organization: the case for realism and balance. *Academy of Management Review* 21(1): 58–72.

Murray, J. Y., M. Kotabe, and A. R. Wildt (1995). Strategic and financial implications of global sourcing strategy: a contingency analysis. *Journal of International Business Studies* 26(1): 181–202.

Nelson, R. R., and S. G. Winter (1982). *An Evolutionary Theory of Economic Change*. Cambridge, Mass.: Harvard University Press.

Nickerson, J. A., and R. Vandenbergh (1999). Economizing in a context of strategizing: governance mode choice in Cournot competition. *Journal of Economic Behavior and Organization* 40: 1–15.

Nishiguchi, T. (1994). *Strategic Industrial Sourcing: The Japanese Advantage*. Oxford: Oxford University Press.

Nishiguchi, T., and A. Beaudet (1998). The Toyota group and the Aisin fire. *Sloan Management Review* 39(3): 49–59.

Nooteboom, B. (1998). *Management van partnerships: in toeleveren en uitbesteden*. Schoonhoven: Academic Service.

(1999). *Inter-firm Alliances: Analysis and Design*. London: Routledge.

North, D. C. (1991). Institutions. *Journal of Economic Perspectives* 5(1): 97–112.

Oliver, C. (1997). Sustainable competitive advantage: combining institutional and resource-based views. *Strategic Management Journal* 18(9): 697–713.

Pascale, R. T., and A. G. Athos (1981). *The Art of Japanese Management: Applications for American Executives*. New York: Simon and Schuster.

Peters, T. J., and R. H. Waterman (1982). *In Search of Excellence*. New York: Harper.

Piore, M., and C. Sabel (1984). *The Second Industrial Divide: Possibilities for Prosperity*. New York: Basic Books.

Pisano, G. P. (1990). The R&D boundaries of the firm: an empirical analysis. *Administrative Science Quarterly* 35(1): 153–176.

Poppo, L., and T. Zenger (1998). Testing alternative theories of the firm: transaction cost, knowledge-based, and measurement explanations for make-or-buy decisions in information services. *Strategic Management Journal* 19(9): 853–877.

Porter, M. E. (1980). *Competitive Strategy*. New York: Free Press.

(1985). *Competitive Advantage*. New York: Free Press.

(1990). *The Competitive Advantage of Nations*. New York: Free Press.

(1997). *On Competition*. Boston: Harvard Business School Press.

(1998). Clusters and the new economics of competition. *Harvard Business Review* 76(6): 77–90.

(2001). Strategy and the Internet. *Harvard Business Review*, 79(3): 62–78.

Powell, W. W. (1990). Neither market nor hierarchy: network forms of organization. In *Research in Organizational Behavior*, ed. B. J. Straw and A. L. L. Cummings. Greenwich, Conn.: JAI Press.

Prahalad, C. K., and R. A. Bettis (1986). The dominant logic: a new linkage between diversity and performance. *Strategic Management Journal* 7: 485–501.

Prahalad, C. K., and G. Hamel (1990). The core competence of the corporation. *Harvard Business Review* 68(3): 79–91.

Puranam, P., and K. Srikanth (2006) The seven deadly superstitions in business process outsourcing. Working Paper, London Business School.

Pyndt, J., and T. Pedersen (2006). *Managing Global Offshoring Strategies: A Case Approach*. Copenhagen: Copenhagen Business School Press.

Quinn, J. B. (1992). *Intelligent Enterprise: A Knowledge and Service-Based Paradigm for Industry*. New York: Free Press.

(1999). Strategic outsourcing: leveraging knowledge capabilities. *Sloan Management Review* 40(3): 9–21.

(2000). Outsourcing innovation: the new engine of growth. *Sloan Management Review* 41(4): 13–28.

Quinn, J. B., J. J. Baruch, and K. A. Zien (1997). *Innovation Explosion: Using Intellect and Software to Revolutionize Growth Strategies.* New York: Free Press.

Quinn, J. B., T. I. Doorley, and P. C. Paquette (1990). Technology in services: rethinking strategic focus. *Sloan Management Journal* 31(2): 79–87.

Quinn, J. B., and F. G. Hilmer (1994). Strategic outsourcing. *Sloan Management Review* 35(4): 43–55.

Quintens, L. (2006). Global purchasing strategy: determinants, dimensions and performance outcome. Ph.D. dissertation, University of Hasselt.

Rangan, S. (2000). The problem of search and deliberation in international exchange: microfoundations to some macro patterns. *Journal of International Business Studies* 31(2): 205–222.

Reed, R., and R. J. DeFillippi (1990). Causal ambiguity, barriers to imitation, and sustainable competitive advantage. *Academy of Management Review* 15: 88–102.

Reuer, J. J., M. Zollo, and H. Singh (2002). Post-formation dynamics in strategic alliances. *Strategic Management Journal* 23(2): 135–151.

Richardson, G. B. (1972). The organisation of industry. *Economic Journal* 82: 883–892, 895–896.

Richardson, J. (1993). Parallel sourcing and supplier performance in the Japanese automobile industry. *Strategic Management Journal* 14(5): 339–350.

Ring, P. S., and A. H. Van de Ven (1994). Developmental processes of co-operative interorganizational relationships. *Academy of Management Review* 19(1): 90–118.

Rosenzweig, P. M. (1994). When can management science research be generalized internationally? *Management Science* 40(1): 28–39.

Rugman, A. M. (1981). *Inside the Multinationals: The Economics of Internal Markets.* New York: Columbia University Press.

Ruhnke, H. O. (1966). Vertical integration: trend for the future? *SAM Advanced Management Journal* 31(1): 69–73.

Sako, M. (2004). Supplier development at Honda, Nissan and Toyota: comparative case studies of organizational capability enhancement. *Industrial and Corporate Change* 132(6): 281–308.

   (2006) Shifting boundaries of the firm: Japanese company – Japanese labour. Oxford: Oxford University Press.

Scott, W. R. (1995). *Institutions and Organizations.* Thousand Oaks, Calif.: Sage Publications.

Semlinger, K. (1993). Small firms and outsourcing as flexibility reservoirs of large firms. In *The Embedded Firm: On the Socioeconomics of Industrial Networks,* ed. G. Grabher. London: Routledge.

Shy, O., and R. Stenbacka (2003). Strategic outsourcing. *Journal of Economic Behavior and Organization* 50(2): 203–224.

(2005). Partial outsourcing, monitoring cost, and market structure. *Canadian Journal of Economics* 38(4): 1173–1190.

Simon, H. A. (1991). Organizations and markets. *Journal of Economic Perspectives* 5(2): 25–44.

(1998). *Administrative Behavior*. New York: Free Press.

Smith, A. (1976). *An Inquiry into the Nature and Causes of the Wealth of Nations*. Oxford: Clarendon Press.

Snijders, C., and F. Tazelaar (2005). Five counterintuitive findings in IT-purchasing. *Journal of Purchasing and Supply Management* 11(2/3): 83–96.

Staw, B. M. (1981). The escalation of commitment to a course of action. *Academy of Management Review* 6(4): 577–587.

Stigler, G. J. (1951). The division of labor is limited by the extent of the market. *Journal of Political Economy* 59(2): 185–193.

Stinchcombe, A. L. (1965). Social structure and organizations. In *Handbook of Organizations*, ed. J. G. March. Chicago: Rand-McNally.

Swamidass, P. M., and M. Kotabe (1993). Component sourcing strategies of multinationals: an empirical study of European and Japanese multinationals. *Journal of International Business Studies* 24(1): 81–99.

Takeishi, A. (2001). Bridging inter- and intra-firm boundaries: management of supplier involvement in automobile product development. *Strategic Management Journal* 22(5): 403–433.

Tayles, M., and C. Drury (2001). Moving from make/buy to strategic sourcing: the outsource decision process. *Long Range Planning* 34(5): 605–622.

Tecson, G. (1998). The "global" sourcing of core firms. Management Report, ERASM, Rotterdam.

Teece, D. J. (1980). The diffusion of an administrative innovation. *Management Science* 26(5): 464–470.

(1986). Profiting from technological innovation: implications for integration, collaboration, licensing, and public policy. *Research Policy* 15: 285–305.

Teece, D. J., G. Pisano, and A. Shuen (1997). Dynamic capabilities and strategic management. *Strategic Management Journal* 18(7): 509–533.

Thompson, J. D. (1967). *Organizations in Action: Social Science Bases of Administrative Theory*. New York: McGraw-Hill.

Toulan, O. (2002). The impact of market liberalization on vertical scope: the case of Argentina. *Strategic Management Journal* 23(6): 551–560.

Trent, R. J., and R. M. Monczka (2003). International purchasing and global sourcing: what are the differences? *Journal of Supply Chain Management* 39(4): 26–37.

Tushman, M. L., and P. Anderson (1986). Technological discontinuities and organizational environments. *Administrative Science Quarterly* 31(3): 439–465.

Uzzi, B. (1996). The sources and consequences of embeddedness for the economic performance of organizations: the network effect. *American Sociological Review* 61(August): 674–698.

(1997). Social structure and competition in interfirm networks: the paradox of embeddedness. *Administrative Science Quarterly* 42(1): 35–67.

Van de Ven, A., and P. Johnson (forthcoming). Knowledge for theory and practice. *Academy of Management Review*.

Van Tulder, R. J. M., and M. J. Mol (2002). Reverse auctions or auctions reversed: first experiments by Philips. *European Management Journal* 20(5): 1–12.

Van Weele, A. J. (2002). *Purchasing and Supply Chain Management: Analysis, Planning and Practice*. London: Thomson Learning.

Venkatesan, R. (1992). Strategic sourcing: to make or not to make. *Harvard Business Review* 70(6): 98–107.

Venkatraman, N., and V. Ramanujam (1986). Measurement of business performance in strategy research: a comparison of approaches. *Academy of Management Review* 11(4): 801–813.

Walker, G., and D. Weber (1984). A transaction cost approach to make–buy decisions. *Administrative Science Quarterly* 29(3): 373–391.

Wernerfelt, B. (1984). A resource-based view of the firm. *Strategic Management Journal* 5(2): 171–180.

Willcocks, L. P., and T. Kern (1998). IT outsourcing as strategic partnering: the case of the UK Inland Revenue. *European Journal of Information Systems* 7(1): 29–45.

Williamson, O. E. (1975). *Markets and Hierarchies: Analysis and Antitrust Implications*. New York: Free Press.

(1979). Transaction cost economics: the governance of contractual relations. *Journal of Law and Economics* 22(October): 233–261.

(1981). The economics of organization: the transaction cost approach. *American Journal of Sociology* 87(3): 548–577.

(1985). *The Economic Institutions of Capitalism*. New York: Free Press.

(1991a). Strategizing, economizing and economic organization. *Strategic Management Journal* 12(Winter Special Issue): 75–94.

(1991b). Comparative economic organization: the analysis of discrete structural alternatives. *Administrative Science Quarterly* 36: 269–296.

(1995). *The Mechanisms of Governance*. Oxford: Oxford University Press.

(1999). Strategy research: governance and competence perspectives. *Strategic Management Journal* 20(12): 1087–1108.

Womack, J. P., D. T. Jones, and D. Roos (1990). *The Machine that Changed the World*. New York: Harper-Perennial.

Woodward, J. (1965). *Industrial Organization: Theory and Practice*. Oxford: Oxford University Press.

Wouters, M., J. C. Anderson, and F. Wynstra (2005). The adoption of total cost of ownership for sourcing decisions – a structural equations analysis. *Accounting, Organizations and Society* 30(2): 167–191.

Wynstra, F., and M. Weggemann (2001). Managing supplier involvement in product development: three critical issues. *European Management Journal* 19(2): 157–167.

Zaheer, A., B. McEvily, and V. Perrone (1998). Does trust matter? Exploring the effects of interorganizational and interpersonal trust on performance. *Organization Science* 9(2): 141–159.

Zajac, E. J., and C. P. Olsen (1993). From transactional cost to transactional value analysis: implications for the study of interorganizational strategies. *Journal of Management Studies* 30(1): 131–145.

Zucker, L. G. (1983). Organizations as institutions. In *Research in the Sociology of Organizations*, ed. S. B. Bacharach. Greenwich, Conn.: JAI Press.

# Index